D1072056

ARMOURED
FIGHTING VEHICLES

ARMOURED
FIGHTING VEHICLES

PHILIP TREWHITT

PROSPERO
B·O·O·K·S
A DIVISION OF CHAPTERS INC.

Published by Prospero Books
a division of Chapters Inc.
90 Ronson Drive
Etobicoke
Ontario
Canada M9W 1C1

ISBN 1-89410-281-9

Editorial and design by Brown Packaging Books Ltd
Bradley's Close
74–77 White Lion Street
London N1 9PF

Design: Wilson Design Associates

Printed in Singapore

CONTENTS

Introduction

Despite the fact that, at the beginning of World War I, all the combatant armies relied heavily on horses (many continued to do so at the beginning of World War II, and many would continue to use horses for general transport duties), the benefits of using the relatively recent innovation of the combustion engine to provide mobility, firepower and protection were evident from the first days of the conflict. The British Admiralty was soon pressing commercial motor cars such as the Lanchester and Rolls-Royce into service, with the British Army taking over these armoured units by the beginning of 1915. Their well-made suspensions needed little reinforcing, and with a machine gun mounted on the top and some additional armour these vehicles proved versatile and useful, albeit for reconnaissance and not direct attacks against enemy positions. They were particularly valued in the desert campaigns of World War I, in Africa and in the Middle East, where they proved themselves in difficult terrain.

Above: The most powerful main battle tank in the world – the American Abrams.

But even armoured cars could not operate effectively against entrenched and well-defended positions, and it was the murderous stalemate of the Western Front which gave the impetus to serious development of armoured fighting vehicles. When the trench network began to spread to eventually form a continuous line between the English Channel and the Swiss frontier, it was realised that barbed wire and machine guns were spelling the end of the horse in a combat role, and a new form of mobile strike force was needed to cope with a new type of war. The 'tank',

Above: The crude Russian T-62, one of the tanks that made up the massed Warsaw Pact armoured force during the Cold War, and which was inferior to NATO rivals.

as it was codenamed for reasons of security, carried the hope that it might break the deadlock. Well armoured and bristling with weapons, the idea was to cross trenches with ease using the all-round tracks of the early vehicles (such as the Tank Mk V) and destroy enemy resistance with impunity.

The idea was sound enough, and when they first appeared at the Battle of the Somme in 1916 they proved effective in frightening German conscripts, if not in fulfilling their intended role. Early models were highly unreliable and the tactics employed – using them singly to support infantry attacks – did not make the most effective use of them. However, by the time of their first significant action at Cambrai in 1917, improvements had been made. German efforts to catch up with the Allies, in the shape of the Sturmpanzerwagen A7V, a truly monstrous vehicle, proved unsuccessful, and by the end of the war tanks were being produced and used in considerable quantities by the Allies only. It would be inappropriate to suggest that the tank was in any way a war winner. German stormtrooper attacks during the offensives of March 1918 proved more effective in breaking the trench stalemate than tanks. However, it proved that the idea of armoured machines was workable.

If Germany lagged behind the Allies in armoured warfare at the end of World War I, it would labour under less of a disadvantage by the advent of the next global war. Despite the restrictions of the Treaty of Versailles, Germany developed an armoured force during the interwar period which was to have an impact on warfare the like of which had rarely been seen. It was not the quality of the armoured vehicles – the French Char B1 bis was superior to most German tanks in May 1940, for example – but the way in which they were used that proved the value of the armoured fighting vehicle. Whereas the French, and the British to some extent, used their armour in dribs and drabs in an infantry support role (as they had been used in World War I), the German Army believed in the value of massed armoured formations. They were right to do so. The early panzers, many based on Czech designs appropriated after the 1938 annexation of Czechoslovakia by Germany, proved too much for the Allies. It was at a price, though. The German panzer divisions suffered heavy casualties in the early campaigns, and all sides realised that the future of armoured warfare lay in bigger, better-armed and better-armoured vehicles. Any complacency felt by the German High Command over the early victories evaporated when the first T-34s appeared on the Russian Front.

HEAVIER AND MORE POWERFULLY ARMED TANKS

With the development of the superb Panzer V Panther, developed in response to the T-34's challenge, and then the Tiger and King Tiger tanks, the Germans maintained a slight armoured advantage throughout the war, despite the excellent qualities of Allied tanks such as the M4 Sherman. Evidence of this advantage can be found in the combat records for the Normandy campaign of 1944, where the exploits of Tiger aces such as Michael Wittmann speak for themselves. The Tiger proved an awesome vehicle on the battlefield, respected and feared by the Allies. However, no matter how powerful and how invulnerable a vehicle was, if it was not mechanically reliable and not available in numbers, then its value was limited. The brilliant German counterattack through the Ardennes forest in late 1944 was impeded through lack of fuel, which rendered the tank force impotent and immobile.

Increasing use of tanks led to development of specialist tank destroyers, which had the advantage of being much cheaper and easier to build as a rule than tanks themselves. The German Marder, for example, was a superb vehicle/weapon combination, so good in fact that it found itself being used more and more in a tank role and being attached to mobile panzer divisions, a job for which it was unsuited. The ensuing high attrition rate left the Marder a victim of its own success. The concept of mobile firepower continued with self-propelled artillery, with any useful artillery weapon being mounted on a mobile tracked chassis. The StuG III was perhaps the most famous of the type in World War II, though in terms of numbers employed the American M7 Priest would certainly rank first. Like the tank destroyer, the self-propelled gun was not designed for the all-purpose fighting vehicle role. Its job was to move to a spot, fire and then move again when required. Superficially similar to tanks, both self-propelled guns and tank destroyers were inferior to tanks in terms of mobility and armour protection, and thus suffered when called upon to fill the role of a tank.

VARIANTS OF THE MAIN BATTLE TANK

One of the more startling aspects of the development in armoured vehicles is the number of variants of the vehicles produced. Most main battle tanks since World War II have been adapted for a number of different roles, such as flamethrower and combat engineer tank. For example, the Centurion could be adapted to carry dozer blades, mine-clearing flails, demolition charges, cranes and fascine-laying equipment amongst other equipment. Most vehicles since World War II have been equipped with an amphibious capability, with widely varying levels of sophistication. The World War II Sherman BARV, for example, was designed as a recovery vehicle during amphibious landings, and thus needed to be able to operate in open water. This vehicle was fully sealed and equipped with periscopes and breathing apparatus for the crew. It came as a severe shock to the Germans when it made its debut, as they had been trying to perfect a similar vehicle for a considerable time. Other vehicles were given more rudimentary amphibious capability, in the form of flotation bags. Some had propellers or water jets fitted. Vehicles designed specifically for amphibious operations included the famous American-built DUKW, known universally as the 'Duck'. This vehicle operated well on land or in the water, and proved a magnificent transport carrier for the Americans and British.

Above: The right blend of armament, powerplant, design and armour produces an outstanding main battle tank, such as the British Centurion, in service for over 50 years.

For transporting personnel or equipment across difficult terrain, the halftrack, which was first used on a significant scale by the German Army in World War II but soon adopted by all armies, has proved an excellent and lasting innovation. The American M3 and the German SdKfz 251 were the forefathers of modern tracked personnel carriers such as the Bradley M2 Infantry Fighting Vehicle. Interestingly enough, modern developments in wheeled vehicles, such as effective tyre-pressure regulation systems, has cut the mobility deficit between the tracked and wheeled vehicle over rough terrain, and the greater speed and lower maintenance of the latter vehicle may well spell the end for tracked personnel carriers on the modern battlefield.

Most armoured fighting vehicles during the twentieth century have been hurried improvisations, labouring under all the deficiencies which such vehicles are prone to. However, some vehicles have seemed so dominant that they have become synonymous with their theatre of operations. The lumbering Mk V crashing over the barbed wire on the Western Front during World War I; the King Tiger during the Ardennes counterattack in 1944; and the Abrams chasing across the desert during Operation 'Desert Storm' in 1991. There have been few constants in armoured warfare. One has been that tactics can compensate for deficiencies in the quality or quantity of equipment (as shown by Germany in 1940 when routing the British and other Allied armies, and Israel during the 1960s and 1970s when fighting against superior numbers of Arab tanks), but only so far. With the complexities of modern tanks, such as the Leclerc, the M1 Abrams and the Challenger, crews must be ever more expert and ever more specialist. The dangers of throwing inadequately trained crews in inferior equipment into battle against such specialists in the best vehicles available was fully illustrated in the 1991 Gulf War. The Iraqi armoured divisions were decimated by the Coalition forces with practically no loss to the latter. The second constant is that no matter how big, how devastating its firepower and how invulnerable an armoured vehicle may seem, within a short space of time the opposition will have come up with its match and probably its successor. Experiences on the Eastern Front during World War II show this,

Above: The Bradley infantry fighting vehicle, designed to transport infantry close to the enemy. Fast and reliable, it is designed to operate with Abrams tanks.

with both sides battling for advantage and constantly increasing armour and armament.

Fighting vehicles cannot operate independently. The most formidable tank will fail if the trucks are not there to provide logistical support; if armoured personnel carriers (APCs) cannot get troops to the area to support and consolidate the breakthroughs. In turn APCs cannot operate if protection is not provided for them and if reconnaissance vehicles have not surveyed the terrain. Advances will falter if bridgelayers and combat engineer vehicles are not there to provide support. The concept of mutual protection is vital for the success of an armoured battle group.

THE ALL-ARMS BATTLEFIELD

Armoured warfare has made war faster and seemingly more destructive. The same problems encountered in the early days of armoured warfare remain, though. The first tanks were only effective when used in significant numbers, over open terrain, with secure and efficient logistical support. The rules are the same in modern times. The vast resources of the Soviet Army were unable to defeat small numbers of *Mujahideen* guerrillas in Afghanistan. The terrain and conditions prevented effective use of armoured resources.The same applied during the Vietnam War. Fighting vehicles are useful but not all-powerful. However, they have done what the first tank was intended to do: make attritional trench warfare impractical and perhaps, perversely, saved a few lives in the process.

The vehicles included in this book are the most influential and important fighting machines to have taken part in land warfare since World War I. Trucks have been included because they have played, and continue to play, an essential role in armoured warfare. Though most are not tracked and do not carry a main gun, they transport ammunition and troops to and from the battlefield; they are the lifeblood of mechanised armies. Similarly, light vehicles are also included because they too are essential to the success of mechanised armies. In addition, many of these light vehicles are armed and armoured to take part in hit-and-run operations (such as the converted British Special Air Service Jeeps that operated behind Axis lines in North Africa in World War II). The modern American M998 'Hummer', for example, can be armed with numerous weapons ranging from machine guns to anti-tank missiles. In this way it becomes a fighting vehicle, one that can knock out many tanks currently in service around the world.

Medium Tank Mk A

The World War I Medium Tank Mk A light tank was designed not so much for crossing obstacles as for exploiting breakthroughs brought about by heavier tanks. The emphasis was thus on speed and mobility. Designed by William Tritton, the Mk A was soon nicknamed 'Whippet'. The prototype was powered by London bus engines and was ready in February 1917, but it was not until late 1917 that the first production models appeared. The Whippet first saw combat in March 1918, being used initially to plug gaps in the line. Its worth was proved in counterattacks, making deep forays behind the lines and creating havoc in the German rear areas. After the war, the Mk A saw service in Ireland and a number were exported to Japan in the 1920s.

Country of origin:	UK
Crew:	3 or 4
Weight:	14,300kg (31,460lb)
Dimensions:	length 6.10m (20ft); width 2.62m (8ft 7in); height 2.74m (9ft)
Range:	257km (160 miles)
Armour:	5-14mm (0.2-0.55in)
Armament:	two Hotchkiss machine guns
Powerplant:	two 45hp (33.6kW) Tylor four-cylinder petrol engines
Performance:	maximum road speed 13.4km/h (8.3mph)

Tank Mk V

T he Tank Mk V was the last of the lozenge-shaped tanks to see service in any number. It was designed to take part in the massive armoured thrusts envisaged for 1919. Improvements on earlier models included a Wilson epicyclic gearbox which allowed the tank to be driven by one man as opposed to two in earlier models. There was a cupola for the commander. Semaphore arms were mounted to give effective communication for the first time. The Tank Mk V* variant had a new 1.83m (6ft) section introduced into the hull to improve trench-crossing capability and provide extra internal space. From mid-1918, the tank saw action with the British and Americans. Post-war variants included bridge-laying and mine-clearing versions, and it remained in service with the Canadians until the early 1930s.

Country of origin:	UK
Crew:	8
Weight:	29,600kg (65,120lb)
Dimensions:	length 8.05m (26ft 5in); width over sponsons 4.11m (13ft 6in); height 2.64m (8ft 8in)
Range:	72km (45 miles)
Armour:	6-14mm (0.24-0.55in)
Armament:	two 6-pounder guns, four Hotchkiss machine guns
Powerplant:	one 150hp (112kW) Ricardo petrol engine
Performance:	maximum road speed 7.4km/h (4.6mph)

Char d'Assaut Schneider

The Char d'Assaut Schneider was developed as an armoured tractor for towing armoured troop sledges across to the German trenches on the Western Front. Based on the American Holt agricultural tractor, the first were available in the middle of 1917. The petrol tanks were very vulnerable to enemy fire and burned easily. Used mainly for infantry support rather than as personnel carriers, they were restricted by poor cross-country mobility, mainly due to their short tracks and long body which hindered the vehicle when crossing obstacles. The gun version ceased production in May 1917, to be replaced by the Char de Ravitaillement variant, used for carrying stores. Attrition and poor reliability led to less than 100 being in service at the end of the war.

Country of origin:	France
Crew:	7
Weight:	14,800kg (32,560lb)
Dimensions:	length 6.0m (19ft 8in); width 2.0m (6ft 6.66in); height 2.39m (7ft 10in)
Range:	48km (30 miles)
Armour:	11.5mm (0.45in)
Armament:	one 75mm gun, two additional machine guns
Powerplant:	one 55hp (41kW) Schneider four-cylinder petrol engine
Performance:	maximum road speed 6km/h (3.7mph)

Char d'Assaut St Chamond

The St Chamond was the French Army's own development. The first prototype appeared in 1916 and the vehicle entered service a year later. Like the Schneider, the St Chamond was based on the Holt tractor. An unusual petrol engine-driven electric transmission added an extra 5.1 tonnes (five tons) to the design weight. The hull extended both forward and rear of the track which, when combined with the weight, caused the St Chamond to become stuck on rough ground or over trenches. Its poor cross-country performance restricted its use in action, its last major action being a counterattack near Reims in July 1918. Many were converted into Char de Ravitaillement supply carriers. By the end of the war, only 72 out of 400 produced were still in service.

Country of origin:	France
Crew:	9
Weight:	23,400kg (51,480lb)
Dimensions:	length with gun 8.83m (28ft 11.75in); length of hull 7.91m (25ft 11.5in); width 2.67m (8ft 9in); height 2.34m (7ft 5.66in)
Range:	59km (36.7 miles)
Armour:	17mm (0.67in)
Armament:	one Modèle 1897 75mm gun; up to four machine guns
Powerplant:	one 90hp (67kW) Panhard four-cylinder petrol engine powering a Crochat-Collardeau electric transmission
Performance:	maximum road speed 8.5km/h (5.3mph)

Renault FT 17

The FT 17 was one of the most successful of all World War I tanks. It was the first of the classic tank design with features mounted directly onto the hull and a turret with a 360-degree traverse. They were ordered in large numbers (over 3000 during World War I) and needed to be, for they had been designed with little thought for maintenance and repair and as a result were often out of action. A self-propelled gun version and a radio-equipped version were among variants produced. In action, they were used *en masse*. For example, 480 being used in a counterattack near Soissons in July 1918 alone. They remained in service right up until 1944, when the Germans used captured FT 17s for street-fighting in Paris. By this time, of course, they were hopelessly out of date.

Country of origin:	France
Crew:	2
Weight:	6600kg (14,520lb)
Dimensions:	length with tail 5.0m (16ft 5in); width 1.71m (5ft 7.33in); height 2.133m (7ft in)
Range:	35.4km (22 miles)
Armour:	16mm (0.63in)
Armament:	one 37mm gun or one machine gun
Powerplant:	one 35hp (26kW) Renault four-cylinder petrol engine
Performance:	maximum road speed 7.7km/h (4.8mph)

Sturmpanzerwagen A7V

The Sturmpanzerwagen A7V was an enormous vehicle, hurriedly designed following the appearance of British tanks in 1916. Ground clearance was only 40mm (1.57in) and the length of track on the ground was too short for a vehicle of its size. The result was an unstable vehicle with poor cross-country performance. 100 A7Vs were ordered in December 1917, but the German war machine was already stretched and only about 20 were ever produced. Their shortcomings over rough ground were manifested in March 1918 when they first saw action, and they often lagged behind the infantry they were designed to support. Variants included the Uberlandwagen, an open-topped, unarmoured supply version, and the A7V/U with 'all-round' tracks. Post-war, they were used by the Polish Army for some years.

Country of origin:	Germany
Crew:	18
Weight:	33,500kg (73,700lb)
Dimensions:	length 8.0m (26ft 3in); width 3.06m (10ft 0.5in); height 3.30m (10ft 10in)
Range:	40km (25 miles)
Armour:	10-30mm (0.39-1.18in)
Armament:	one 57mm gun; six machine guns
Powerplant:	two 100hp (74.6kW) Daimler petrol engines
Performance:	maximum road speed 12.9km/h (8mph)

PzKpfw 38(t)

The Panzerkampfwagen (PzKpfw) – armoured fighting vehicle – 38(t) began life as the Czech-designed LT vz 38, although none had entered service with the Czech Army prior to the German occupation of Czechoslovakia in 1938. More than 1400 were built for the Axis forces between 1939-42. When it became outclassed as a light tank, the type was used widely as a reconnaissance vehicle and the chassis was used as the basis for a large number of vehicles, including the Marder tank destroyer, several self-propelled anti-aircraft guns, a weapons carrier and the Hetzer tank destroyer, which continued in service with the Swiss Army until the late 1960s. During its combat career its armour thickness was steadily increase. For example, the Ausf E version onwards had armour 50mm (2in) thick.

Country of origin:	Germany
Crew:	4
Weight:	9700kg (21,340lb)
Dimensions:	length 4.546m (14ft 11in); width 2.133m (7ft); height 2.311m (7ft 7in)
Range:	200km (125miles)
Armour:	10-25mm (0.4-1in); later increased from Ausf E version onwards to 50mm (2in)
Armament:	one 37.2mm Skoda A7 gun; two 7.92mm machine-guns
Powerplant:	one Praga EPA six-cylinder water-cooled inline petrol engine developing 150hp (112kW)
Performance:	maximum road speed 42km/h (26mph); fording 0.9m (3ft); vertical obstacle 0.787m (2ft 7in); trench 1.879m (6ft 2in)

Panzer I

The Panzer I was the first German tank to go into mass production, with nearly 600 having being ordered by July 1934. Three separate companies were engaged to build the tank (deliberately to spread experience of tank manufacture as widely as possible) and over 800 had been produced by June 1936, when production ceased. To avoid being seen to break the Treaty of Versailles, which prohibited the Germans from building tanks, the design was disguised as an 'agricultural tractor'. The Panzer I Ausf A was found in varying numbers in all panzer units and served extensively during the early campaigns of World War II. However, its limitations in armour and armament were soon evident, and it had been withdrawn from frontline service by 1941.

Country of origin:	Germany
Crew:	2
Weight:	5500kg (12,100lb)
Dimensions:	length 4.02m (13.2ft); width 2.06m (6ft 7in); height 1.72m (5ft 7in)
Range:	145km (81 miles)
Armour:	6-13mm (0.2-0.5in)
Armament:	two 7.92mm MG13 machine guns
Powerplant:	one Krupp M305 petrol engine developing 60hp (45kW)
Performance:	maximum road speed 37 km/h (21mph); fording 0.85m (2ft 10in); vertical obstacle 0.42m (1ft 5in); trench 1.75m (5ft 9in)

Panzer II Light Tank

The first production model PzKpfw II Ausf A appeared in 1935, having been designated as a tractor since German rearmament was hindered by the restrictions of the Treaty of Versailles. The initial tanks were a collaboration between the firms of MAN and Daimler-Benz. The Ausf B, C, D, E, and F versions were built during the years up to 1941, the main improvements being in the thickness of the armour. The tank formed the backbone of the invasions of Poland and France, with around 1000 seeing service. By the time of the invasion of the USSR in 1941, the tank was obsolete but was used as the basis for the Luchs reconnaissance tank. Other variants included an amphibious version designed for the invasion of Britain and the Flammpanzer II flame-throwing tank.

Country of origin:	Germany
Crew:	3
Weight:	10,000 kg (22,046lb)
Dimensions:	length 4.64m (15ft 3in); width 2.30m (7ft 6.5in); height 2.02m (6ft 7.5in)
Range:	200km (125miles)
Armour:	(Ausf F version) 20-35mm (0.8-1.38in)
Armament:	one 20mm cannon; one 7.92mm machine gun
Powerplant:	one Maybach six-cylinder petrol engine developing 140hp (104kW)
Performance:	maximum road speed 55km/h (34mph); fording 0.85m (2ft 10in); vertical obstacle 0.42m (1ft 5in); trench 1.75m (5ft 9in)

Panzer III Medium Tank

Following a 1935 German Army requirement for a light medium tank design, Daimler-Benz began mass production of the Pzkpfw III in September 1939. The early Ausf A, B and C models saw action in Poland, and in 1940 the Ausf F entered production, with heavier armour and an uprated engine. By the time the final version, the Ausf N, ceased production in August 1943, when the army was fighting in Russia, the tank carried twice as big a gun and weighed twice as much as the original prototype. Variants included an amphibious version, a command vehicle, an armoured recovery vehicle, an observation vehicle and one adapted for desert warfare. In addition, the chassis was used for a number of self-propelled guns right to the end of World War II in 1945.

Country of origin:	Germany
Crew:	5
Weight:	22,300kg (49,060lb)
Dimensions:	length 6.41m (21ft); width 2.95m (9ft 8in); height 2.50m (8ft 2.5in)
Range:	175km (110 miles)
Armour:	30mm (1.18in)
Armament:	(Ausf M version) one 75mm L/24 gun; one 7.92mm machine gun
Powerplant:	one Maybach HL 120 TRM 12-cylinder petrol engine developing 300hp (224kW)
Performance:	maximum road speed 40km/h (25mph); fording 0.8m (2ft 8in); vertical obstacle 0.6m (2ft); trench 2.59m (8ft 6in)

Panzer IV Medium Tank

The PzKpfw IV was built under a 1934 requirement from the German Army Weapons Department and was later to become the backbone of the Wehrmacht's panzer arm. The tank was in production right throughout the war, with the final version, the Ausf J, appearing in March 1944. In total, nearly 9000 vehicles were built by Krupp, with the basic chassis remaining the same in all models, but with heavier armour and armament being added as requirements changed. Despite the extra weight, the PzKpfw IV retained a good power-to-weight ratio throughout its production life and thus had good mobility. Like the Panzer III, the chassis was used as the basis for various self-propelled guns as well as armoured recovery vehicles and bridge-layers and the Jagdpanzer IV tank destroyer.

Country of origin:	Germany
Crew:	5
Weight:	25,000kg (55,000lb)
Dimensions:	length 7.02m (23ft); width 3.29m (10ft 9.5in); height 2.68m (8ft 9.5in)
Range:	200km (125miles)
Armour:	50-60mm (1.97-2.4in)
Armament:	(Ausf H version) one 75mm gun; two 7.92mm MG 34 machine guns
Powerplant:	one Maybach HL 120 TRM 12-cylinder petrol engine developing 300hp (224kW)
Performance:	maximum road speed 38km/h (24mph); fording 1.0m (3ft 3in); vertical obstacle 0.6m (2ft); trench 2.20m (7ft 3in)

Panzer V Panther

The Panther is widely considered to be one of the best tanks of World War II. Designed to combat the Soviet T-34 tanks which were outclassing the PzKpfw IV on the Eastern Front in early 1942, the Panther fulfilled the requirement for a tank with a powerful gun, good mobility and good protection. MAN completed the first production models in September 1942. The early versions suffered from mechanical problems, particularly at the Battle of Kursk in July 1943, borne from a lack of proper testing. However, once the problems were ironed out, the Panther saw action in all theatres and proved to be very effective. Over 4500 were built up to early 1945, and they continued to see service with the French Army in the immediate post-war period.

Country of origin:	Germany
Crew:	4
Weight:	45,500kg (100,100lb)
Dimensions:	length 8.86m (29ft 0.75in); width 3.43m (11ft 3in); height 3.10m (10ft 2in)
Range:	177km (110miles)
Armour:	30-110mm (1.2-4.3in)
Armament:	one 75mm gun; three 7.92mm MG34 machine guns (one coaxial, one anti-aircraft, one on hull front)
Powerplant:	one Maybach HL 230 12-cylinder diesel developing 700hp (522kW)
Performance:	maximum road speed 46km/h (29mph); fording 1.70m (5ft 7in); vertical obstacle 0.91m (3ft 0in); trench 1.91m (6ft 3in)

Panzer VI Tiger

The Tiger heavy tank was produced by Henschel based on a 1941 design and entered production in August 1942. A total of 1350 were built before production ceased in August 1944 and the type was replaced by the King Tiger. There were three main variants: a command tank, a recovery vehicle fitted with a winch and the Sturmtiger, which was fitted with a rocket launcher. The Tiger was an excellent tank, but complicated and therefore difficult to produce in large numbers and maintain. The overlapping wheel suspension had a tendency to clog with mud and stones which, if it froze in cold conditions such as during the Russian winter, could immobilise the vehicle. It first saw action against the British in Tunisia in 1942 and thereafter appeared on all fronts.

Country of origin:	Germany
Crew:	5
Weight:	55,000kg (121,000lb)
Dimensions:	length 8.24m (27ft); width 3.73m (12ft 3in); height 2.86m (9ft 3.25in)
Range:	100km (62miles)
Armour:	25-100mm (1-3.94in)
Armament:	one 88mm KwK 36 gun; one 7.92 coaxial MG 34 machine gun
Powerplant:	one Maybach HL 230 P45 12-cylinder petrol engine developing 700hp (522kW)
Performance:	maximum road speed 38km/h (24mph); fording 1.20m (3ft 11in); vertical obstacle 0.79m (2ft 7in); trench 1.8m (5ft 11in)

Panzer VI Tiger II

The Henschel design for the Tiger II (King Tiger) was completed in October 1943. Early production models carried a turret designed by Porsche, but after the first 50 models had been built, the tanks were wholly produced by Henschel. The tank was similar to the Panther and used the same engine, although its heavier armour, impenetrable to most Allied weapons, resulted in a lower power-to-weight ratio and consequent loss of speed and mobility. The main problem with the Tiger II was unreliability. Many were abandoned by their crews when they broke down or ran out of fuel, as their bulk made them difficult to move or conceal. The Tiger II first saw combat on the Eastern Front in May 1944 and in the battles in Normandy in the autumn of that year.

Country of origin:	Germany
Crew:	5
Weight:	69,700kg (153,340lb)
Dimensions:	length 10.26m (33ft 8in); width 3.75m (12ft 3.5in); height 3.09m (10ft 1.5in)
Range:	110km (68miles)
Armour:	100-150mm (3.94-5.9in)
Armament:	one 88mm KwK 43 gun; two 7.92 MG34 machine guns (one coaxial, one on hull front)
Powerplant:	one Maybach HL 230 P30 12-cylinder petrol developing 700hp (522kW)
Performance:	maximum road speed 38km/h (24mph); fording 1.60m (5ft 3in); vertical obstacle 0.85m (2ft 10in); trench 2.5m (8ft 2in)

Fiat L6/40 Light Tank

The Fiat L6/40 arose from a 1930s design based on the British Carden-Loyd Mark VI tankette. Intended primarily for export, the first production models arrived in 1939 and a total of 283 were built. At the time of its introduction, the L6/40 was roughly equivalent to the German PzKpfw II, but was never really suitable for frontline service. However, it saw service with reconnaissance and cavalry units in Italy, North Africa and Russia. Variants included a flame-thrower version and a command tank, the latter having extra communications equipment and an open-topped turret. In addition, a number of L6/40s were converted into Semovente L40 self-propelled anti-tank guns. Like most Italian tanks in World War II, it was hopelessly outclassed when it came up against Allied armour.

Country of origin:	Italy
Crew:	2
Weight:	6800kg (14,960lb)
Dimensions:	length 3.78m (12ft 5in); width 1.92m (6ft 4in); height 2.03m (6ft 8in)
Range:	200km (124miles)
Armour:	6-40mm (0.23-1.57in)
Armament:	one Breda Model 35 20mm cannon; one coaxial Breda Model 38 8mm machine gun
Powerplant:	one SPA 18D four-cylinder petrol engine developing 70hp (52kW)
Performance:	maximum road speed 42km/h (26mph); fording 0.8m (2ft 8in); vertical obstacle 0.7m (2ft 4in); trench 1.7m (5ft 7in)

Fiat M 13/40 Medium Tank

The M 13/40 was based on an earlier design, the M 11/39, which was not produced in numbers as it was considered already obsolete by the time of its introduction. The M 13/40 used the same chassis but had a redesigned hull with better armour. Nearly 800 were produced in total and the tank was widely used in North Africa during Italian attempts to drive British and Commonwealth forces out of the region. In combat the M 13/40's shortcomings became very apparent: it was cramped, unreliable and caught fire easily when hit by anti-tank rounds. Many abandoned and captured M 13/40s were pressed into service by the British and Australian forces and used to fill a serious shortage of Allied tanks in early 1941. They did not remain in Allied service for long.

Country of origin:	Italy
Crew:	4
Weight:	14,000kg (30,800lb)
Dimensions:	length 4.92m (16ft 2in); width 2.2m (7ft 3in); height 2.38m (7ft 10in)
Range:	200km (125miles)
Armour:	6-42mm (0.24-1.65in)
Armament:	one 47mm gun; two Modello 38 8mm machine guns (one coaxial, one anti-aircraft)
Powerplant:	one SPA TM40 eight-cylinder diesel engine developing 125hp (93kW)
Performance:	maximum road speed 32km/h (20mph); fording 1.0m (3ft 3in); vertical obstacle 0.8m (2ft 8in); trench 2.1m (6ft 11in)

Type 95 Light Tank

The Type 95, known as the KE-GO, was developed in the early 1930s to meet the requirements of the Japanese Army at that time. When production ceased in 1943, over 1100 had been built. The major drawback of the vehicle was that the commander had to operate the gun in addition to his normal duties, which impeded combat effectiveness. While this was acceptable when faced with infantry in Manchuria, it proved disastrous when up against American armour in the later years of the war. Despite later upgunning, the tank's poor armour and lack of firepower ensured that it was wholly inadequate. The Type 95 also served as the basis for the Type 2 KA-MI amphibious tank which was widely used in the early Pacific campaigns of World War II.

Country of origin:	Japan
Crew:	4
Weight:	7400kg (16,280lb)
Dimensions:	length 4.38m (14ft 4in); width 2.057m (6ft 9in); height 2.184m (7ft 2in)
Range:	250km (156miles)
Armour:	6-14mm (0.25-0.6in)
Armament:	one 37mm gun; two 7.7mm machine guns
Powerplant:	one Mitsubishi NVD 6120 six-cylinder air-cooled diesel engine developing 120hp (89kW)
Performance:	maximum road speed 45km/h (28mph); fording 1.0m (3ft 3in); vertical obstacle 0.812m (2ft 8in); trench 2.0m (6ft 7in)

Light Tank M3

Having followed the battles of 1940 on the European mainland closely, the American military realised that its main light tank, the M2, was obsolete, and that a more heavily armoured version was required. The result was the M3 which entered full-scale production in 1941, and nearly 6000 were built. Many were passed to the Soviet Red Army and to British forces where they were known as Stuarts. Their reliability and mobility were impressive and they were popular with crews, being used in all theatres of the war. Obsolete as a combat tank by 1944, many were converted to command and reconnaissance vehicles with the turrets removed and extra machine guns added instead. Variants included mine-clearing, flame-throwing and anti-aircraft versions.

Country of origin:	USA
Crew:	4
Weight:	12,927kg (28,440lb)
Dimensions:	length 4.54m (14ft 10.75in); width 2.24m (7ft 4in); height 2.30m (7ft 6.5in)
Range:	112.6km (70 miles)
Armour:	15-43mm (0.59-1.69in)
Armament:	one 37mm gun; two 7.7mm machine guns
Powerplant:	one Continental W-970-9A six-cylinder radial petrol engine developing 250hp (186.5kW)
Performance:	maximum road speed 58km/h (36mph); fording 0.91m (3ft 0in); vertical obstacle 0.61m (2ft); trench 1.83m (6ft 0in)

Light Tank M24 Chaffee

By 1942 it was evident that the 37mm gun was inadequate for the needs of America's light tanks, and indeed as a main armament of any tank. Attempts to install larger weapons in M5 tanks failed and so a new tank was designed by Cadillac, the first being ready by late 1943. Known as the Chaffee, the M24 entered full service with the US Army in late 1944, too late in the war to make a big impression. It was in Korea that the M24 realised its full combat value, with the agility for reconnaissance, but well-armed for battle. Its biggest contribution was in its concept. It was designed to be part of a combat family of vehicles, all using the same chassis, including self-propelled guns and anti-aircraft tanks. The tank continues to see service with some nations to this day.

Country of origin:	USA
Crew:	5
Weight:	18,370kg (40,414lb)
Dimensions:	length 5.49m (18ft); width 2.95m (9ft 8in); height 2.48m (8ft 1.5in)
Range:	161km (100 miles)
Armour:	12-38mm (0.47-1.5in)
Armament:	one 75mm gun; two 7.62mm machine guns; one 12.7mm gun on turret; one 51mm smoke mortar
Powerplant:	two Cadillac Model 44T24 V-8 petrol engines developing 110hp (82kW) each
Performance:	maximum road speed 56km/h (35mph); fording 1.02m (3ft 4in); vertical obstacle 0.91m (3ft); trench 2.44m (8ft)

Medium Tank M3

The M3 was developed by the Americans following the realisation, based on observation of the armoured battles in France in 1940, that a more powerful armament would be required than that mounted on the M2 in development at the time. The M3 was shipped to British forces with minor modifications and was known as the General Grant. The Grant proved highly effective against the *Afrika Korps* in North Africa in its first actions in May 1942, and was popular with the tank crews of hard-pressed British forces. The original version retained by US forces was known as the General Lee. Reliable and hard-wearing, its only drawback was the limited traverse of the hull-mounted main gun. The M3 saw action on all fronts and was widely exported after the war.

Country of origin:	USA
Crew:	6
Weight:	27,240kg (59,928lb)
Dimensions:	length 5.64m (18ft 6in); width 2.72m (8ft 11in); height 3.12m (10ft 3in)
Range:	193km (120 miles)
Armour:	12-38mm (0.47-1.5in)
Armament:	one 75mm hull-mounted gun; one 35mm gun on turret; four 7.62mm machine guns
Powerplant:	one Continental R-975-EC2 radial petrol engine developing 340hp (253.5kW)
Performance:	maximum road speed 42km/h (26mph); fording 1.02m (3ft 4in); vertical obstacle 0.61m (2ft); trench 1.91m (6ft 3in)

Medium Tank M4A2

The M4 Sherman used the same basic hull and suspension as the M3, but mounted the main armament on the gun turret rather than the hull. Easy to build and an excellent fighting platform, it proved to be a war-winner for the Allies. By the time production ceased in 1945, over 40,000 had been built. There were many variants, including engineer tanks, assault tanks, rocket launchers, recovery vehicles and mine-clearers. The British employed the Sherman extensively, notably at El Alamein in 1942. Though outgunned by German tanks and with insufficient armour to compete in the later stages of the war, the sheer numbers produced overwhelmed enemy armoured forces. Its hardiness kept it in service with some South American countries until very recently.

Country of origin:	USA
Crew:	5
Weight:	31,360kg (69,000lb)
Dimensions:	length 5.9m (19ft 4in); width 2.6m (8ft 7in); height 2.74m (9ft)
Range:	161km (100 miles)
Armour:	15-76mm (0.59-2.99in)
Armament:	one 75mm gun; one coaxial 7.62mm machine gun; 12.7mm anti-aircraft gun on turret
Powerplant:	twin General Motors 6-71 diesel engines developing 500hp (373kW)
Performance:	maximum road speed 46.4km/h (29mph); fording 0.9m (3ft); vertical obstacle 0.61m (2ft); trench 2.26m (7ft 5in)

Medium Tank M4A3

The M4A3 was one of the most developed of all the Sherman variants used during World War II. It differed from the M4A2 mainly in the design of its turret and suspension (using a more effective horizontal volute spring system) and in its armament, employing the larger and more powerful 76mm gun as well as having thicker armour. This particular model was the production type most favoured by the US Army. Ford built 1690 A3s between June 1942 and September 1943, before ceasing tank production. Manufacture was then taken over by Grand Blanc from February 1944. Improved features included a vision cupola for the commander, a loader's hatch and so-called 'wet stowage' for the ammunition. In addition, its petrol engine was specifically developed for the vehicle.

Country of origin:	USA
Crew:	5
Weight:	32,284kg (71,024lb)
Dimensions:	length, with gun 7.52m (24ft 8in), and over hull 6.27m (20ft 7in); width 2.68m (8ft 9.5in); height 3.43m (11ft 2.875in)
Range:	161km (100 miles)
Armour:	15-100mm (0.59-3.94in)
Armament:	one 76mm gun; one 7.62mm coaxial machine gun
Powerplant:	one Ford GAA V-8 petrol engine developing 400 or 500hp (335.6 or 373kW)
Performance:	maximum road speed 47km/h (29mph); fording 0.91m (3ft); vertical obstacle 0.61m (2ft); trench 2.26m (7ft 5in)

T-70 Light Tank

The Soviet military had spent a great deal of time and effort in the development of a series of light tanks during the 1930s. The T-70 was the culmination of this effort at the time of the German invasion of Russia in June 1941. Reasonably armoured, the T-70's armament was of limited use against heavier tanks, especially as the commander of the tank had to operate the gun single-handed, thus reducing his combat effectiveness. Its service record was unremarkable, mainly being used for reconnaissance and close infantry support. Over 8000 were produced up to 1943, but despite the numbers, the T-70 was at best only an adequate combat tank. It was certainly better than the tank it superseded, the T-60, but was outgunned by the German panzers in 1941-42.

Country of origin:	USSR
Crew:	2
Weight:	9367kg (20,608lb)
Dimensions:	length 4.29m (14ft 0.9in); width 2.32m (7ft 7.3in); height 2.04m (6ft 8.3in)
Range:	360km (223.7 miles)
Armour:	10-60mm (0.39-2.36in)
Armament:	one 45mm gun; one 7.62mm machine gun
Powerplant:	two GAZ-202 petrol engines delivering a total of 140hp (104kW)
Performance:	maximum road speed 45km/h (28mph); fording not known; vertical obstacle 0.70m (2ft 3.6in); trench 3.12m (10ft 2.8in)

T-28 Medium Tank

Inspired by British and German tank designs, the T-28 medium tank had a centrally mounted main turret and two auxiliary machine-gun turrets in front. The vehicle's suspension was directly copied from the British Vickers vehicle, and though the prototype was armed with a 45mm main gun, production models were equipped with the more powerful 76.2mm low-velocity gun. There were a number of different models and variants, some of which were produced as a result of combat experience. The T-28C, for example, was given additional armour on the hull front and turret as a result of the Red Army's unhappy time in the Russo-Finnish War. An interesting variant was the T-28(V), a commander's tank fitted with a radio which had a frame aerial round the turret.

Country of origin:	USSR
Crew:	6
Weight:	28,509kg (62,720lb)
Dimensions:	length 7.44m (24ft 4.8in); width 2.81m (9ft 2.75in); height 2.82m (9ft 3in)
Range:	220km (136.7 miles)
Armour:	10-80mm (0.39-3.15in)
Armament:	one 76.2mm gun; three 7.62mm machine guns
Powerplant:	one M-17 V-12 petrol engine developing 500hp (373kW)
Performance:	maximum road speed 37km/h (23mph); fording not known; vertical obstacle 1.04m (3ft 5in); trench 2.90m (9ft 6in)

T-34/76A Medium Tank

The T-34 was an advanced tank for its era, produced in vast numbers to an excellent design, a design borne from two decades of Soviet experimentation and a readiness to embrace the best of foreign ideas. Mass production began in 1940 and its powerful gun and thick armour came as a nasty surprise to the Germans in 1941-42. Finesse was sacrificed for speed of production, but their rough and ready appearance belied their effectiveness. The T-34 was used in every role from recovery vehicle to personnel carrier and reconnaissance, and distinguished itself at every turn forcing the Germans back on the defensive. It is no exaggeration to say that the T-34 was the most decisive tank of World War II. The upgunned T-34/85 tank introduced in 1944 is still in use with many armies today.

Country of origin:	USSR
Crew:	4
Weight:	26,000kg (57,200lb)
Dimensions:	length 5.92m (19ft 5.1in); width 3.0m (9ft 10in); height 2.44m (8ft)
Range:	186km (115 miles)
Armour:	18-60mm (0.71-2.36in)
Armament:	one 76.2mm gun; two 7.62mm machine guns
Powerplant:	one V-2-34 V-12 diesel engine developing 500hp (373kW)
Performance:	maximum road speed 55km/h (34mph); fording 1.37m (4ft 6in); vertical obstacle 0.71m (2ft 4in); trench 2.95m (9ft 8in)

KV-1 Heavy Tank

Design on the KV-1 began in 1938, with the intention that it should be the successor to the T-35 heavy tank. The first models were field-tested during the Red Army's disastrous 1940 campaign in Finland. Nevertheless, the KV-1 set the standard for Soviet tank design for several years to come and proved to be a formidable vehicle, being used as an assault tank or to spearhead breakthroughs. However, the tank was not particularly mobile and suffered from automotive problems. In addition, it was uparmoured progressively without any increase in power being allotted, which resulted in poor power-to-weight ratio and performance. The importance of the KV-1 is that it paved the way for later generations of Russian heavy tanks, such as the Josef Stalin.

Country of origin:	USSR
Crew:	5
Weight:	43,000kg (94,600lb)
Dimensions:	length 6.68m (21ft 11in); width 3.32m (10ft 10.7in); height 2.71m (8ft 10.7in)
Range:	150km (93.2 miles)
Armour:	100mm (3.94in)
Armament:	one 76.2mm gun; four 7.62mm machine guns
Powerplant:	one V-2K V-12 diesel engine developing 600hp (448kW)
Performance:	maximum (rarely achieved) road speed 35km/h (21.75mph); fording not known; vertical obstacle 1.20m (3ft 8in); trench 2.59m (8ft 6in)

IS-2 Heavy Tank

The IS-2 (Josef Stalin) was a development of the earlier KV series of Russian tanks. It was a lighter tank than the KVs with improved transmission and suspension and a redesigned hull and turret. The first examples appeared in 1944, helping to exploit the strategic initiative which the Red Army had achieved by that stage of World War II on the Eastern Front. A massive vehicle, the tank was well-armed and armoured, the only drawback of the early versions was a slow rate of fire using separate charges and shells. This was remedied by the time the IS-3 entered production. Symbolically, Josef Stalin tanks were at the head of the advance to Berlin in 1945 and remained in production after the war being the world's most powerful tank for well over a decade.

Country of origin:	USSR
Crew:	4
Weight:	46,000kg (101,200lb)
Dimensions:	length 9.9m (32ft 5.8in); width 3.09m (10ft 1.6in); height 2.73m (8ft 11.5in)
Range:	240km (149 miles)
Armour:	132mm (5.2in)
Armament:	one 122mm gun; one 12.7mm machine gun; one 7.62mm machine gun
Powerplant:	one V-2-IS (V-2K) V-12 diesel developing 600hp (447kW)
Performance:	maximum road speed 37km/h (23mph); fording not known; vertical obstacle 1.0m (3ft 3in); trench 2.49m (8ft 2in)

Hotchkiss H-39 Light Tank

The Hotchkiss H-39 first appeared in 1939, intended for use by French cavalry formations. Despite production problems common to all French tanks in the period before World War II, about 1000 were built. The tank gave a good account of itself in combat during the German invasion of France in 1940, but had too little firepower to compete with enemy armour. In addition, French tactics at the time envisaged tanks being used as infantry support rather than in mass formations, diminishing its effectiveness. After the surrender, the Germans employed the H-39 for occupation duties. Some saw action with the Free French and Vichy French forces in the Middle East, where they were later used by the Israelis, remaining in service until 1956.

Country of origin:	France
Crew:	2
Weight:	12,100kg (26,620lb)
Dimensions:	length 4.22m (13ft 10in); width 1.95m (6ft 4.8in); height 2.15m (7ft 0.6in)
Range:	120km (74.5 miles)
Armour:	40mm (1.57in)
Armament:	one 37mm gun; one coaxial 7.5mm machine gun
Powerplant:	one Hotchkiss six-cylinder petrol engine developing 120hp (89.5kW)
Performance:	maximum road speed 36km/h (22.3mph); fording 0.85m (2ft 10in); vertical obstacle 0.50m (1ft 8in); trench 1.80m (5ft 11in)

Renault R-35 Light Tank

The Renault R-35 was designed in the mid-1930s to replace the ageing World War I-vintage Renault FT 17. By 1940, some 1600 had been built and it was the most numerous French tank in service, even though it never managed to fulfil its role as the FT 17's replacement. An adequate vehicle, it was no match for German panzers, particularly as it was deployed piecemeal against their massed formations. The gun was unable to penetrate even light German armour and many were abandoned during the French retreat in May 1940. The Germans used the R-35 as a garrison and training tank and adapted many for use as artillery tractors, ammunition carriers and self-propelled artillery carriages. For the latter, the turrets were removed and used for coastal defences.

Country of origin:	France
Crew:	2
Weight:	10,000kg (22,046lb)
Dimensions:	length 4.20m (13ft 9.25in); width 1.85m (6ft 0.75in); height 2.37m (7ft 9.25in)
Range:	140km (87 miles)
Armour:	40mm (1.57in)
Armament:	one 37mm gun; one coaxial 7.5mm machine gun
Powerplant:	one Renault four-cylinder petrol engine developing 82hp (61kW)
Performance:	maximum road speed 20km/h (12.4mph); fording 0.80m (2ft 7in); vertical obstacle 0.50m (1ft 7.7in); trench 1.60m (5ft 3in)

SOMUA S-35 Medium Tank

The SOMUA S-35 was one of the first tanks used to mechanise the French cavalry in the mid-1930s. It was a very advanced vehicle for its time and many of its features were to become standard for future tank designs, such as cast, rather than rivetted, armour. A radio was fitted as standard and the tank was supplied with a sufficiently powerful main armament to be still in service in German hands on D-Day in June 1944. Production was slow and there were only around 250 in frontline service by the time the Germans invaded in 1940. The major drawback was that the commander was required to operate the gun and the radio as well as his normal duties. Despite this reduced effectiveness, the S-35 was still the best Allied tank in service in 1940 (which says a lot about Allied armoured strength).

Country of origin:	France
Crew:	3
Weight:	19,500kg (42,900lb)
Dimensions:	length 5.38m (17ft 7.8in); width 2.12m (6ft 11.5in); height 2.62m (8ft 7in)
Range:	230km (143 miles)
Armour:	20-55mm (0.8-2.2in)
Armament:	one 47mm gun; one coaxial 7.5mm machine gun
Powerplant:	one SOMUA V-8 petrol engine developing 190hp (141.7kW)
Performance:	maximum road speed 40km/h (24.85mph); fording 1.0m (3ft 3in); vertical obstacle 0.76m (2ft 6in); trench 2.13m (7ft)

Char B1 Heavy Tank

The first B1s appeared in 1937. Despite its appearance, which was reminiscent of World War I tanks, the Char B1 was a powerful tank for the time and carried a range of advanced design features such as self-sealing fuel tanks. The crew were seated some way from each other, however, which made internal communication difficult. These crews needed to be highly trained to operate the B1 to full advantage, and such crews were rare in 1940. In addition, the tank's complexities made maintenance difficult and many broke down in combat. Those that entered the fray were really too cumbersome for their powerful armament to have much effect. The Germans later employed captured Char B1s as training tanks or self-propelled artillery carriages.

Country of origin:	France
Crew:	4
Weight:	31,500kg (69,300lb)
Dimensions:	length 6.37m (20ft 10.8in); width 2.50m (8ft 2.4in); height 2.79m (9ft 1.8in)
Range:	180km (112 miles)
Armour:	14-65mm (0.6-2.6in)
Armament:	one 75mm gun; one 45mm gun
Powerplant:	one Renault six-cylinder petrol engine developing 307hp (229kW)
Performance:	maximum road speed 28km/h (17.4mph); fording not known; vertical obstacle 0.93m (3ft 1in); trench 2.74m (9ft)

Vickers Light Tank

Originally based on the Carden-Loyd tankette of the 1920s, the Vickers light tanks were developed in the 1930s. Mobile and fast across country, the Vickers was widely used in the 1930s for policing the British Empire and in the early years of World War II. However, World War II combat experience proved them to be virtually useless. Their thin armour was easily pierced and their machine-gun armament was utterly inadequate on the battlefield. Lack of equipment forced the British to use them in combat rather than for reconnaissance, as they were designed to be used, and the consequences were disastrous. Attempts to convert them into anti-aircraft tanks failed, although the Germans managed to employ some captured vehicles as anti-tank gun carriers.

Country of origin:	UK
Crew:	3
Weight:	4877kg (10,729lb)
Dimensions:	length 3.96m (13ft); width 2.08m (6ft 10in); height 2.235m (7ft 6in)
Range:	range 201km (215 miles)
Armour:	10-15mm (0.4-0.6in)
Armament:	one 7.7mm/12.7mm machine gun
Powerplant:	one Meadows ESTL six-cylinder petrol engine developing 88hp (66kW)
Performance:	maximum road speed 51.5km/h (32mph); fording 0.6m (2ft); vertical obstacle – ; trench –

Light Tank Mk VII Tetrarch

When the prototype of the Tetrarch, known at the time as the Purdah, appeared in 1938, it was received without enthusiasm as it had no outstanding attributes. Like other light tanks, it fared badly in combat in the early years of the war, being poorly armed and armoured and lacking a specified purpose. It was withdrawn quickly, although some were passed on to the Soviet Union (where it was greeted with a similar lack of enthusiasm). However, it was given new life as an airborne tank and the Hamilcar glider was specifically designed to carry it. Fitted with a more powerful armament, the tank landed with British airborne forces on D-Day, but proved no match for enemy armour and its role was later assumed by the American M22 Locust.

Country of origin:	UK
Crew:	3
Weight:	7620kg (16,764lb)
Dimensions:	length overall 4.305m (14ft 1.5in); length of hull 4.115m (13ft 6in); width 2.31m (7ft 7in); height 2.121m (6ft 11.5in)
Range:	224km (140 miles)
Armour:	4-16mm (0.16-0.63in)
Armament:	one 2-pounder gun; one coaxial 7.92mm machine gun
Powerplant:	one Meadows 12-cylinder petrol engine developing 165hp (123kW)
Performance:	maximum road speed 64km/h (40mph); maximum cross-country speed 45km/h (28mph); fording 0.914m (3ft 0in); trench 1.524m (5ft)

Cruiser Tank Mk VI Crusader

The Crusader's attractive design belied the fact that by the time it first appeared in 1941 it was already outdated. Fast and mobile (their suspension was so tough that theoretical maximum speed was often exceeded), they were thinly armoured and lacked firepower, being no match for their German counterparts. Reliability was also a problem. Even with gradual improvements, the Crusader failed to prove itself in the North African campaigns and was replaced as quickly as possible by the M4 Sherman. Once withdrawn from frontline combat duties, the Crusader was adapted for a variety of roles, such as anti-aircraft tank, recovery vehicle and combat engineer tank with a dozer blade. Many saw service in the last years of the war as artillery tractors, pulling the 17-pounder gun.

Country of origin:	UK
Crew:	3
Weight:	20,067kg (44,147lb)
Dimensions:	length 5.994m (19ft 8in); width 2.64m (8ft 8in); height 2.235m (7ft 4in)
Range:	204km (127 miles)
Armour:	40mm (1.57in)
Armament:	one 2-pounder gun; one coaxial 7.62mm machine gun
Powerplant:	one Nuffield Liberty Mk III petrol engine developing 340hp (254kW)
Performance:	maximum road speed 43.4km/h (27mph); maximum cross-country speed 24km/h (15mph); fording 0.99m (3ft 3in); vertical obstacle 0.686m (2ft 3in); trench 2.59 (8ft 6in)

Cruiser Tank Mk VIII Cromwell

The Cromwell was produced in response to a requirement for a more heavily armed and armoured tank to replace the Crusader. The first Cromwells appeared in 1943 armed with a 6-pounder gun. However, it was realised that this would be inadequate and the tanks were soon being equipped with heavier weaponry, which gave some parity with contemporary German tanks. That said, most units were equipped with the M4 Sherman, but the Cromwell gave valuable service as a training tank in the run-up to D-Day and was used for many other roles, such as mobile observation posts and armoured recovery vehicles. Although not quite equal to German tanks, the Cromwell was at least better than previous British efforts and fared reasonably well in combat.

Country of origin:	UK
Crew:	5
Weight:	27,942kg (61,472lb)
Dimensions:	length 6.42m (21ft 0.75in); width 3.048m (10ft); height 2.51m (8ft 3in)
Range:	278km (173 miles)
Armour:	8-76mm (0.3-3in)
Armament:	one 75mm gun; one coaxial 7.62mm machine gun
Powerplant:	one Rolls-Royce Meteor V-12 petrol engine developing 570hp (425kW)
Performance:	maximum speed 61km/h (38mph); fording 1.219m (4ft); vertical obstacle 0.914m (3ft); trench 2.286 (7ft 6in)

Infantry Tank Matilda

The Mk I Matilda was developed in response to a 1934 requirement for an infantry tank. Well armoured for its day, it was a small, simple tank. However, despite being sturdy enough to withstand hits from most German tank guns in the early stages of World War II, it was too poorly armed to be of much use as the war progressed. The Mk II had improved armament and this helped the Matilda to fare reasonably well in combat, particularly in North Africa where it was widely used in the run-up to El Alamein in 1942. Following its replacement in frontline service, the Matilda was used for a variety of specialised roles, such as mine-clearing (the Baron); as a flame-thrower tank (the Frog); and as the basis of a Canal Defence Light for illuminating night operations.

Country of origin:	UK
Crew:	4
Weight:	26,926kg (59,237lb)
Dimensions:	length 5.613m (18ft 5in); width 2.59m (8ft 6in); height 2.51m (8ft 3in)
Range:	257km (160 miles)
Armour:	20-78mm (0.8-3.1in)
Armament:	one 2-pounder gun; one 7.92mm Besa machine gun
Powerplant:	two Leyland six-cylinder petrol engines each developing 95hp (71kW) or two AEC diesels each developing 87hp (65kW)
Performance:	maximum speed 24km/h (15mph); maximum cross-country speed 12.9km/h (8mph); fording 0.914m (3ft 0in); vertical obstacle 0.609m (2ft); trench 2.133 (7ft)

Infantry Tank Mk III Valentine

In 1938 Vickers was asked to produce an infantry tank based upon their A10 Cruiser tank. There were initial doubts about the new Valentine's two-man turret, which would limit the possibility of increased armament at a later date, but as war was imminent necessity overcame this caution. Mass production began in 1940 and the Valentine soon proved to be a sturdy, reliable vehicle, if a little slow. Armament was gradually improved as the war progressed, and the Valentine saw service in all theatres. Variants included a mobile bridge, a flame-thrower tank, a mine-clearing tank and a self-propelled gun. Over 8000 Valentines were built before production ceased in 1944, thus making the Valentine one of the most important British tanks in numbers if nothing else.

Country of origin:	UK
Crew:	3
Weight:	17,690kg (38,918lb)
Dimensions:	length 5.41m (17ft 9in); width 2.629m (8ft 7.5in); height 2.273m (7ft 5.5in)
Range:	145km (90 miles)
Armour:	8-65mm (0.3-2.6in)
Armament:	one 2-pounder gun; one 7.62mm machine gun
Powerplant:	one AEC diesel developing 131hp (98kW) in Mk III or GMC diesel developing 138hp (103kW) in Mk IV
Performance:	maximum speed 24km/h (15mph); fording 0.914m (3ft); vertical obstacle 0.838m (2ft 9in); trench 2.286 (7ft 6in)

Infantry Tank Mk IV Churchill

The Churchill began life as a 1939 requirement which envisaged a return to trench-warfare, and was thus slow and heavily armoured. The final prototype, however, was a much lighter vehicle than had first been thought of, not unlike a World War I tank in appearance. Rushed into production at a time when invasion seemed imminent, it suffered early reliability problems and was not fully introduced until 1943. Early combat experience during the Dieppe raid in 1942 was disappointing, but the Cromwell proved mobile over rough terrain in North Africa. The tank excelled in its specialised variants, such as the AVRE, the Crocodile flame-thrower tank, the bridgelayer and many more. The tank gave excellent service and the final Churchill was not retired until the 1960s.

Country of origin:	UK
Crew:	5
Weight:	40,642kg (89,412lb)
Dimensions:	length 7.442m (24ft 5in); width 2.438m (8ft); height 3.454m (11ft 4in)
Range:	144.8km (90 miles)
Armour:	16–102mm (0.6–4in)
Armament:	one 6-pounder gun; one coaxial 7.62mm machine gun
Powerplant:	one Bedford twin-six petrol engine developing 350hp (261kW)
Performance:	maximum speed 20km/h (12.5mph); maximum cross-country speed about 12.8km/h (8mph); fording 1.016m (3ft 4in); vertical obstacle 0.76m (2ft 6in); trench 3.048m (10ft)

Tanks

Cruiser Tank Ram Mk I

A t the start of World War II, Canada had no tank units. With no possibility of obtaining tanks from a desperate Britain, the Canadians were forced to build their own. The decision was taken to use the basic components of the American M3, but swap the sponson-mounted main gun for a turret mounting the readily available 40mm gun, with the option of upgunning later. Production began at the end of 1941, but the tank never saw action as by the time it arrived in Europe, the M4 Sherman was being produced in numbers and it was decided to adopt this as the standard for Canadian units. Many Rams had their turrets removed and were used as armoured personnel carriers. The Ram's greatest contribution to the Allied victory was as the basis for the Sexton self-propelled gun.

Country of origin:	Canada
Crew:	5
Weight:	29,484kg (64,864lb)
Dimensions:	length 5.79m (19ft); width 2.895m (9ft 6in); height 2.667m (8ft 9in)
Range:	232km (144 miles)
Armour:	25-89mm (1-3.5in)
Armament:	one 2-pounder gun; two coaxial 7.62mm machine guns
Powerplant:	one Continental R-975 radial petrol engine developing 400hp (298kW)
Performance:	maximum road speed 40.2km/h (25mph); vertical obstacle 0.61m (2ft); trench 2.26m (7ft 5in)

Sherman Crab Mine-Clearing Flail

Invented by a South African, the concept of using flails to clear mines was developed in the UK culminating in the development of the Crab, usually fitted to Sherman tanks. Some 43 chains were mounted on a revolving drum powered by the main tank engine. Further developments included the addition of barbed wire-cutting disks and a contour-following device to allow the flails to operate effectively over rough ground. The Crab carried the standard Sherman armament and could thus be used in a combat role if the need arose. The drive for the rotor was taken by roller chain from the tank propeller shaft, through an aperture in the hull off-side armour, to a carden shaft. The drive from this shaft was taken by another carden shaft to a spiral bevel double reduction gear on the off-side end of the rotor.

Country of origin:	UK
Crew:	5
Weight:	31,818kg (70,000lb)
Dimensions:	length 8.23m (27ft); width 3.5m (11ft 6in); height 2.7m (9ft)
Range:	62km (100 miles)
Armour:	15-76mm (0.59-2.99in)
Armament:	one 75mm gun; one 7.62mm machine gun
Powerplant:	one Ford GAA V-8 petrol engine developing 500hp (373kW)
Performance:	maximum road speed 46km/h (28.75mph); fording 0.9m (3ft); vertical obstacle 0.6m (2ft); trench 2.26m (7ft 5in)

Churchill AVRE

The Churchill Assault Vehicle Royal Engineers (AVRE) was borne out of the failure of the 1942 Dieppe raid where engineers were prevented from clearing obstacles by enemy fire. The tank was developed to transport engineers to the required spot and give protection, as well as carrying a heavy demolition weapon (special fittings were placed on the sides at the front for attaching devices). With a stripped interior to give extra storage space and a mortar capable of firing a heavy demolition charge, they performed excellently during their first action, clearing the way for the Normandy landings on D-Day (6 June 1944). They remained in service with the British Army until the 1960s but the concept was so successful that AVREs are still used, the current model being the Centurion AVRE.

Country of origin:	UK
Crew:	6
Weight:	38,000kg (83,600lb)
Dimensions:	length 7.67m (25ft 2in); width 3.25m (10ft 8in); height 2.79m (9ft 2in)
Range:	193km (120 miles)
Armour:	16-102mm (0.6-4in)
Armament:	one Petard 290mm spigot mortar; one 7.92mm Besa machine-gun
Powerplant:	one Bedford Twin-Six petrol engine developing 350hp (261kW)
Performance:	maximum road speed 24.9km/h (15.5mph); fording 1.016m (3ft 4in); vertical obstacle 0.76m (2ft 6in); trench 3.048m (10ft)

Canal Defence Light

The basic idea behind the the Canal Defence Light (a name chosen to preserve secrecy) was to replace the turret of a tank with a powerful searchlight to illuminate battlefields at night. The idea was first mooted in the mid-1930s, and by late 1939 a turret was ready for production. Initially attached to Matilda II tanks and then Grants, some 300 turrets were ordered. Two British brigades were equipped, one in the UK and one in North Africa. The light was positioned behind a shutter which was opened and closed to provide a flickering impression. Somehow, the opportunity to use the CDL never arose and they were confined to providing light for night river crossings and the like. This was probably just as well, for similar Russian experiments proved disastrous in battle.

Country of origin:	UK
Crew:	3 or 4
Weight:	26,000kg (57,200lb)
Dimensions:	length 5.61m (18ft 5in); width 2.59m (8ft 6in); height 2.51m (8ft 3in)
Range:	257km (160 miles)
Armour:	12-38mm (0.47-1.5in)
Armament:	one 7.92mm Besa machine gun
Powerplant:	two Leyland E148/E149 diesel engines each developing 95hp (70.8kW)
Performance:	maximum road speed 24km/h (15mph); fording 1.02m (3ft 4in); vertical obstacle 0.61m (2ft); trench 1.91m (6ft 3in)

ARK

The British Army produced its first bridging tank at the end of World War I and experimented throughout the inter-war period, seeing the need to have vehicles to facilitate the crossing of obstacles. The first Armoured Ramp Carrier, the ARK Mk I, appeared in 1943. This was a converted Churchill tank with the turret removed and a blanking plate welded over the aperture and timbered trackways across the top. The ARK could be driven into ditches or against obstacles and when the two folding ramps were lowered it could be used as a bridge for other vehicles. Variants included the Churchill Woodlark, which used rockets to open up the ramps and put them into position, and the Churchill Great Eastern which used a raised ramp system, but neither was very successful.

Country of origin:	UK
Crew:	4
Weight:	38,385kg (84,450lb)
Dimensions:	length 7.442m (24ft 5in); width 2.43m (8ft); height 2.13m (7ft)
Range:	144km (90 miles)
Armour:	16mm (0.6in)
Armament:	none
Powerplant:	one Bedford twin-six petrol engine developing 350hp (261kW)
Performance:	maximum road speed 20km/h (12.5mph); maximum cross-country speed about 12.8km/h (8mph); fording 1.016m (3ft 4in); vertical obstacle 0.76m (2ft 6in); trench 3.048m (10ft)

Churchill AVRE Fascine-and Mat-Layer

The fascine-layer was developed from a technique used in ancient times and resurrected during World War I to allow tanks and other vehicles to cross ditches or soft ground, generally using bundles of brushwood to fill gaps or mats made of bundles of chespaling or hessian, linked up and laid out behind the tank using a roller mechanism. The tank was a standard Churchill AVRE with the devices attached to the front. The Bobbin Carpet used a hessian mat to cover wire obstacles and allow troops forward to assault the defences. The bobbins were carried well above the ground. When required the weighted free end of the carpet was dropped to the ground, the bobbin automatically unwinding itself as the tank rolled forward. This was first used during the 1942 Dieppe raid.

Country of origin:	UK
Crew:	5
Weight:	42,000kg (92,400lb)
Dimensions:	length 7.442m (24ft 5in); width 2.438m (8ft); height 5.49m (18ft)
Range:	130km (81.25 miles)
Armour:	16-102mm (0.6-4in)
Armament:	one Petard 290mm spigot mortar; one 7.92mm Besa machine gun
Powerplant:	one Bedford twin-six petrol engine developing 350hp (261kW)
Performance:	maximum road speed 20km/h (12.5mph); maximum cross-country speed about 12.8km/h (8mph); fording 1.016m (3ft 4in); vertical obstacle 0.76m (2ft 6in); trench 3.048m (10ft)

Churchill AVRE with Log Carpet

A similar arrangement was developed using linked logs. The roadway was laid under the front tracks and was pulled from its carrying frame as the AVRE moved forward. Like the Bobbin Carpet, the Log Carpet was intended to be a temporary measure only. After World War II, flexible metal roadways were developed to replace these earlier devices. The log carpet itself consisted of 100 152mm (6in) diameter logs, each 4.26m (14ft) long, bound together with wire rope. A removable steel frame was fitted above the AVRE superstructure carrying the looped mat, which was released over the front of the vehicle by detonating a light charge. The vehicle was one of a number developed for laying tracks over marshy ground or barbed wire for wheeled vehicles and infantry.

Country of origin:	UK
Crew:	5
Weight:	40,727kg (89,600lb)
Dimensions:	length 7.442m (24ft 5in); width 2.438m (8ft); height 3.454m (11ft 4in) – log carpet mounted above tank
Range:	144.8km (90 miles)
Armour:	16-102mm (0.6-4in)
Armament:	one Petard 290mm spigot mortar; one 7.92mm Besa machine gun
Powerplant:	one Bedford twin-six petrol engine developing 350hp (261kW)
Performance:	maximum road speed 20km/h (12.5mph); maximum cross-country speed about 12.8km/h (8mph); fording 1.016m (3ft 4in); vertical obstacle 0.76m (2ft 6in); trench 3.048m (10ft)

Sherman BARV

The BARV was developed during the planning for the D-Day landings when it was deemed prudent to have deep-wading recovery vehicles available to rescue vehicles stranded in the water. Trials in December 1943 were successful, and by D-Day there were 55 ready for action, the rough weather giving them plenty of work to do. The BARV was in essence a standard Sherman, but with the turret replaced by a tall superstructure with extensive waterproofing. The crew generally included a diver for securing towing cables. The BARV could either tow or push but suffered a little from the lack of a winch. The BARV was eventually christened the Sea Lion during a long post-war service record. It was standard procedure for the crew to be issued with life jackets, and for one of their number to be a diver.

Country of origin:	USA
Crew:	5
Weight:	unknown
Dimensions:	length 6.2m (20ft 4in); width 2.68m (8ft 9in); height 2.97m (9ft 9in)
Range:	136-160km (85-100 miles)
Armour:	12-62mm (0.4-2.4in)
Armament:	none
Powerplant:	twin General Motors 6-71 engines
Performance:	maximum road speed 47km/h (29mph); fording amphibious; vertical obstacle 0.61m (2ft); trench 2.26m (7ft 5in)

Bergepanther

With the advent of the heavier Tiger and Panther tanks, standard German recovery vehicles such as the SdKfz 9/1 proved inadequate. The Panther tank was therefore used as the basis for a new heavy recovery vehicle. The Bergepanther first appeared in 1943. The Panther's turret was removed and replaced by an open superstructure containing a winch. A large anchor at the back dug into the ground to give the vehicle extra stability when winching. There was also an open machine-gun mounting on the front of the vehicle for self-defence. Bergepanthers entered full service in the spring of 1944, concentrated in the heavy tank battalions, and by the end of the war almost 300 had been produced. It proved to be the best recovery vehicle of World War II.

Country of origin:	Germany
Crew:	5
Weight:	42,000kg (92,400lb)
Dimensions:	length 8.153m (26ft 9in); width 3.276m (10ft 9in); height 2.74m (9ft)
Range:	169km (105 miles)
Armour:	8-40mm (0.3-1.57in)
Armament:	one 20mm cannon and one 7.92mm machine gun
Powerplant:	one Maybach HL210 P.30 petrol engine developing 642hp (478.7kW)
Performance:	maximum road speed 32km/h (20mph); fording 1.70m (5ft 7in); vertical obstacle 0.91m (3ft 0in); trench 1.91m (6ft 3in)

Karl Ammunition Carrier

The Karl Ammunition Carrier was designed to supply the massive Karl Siege Howitzers, the sheer weight of the projectiles (over two tonnes [1.96 tons] each) necessitating a new vehicle. The basic tank hull of the PzKpfw IV Ausf D was used, with a platform for the ammunition and a crane added to lift the heavy rounds. The carriers were usually moved by train and assembled near to the point of use, before being driven into position. In 1941, 13 PzKpfw IV Ausf F chassis were converted to ammunition carriers. The Karl Howitzers and Carriers were designed to smash fortifications. They were used rarely in World War II, but did see service during the siege of Sevastopol and during the Battle of Warsaw in 1944, where they were put to devastating use against the defenders.

Country of origin:	Germany
Crew:	4
Weight:	25,000kg (55,000lb)
Dimensions:	length 5.41m (17ft 9in); width 2.883m (9ft 5.5in); height not recorded
Range:	209km (130 miles)
Armour:	60mm (2.4in)
Armament:	none
Powerplant:	one Maybach HL120 TRM petrol engine developing 300hp (223.7kW)
Performance:	maximum road speed 39.9km/h (24.8mph); fording 1.0m (3ft 3in); vertical obstacle 0.6m (2ft); trench 2.20m (7ft 3in)

SdKfz 265 kleiner Panzerbefehlswagen

The concept of the Command Tank came about following the realisation that the leaders of massed panzer formations would not only have to travel in tanks themselves, but the vehicles would have to carry extra equipment and personnel to assist the commander in his duties. In 1938, the PzKpfw I training tank was converted. The rotating hull was changed to a box superstructure to give more space and allow room for map boards and paperwork (though even then the space was not voluminous). More powerful radios were installed and a signaller added to the crew. Around 200 conversions were made, and the tank first saw action in the Polish Campaign in September 1939, later being used in France and North Africa, before being replaced by conversions of larger tanks.

Country of origin:	Germany
Crew:	3
Weight:	5800kg (12,768lb)
Dimensions:	length 4.445m (14ft 7in); width 2.08m (6ft 9.9in); height 1.72m (5ft 7.7in)
Range:	290km (180 miles)
Armour:	6-13mm (0.24-0.5in)
Armament:	one 7.92mm machine gun
Powerplant:	one Maybach NL38TR petrol engine developing 100hp (74.6kW)
Performance:	maximum road speed 40km/h (25mph); fording 0.85m (2ft 10in); vertical obstacle 0.42m (1ft 5in); trench 1.75m (5ft 9in)

M48 A3

When the Korean War began, the US military had no medium tanks in production. The M47 appeared as an interim measure but work immediately began on the M48. The first 'Pattons' were completed in July 1952. The speed of development resulted in numerous teething troubles for the early Pattons, including poor reliability and a short operating range. The A3 was a highly modified version designed to rectify these failings, and the M48 served successfully in Vietnam, India and with the Israelis in the Middle East. The M48 has been used as the basis for flame-thrower tanks, recovery vehicles and an AVLB. The A5 was an upgraded version produced in the mid-1970s which extended the M48's shelf-life considerably, and it is still being used in many countries today.

Country of origin:	USA
Crew:	4
Weight:	47,040kg (103,488lb)
Dimensions:	length 8.6m (28ft 6in); width 3.6m (11ft 11in); height 3.2m (10ft 3in)
Range:	463km (288 miles)
Armour:	12.7-120mm (0.5-4.72in)
Armament:	one 90mm gun; one 7.62mm coaxial machine gun; one 12.7mm machine gun in commander's cupola
Powerplant:	one Continental AVDS-1790-2A 12-cylinder diesel engine developing 750hp (560kW)
Performance:	maximum road speed 48.2km/h (30mph); fording 1.219m (4ft); vertical obstacle 0.915m (3ft); trench 2.59m (8ft 6in)

M103 Heavy Tank

The advent of the Cold War saw the Americans begin work on a new tank designed for direct assault and long-range anti-tank support for medium tanks against Soviet armour. Early prototypes of what was to become the M103 showed deficiencies in both the turret and gun control equipment. Despite modifications, the 200 built by Chrysler for deployment in Europe were found to be difficult to employ because of their size (which made concealment difficult), weight and small range, as well as poor reliability. They were phased out during the 1960s. Their bulk required a specialised recovery vehicle, built on the M103's chassis and named the M51. Nevertheless, the M103 was part of a trend for bigger and more heavily armed tanks on NATO's frontline.

Country of origin:	USA
Crew:	5
Weight:	56,610kg (124,544lb)
Dimensions:	length 11.3m (37ft 1.5in); width 3.8m (12ft 4in); height 2.9m (9ft 5.3in)
Range:	130km (80 miles)
Armour:	12.7-178mm (0.5-7in)
Armament:	one 120mm rifled gun; one 7.62mm coaxial machine gun; one 12.7mm anti-aircraft machine gun
Powerplant:	one Continental AV-1790-5B or 7C V-12 petrol engine developing 810hp (604kW)
Performance:	maximum road speed 34km/h (21mph); vertical obstacle 0.91m (3ft); trench 2.29m (7ft 6in)

Conqueror Heavy Tank

The FV214 Conqueror was the result of a requirement for a post-war heavy tank for the British Army for the expected massed armoured clash with the tanks of the Warsaw Pact on the central European plain. The British were determined that the experience of 1940, when their tanks had been out-gunned by the German panzers, would not happen again. Based on the Centurion, nearly 200 Conquerors were built between 1955 and 1958, mostly deployed in support of Centurion squadrons in the British Army of the Rhine. Unfortunately the Conqueror proved too cumbersome and difficult to maintain. Its advantage over the Centurion was limited to a longer-range gun, and when the Centurion was upgunned there was no longer a role for the Conqueror. The type was phased out during the 1960s.

Country of origin:	UK
Crew:	4
Weight:	64,858kg (142,688lb)
Dimensions:	length (gun forwards) 11.58m (38ft 0in); length (hull) 7.72m (25ft 4in); width 3.99m (13ft 1in); height 3.35m (11ft 0in)
Range:	155km (95 miles)
Armour:	17–178mm (0.66–7in)
Armament:	one 120mm rifled gun; one 7.62mm coaxial machine gun
Powerplant:	one 12-cylinder petrol engine developing 810hp (604kW)
Performance:	maximum road speed 34km/h (21.3mph); vertical obstacle 0.91m (3ft); trench 3.35m (11ft 0in)

Centurion

The Centurion Main Battle Tank had its origins in World War II, when it was developed as a cruiser tank. The first prototype appeared in 1945 and the tank entered production shortly after. The Centurion saw action in Korea, Vietnam, Pakistan and the Middle East. Nearly 4500 were built before production ceased in 1962 and it was replaced by the Chieftain. However, its excellent capacity for upgrading ensured that it has remained in service beyond the 1960s with foreign armies. Among the many variants are an armoured recovery vehicle (as well as an amphibious recovery vehicle which was used in the Falklands conflict in 1982), a bridge-layer and an AVRE. It is considered one of the most successful tank designs in the history of warfare.

Country of origin:	UK
Crew:	4
Weight:	51,723kg (113,792lb)
Dimensions:	length 9.854m (32ft 4in); width 3.39m (11ft 1.5in); height 3.009m (9ft 10.5in)
Range:	205km (127 miles)
Armour:	51-152mm (2-6in)
Armament:	one 105mm gun; two 7.62mm machine guns; one 12.7mm machine gun
Powerplant:	Rolls-Royce Meteor Mk IVB V-12 petrol, developing 650hp (485kW)
Performance:	maximum road speed 43km/h (27mph); fording 1.45m (4ft 9in); vertical obstacle 0.91m (3ft); trench 3.352m (11ft)

T-10 Heavy Tank

The T-10 was developed in the USSR after the end of World War II to fulfil the perceived need for a heavy tank, shared by both the USA and UK. At least 2500 were built up to the late 1950s. It was kept purely for the domestic market and was designed to provide long-range fire-support for the T-54/55s, and act as a spearhead for thrusts through heavily defended areas. Its cramped confines required the use of separate-loading ammunition as there was insufficient room for complete shells. After leaving frontline service it was, like all Soviet tanks, kept in reserve for many years. The decrease in speed compared to the earlier T-34 was surprising given the Red Army's emphasis on speed and mass during and after World War II. The Soviets certainly possessed mass, but vehicles such as the T-10 reduced overall speed.

Country of origin:	USSR
Crew:	4
Weight:	49,890kg (109,760lb)
Dimensions:	length (including gun) 9.875m (32ft 4.75in); length (hull) 7.04m (23ft 1in); width 3.566m (11ft 8.5in); height 2.25m (7ft 4.5in)
Range:	250km (155 miles)
Armour:	20-250mm (0.79-9.84in)
Armament:	one 122mm gun; two 12.7mm machine guns (one coaxial, one anti-aircraft)
Powerplant:	one V-12 diesel engine developing 700hp (522kW)
Performance:	maximum road speed 42km/h (26mph); vertical obstacle 0.9m (35.5in); trench 3.0m (9ft 10in)

T-54

The prototype of the T-54 was completed in 1946 and production began some years later. The T-54 and its variants were produced in larger numbers than any other Soviet tank after World War II (around 50,000), also being produced in Czechoslovakia, Poland and China. The T-54 was continually updated prior to the arrival of the T-55, with gun-stabilisers and an infrared capability being added. Variants included flame-throwers, dozers, bridge-layers, mine-clearers, recovery vehicles and a combat engineer vehicle. The tank saw extensive combat in Angola, North Africa, the Far East and in particular the Middle East, where it suffered by comparison to Israeli Centurion and M48 tanks during the Arab-Israeli wars. The T-54 was archetypal Soviet tank: it was simple and produced in mass numbers.

Country of origin:	USSR
Crew:	4
Weight:	35,909kg (79,000lb)
Dimensions:	length 9m (29ft 6.3in); width 3.27m (10ft 8.75in); height 2.4m (7ft 10.5in)
Range:	400km (249 miles)
Armour:	20-250mm (0.79-9.84in)
Armament:	one 100mm gun; two 7.62mm machine guns (one coaxial, one in bow); one 12.7mm anti-aircraft machine gun
Powerplant:	one V-12 diesel engine developing 520hp (388kW)
Performance:	maximum road speed 48km/h (30mph); fording 1.4m (4ft 7in); vertical obstacle 0.8m (2ft 7.5in); trench 2.7m (8ft 10.25in)

Stridsvagn 103 (S-tank)

Immediately after World War II, Sweden's armoured forces consisted mainly of light tanks. To fill this gap, work began on an indigenous heavy tank with the gun fixed to the chassis rather than a turret, with aiming being achieved by turning the vehicle and raising or lowering the suspension – an entirely new concept in tank design. Its only real drawback was that it was unable to fire on the move, but as Sweden was only likely to be engaged in defensive actions, this was not too problematic. Bofors began production in 1966, and 300 were completed by the time they ceased in 1971. The tank included a dozer blade and a flotation screen for amphibious capability. The radical Swedish S-tank generated considerable foreign interest, but few export orders.

Country of origin:	Sweden
Crew:	3
Weight:	38,894kg (85,568lb)
Dimensions:	length (with gun) 8.99m (29ft 6in); length (hull) 7.04m (23ft 1in); width 3.26m (10ft 8.3in); height (overall) 2.5m (8ft 2.5in)
Range:	390km (242 miles)
Armour:	90-100mm (3.54-3.94in)
Armament:	one 105mm gun; three 7.62mm machine guns
Powerplant:	one diesel engine developing 240hp (119kW) and a Boeing 553 gas turbine, developing 490hp (366kW)
Performance:	maximum road speed 50km/h (31mph); fording 1.5m (4ft 11in); vertical obstacle 0.9m (2ft 11.5in); trench 2.3m (7ft 6.5in)

AMX-30

Until the mid-1950s, both France and Germany relied on American M47s for their armour, though France also had a number of the excellent German Panther tanks. A requirement was drawn up for a new main battle tank, lighter and more powerfully armed than the M47, to supply both countries. However, typically, each adopted their own design. The French produced the AMX-30, the first production tanks appearing in 1966, half of which were destined for export. The AMX-30 chassis has been used for a number of other vehicles including the Pluton tactical nuclear missile launcher, as well as a self-propelled anti-aircraft gun, a recovery vehicle, bridge-layer and engineer vehicles. The tank has seen service with the Iraqi, Saudi Arabian and Spanish Armies in addition to the French.

Country of origin:	France
Crew:	4
Weight:	35,941kg (79,072lb)s
Dimensions:	length 9.48m (31ft 1in); width 3.1m (10ft 2in); height 2.86m (9ft 4in)
Range:	600km (373 miles)
Armour:	15-80mm (0.6-3.1in)
Armament:	one 105mm gun; one coaxial 20mm cannon; one 7.62mm machine gun
Powerplant:	one Hispano-Suiza 12-cylinder diesel, developing 720hp (537kW)
Performance:	maximum road speed 65km/h (40mph); vertical obstacle 0.93m (3ft 0.6in); trench 2.9m (9ft 6in)

Chieftain Mk 5

The Chieftain was designed in the late 1950s as a successor to the Centurion, with production beginning in 1963. Over 900 entered service with the British Army, with considerable numbers being sold to Kuwait and Iran (they saw service in the Iran-Iraq War). Until the Leopard 2 entered German service in 1980, the Chieftain was the best armed and armoured main battle tank in the world, and remained the mainstay of British armoured forces on NATO's frontline in Germany, with frequent technological additions such as laser-rangefinders and thermal-imaging devices until being slowly replaced by the Challenger in the late 1980s. It included a bridge-layer, engineer tank and recovery vehicle amongst its variants. The Chieftains in British Army service are now in reserve.

Country of origin:	UK
Crew:	4
Weight:	54,880kg (120,736lb)
Dimensions:	length 10.795m (35ft 5in); width 3.657m (11ft 8.5in); height 2.895m (9ft 6in)
Range:	500km (310 miles)
Armour:	classified
Armament:	one 120mm rifled gun; one 7.62mm coaxial machine gun; six smoke dischargers
Powerplant:	one Leyland six-cylinder multi-fuel engine developing 750hp (560kW)
Performance:	maximum road speed 48km/h (30mph); fording 1.066m (3ft 6in); vertical obstacle 0.914m (3ft); trench 3.149m (10ft 4in)

Leopard 1

Germany's design for the intended 1960s Franco-German joint venture was the Leopard 1 and it was this vehicle that the Germans eventually adopted independently of the French. Built by Krauss-Maffei, the first production vehicles appeared in 1965 and production continued until 1979, a total of 2237 being built for the German Army and many more for export. There were four basic versions, differing in armour, turret-type and fire-control systems. The tank formed the basis of a complete family of vehicles designed to support the vehicle on the battlefield. Optional equipment for the tank included a snorkel for deep-wading and a hydraulic blade to be attached to the front. The Leopard 1 is undoubtedly one of the best tanks designs to have come out of Europe.

Country of origin:	West Germany
Crew:	4
Weight:	39,912kg (87,808lb)
Dimensions:	length 9.543m (31ft 4in); width 3.25m (10ft 8in); height 2.613m (8ft 7in)
Range:	600km (373 miles)
Armour:	classified
Armament:	one 105mm gun; one coaxial 7.62mm machine gun; 7.62mm anti-aircraft machine gun; four smoke dischargers
Powerplant:	one MTU 10-cylinder diesel engine developing 830hp (619kW)
Performance:	maximum road speed 65km/h (40.4mph); fording 2.25m (7ft 4in); vertical obstacle 1.15m (3ft 9.25in); trench 3m (9ft 10in)

Leopard 2

The Leopard 2 was an offshoot of a cancelled joint development between the USA and West Germany in the late 1960s, the project being the MBT-70. The West Germans continued the project, however, first production vehicles were delivered in 1977 and exports were soon equipping the Dutch Army. The Leopard 2 is equipped with laser-rangefinder, thermal-imaging, a nuclear, biological and chemical (NBC) defence system and amphibious capability. Its fire-system is unusual in that the cartridge cases are combustible. When the shell is fired, all that remains is the base of the cartridge, which frees up extra space. It has a 30 percent better power-to-weight ratio than the Leopard 1, which results in increased cross-country mobility and thus survivability.

Country of origin:	West Germany
Crew:	4
Weight:	54,981kg (120,960lb)
Dimensions:	length 9.668m (31ft 8.7in); width 3.7m (12ft 1.7in); height 2.79m (9ft 1.75in)
Range:	550km (342 miles)
Armour:	classified
Armament:	one 120mm gun; one coaxial 7.62mm machine gun; one 7.62mm anti-aircraft machine gun; eight smoke dischargers
Powerplant:	one MTU 12-cylinder multi-fuel, developing 1,500hp (1119kW)
Performance:	maximum road speed 72km/h (45mph); fording 1m (3ft 3in); vertical obstacle 1.1m (3ft 7.25in); trench 3m (9ft 10in)

Tanks

M60A3

The development of the American M60 series of tanks began in 1956 following a decision to create an improved version of the M48. Built by General Dynamics, the M60 entered service in 1960, but was quickly superseded by the A1 to A3 versions. The A3 is notable for its laser fire-control system and thermal sights amongst various other modifications. The two main variants are an AVLB and a Combat Engineer Vehicle, armed with a demolition charge and dozer blade. The M60A3 has been widely exported to Austria, Italy (where it was built under licence), North Africa and many Middle East countries. It is still in frontline service in Africa and the Middle East, particularly in Egypt and Israel, while in the United States it is in National Guard use.

Country of origin:	USA
Crew:	4
Weight:	48,872kg (107,520lb)
Dimensions:	length 9.436m (30ft 11.5in); width 3.631m (11ft 11in); height 3.27m (10ft 8.25in)
Range:	500km (310 miles)
Armour:	25-127mm (0.98-5in)
Armament:	one 105mm gun; one 12.7mm machine gun; one 7.62mm coaxial machine gun
Powerplant:	one Continental 12-cylinder diesel engine developing 750hp (560kW)
Performance:	maximum road speed 48.28km/h (30mph); fording 1.219m (4ft); vertical obstacle 0.914m (3ft); trench 2.59m (8ft 6in)

M1 Abrams

The M1 Abrams was the next stage in American tank development after the M60. Chrysler completed the prototypes in 1978 and the first production vehicles appeared in 1980 with 30 tanks a month being built in following years. Its advanced Chobham armour makes the M1 the best protected US main battle tank yet. Its gas turbine engine is smaller and easier to service than a diesel engine, but the extra fuel requirement negates the space saved, which is perhaps why the idea was rejected for the Leopard 2. Thermal sights, laser rangefinder and gun stabilisation system give the M1 excellent firepower on the move, be it day or night. In the 1991 Gulf War, the Abrams proved itself the best tank in the world, knocking out Iraqi T-72s with impunity – no Abrams were destroyed by enemy fire.

Country of origin:	USA
Crew:	4
Weight:	54,269kg (119,392lb)
Dimensions:	length 9.766m (32ft 0.5in); width 3.655m (12ft); height 2.895m (9ft 6in)
Range:	450km (280 miles)
Armour:	classified
Armament:	one 105mm gun; two 7.62mm machine guns (one coaxial, one on loader's hatch); one 12.7mm machine gun
Powerplant:	Avco Lycoming AGT-1500 gas turbine, developing 1,500hp (1119kW)
Performance:	maximum road speed 72.5km/h (45mph); fording 1.219m (4ft); vertical obstacle 1.244m (4ft 1in); trench 2.743m (9ft)

Merkava

Prior to the Six-Day War in 1967, Israel had relied on Sherman and Centurion tanks for its armoured forces. However, doubts as to future supplies and also concerns that these tanks did not fully meet Israeli requirements prompted development of an indigenous tank. The first production Merkavas appeared in 1980 and saw action for the first time against Syrian forces in Lebanon in 1982. Compared to other modern main battle tanks, the Merkava is slow and has a poor power-to-weight ratio. However, it is designed for specific tactical requirements, which differ from those of most other tank producers. The emphasis is on crew survivability, which explains the Merkava's small cross-section which makes it less of a target, and well-sloped armour for greatest protection.

Country of origin:	Israel
Crew:	4
Weight:	55,898kg (122,976lb)
Dimensions:	length 8.36m (27ft 5.25in); width 3.72m (12ft 2.5in); height 2.64m (8ft 8in)
Range:	500 miles (310 miles)
Armour:	classified
Armament:	one 105mm rifled gun; one 7.62mm machine gun
Powerplant:	one Teledyne Continental AVDS-1790-6A V-12 diesel engine developing 900hp (671kW)
Performance:	maximum road speed 46km/h (28.6mph); vertical obstacle 1m (3ft 3.3in); trench 3m (9ft 10in)

T-62

The Russian T-62 was a development of the T-54/55 series of tanks, but due to the cost of each tank never managed to replace its predecessor which in fact outlived it in production. Produced from 1961 until the early 1970s, the T-62 had an unusual integral shell case ejection system. The recoil of the gun ejected the case out of a trapdoor in the turret, thus saving space but reducing the overall rate of fire. Capable of deep-fording by means of a snorkel over the loader's hatch, the tank was fitted with infrared night-vision equipment, turret-ventilation system, nuclear, biological and chemical (NBC) protection and the ability to create an instant smoke screen by injecting diesel into the exhaust. The tank was first used operationally in the Middle East during the Arab-Israeli wars.

Country of origin:	USSR
Crew:	4
Weight:	39,912kg (87,808lb)
Dimensions:	length 9.34m (28ft 6in); width 3.3m (10ft 1in); height: 2.4m (7ft 5in)
Range:	650km (406 miles)
Armour:	15-242mm (0.59-9.52in)
Armament:	one 115mm U-5TS gun; one 7.62mm coaxial machine gun
Powerplant:	one V-55-5 V-12 liquid-cooled diesel, developing 580hp (432kW)
Performance:	maximum road speed: 60km/h (37.5mph); fording 1.4m (4ft 7in); vertical obstacle 0.8m (2ft 7.5in); trench 2.7m (8ft 10.25in)

T-72

The T-72 came into production in 1971. Smaller and faster than such tanks as the Chieftain, the T-72 was poorly armoured with less versatility and effective firepower than its competitors. This became brutally clear in 1982 when Syrian T-72s proved no match for Israeli Merkava tanks and were knocked out in droves. The T-72 was designed for a conscript army and thus is easy to operate and maintain. This accounts for its export success, being transferred to 14 other countries. It is quite versatile, though, and can be equipped for deep-fording, unlike most other tanks, within a matter of minutes, as well as being fully nuclear, biological and chemical (NBC) protected. Variants include a command vehicle, an anti-tank Cobra missile launcher and an armoured recovery vehicle.

Country of origin:	USSR
Crew:	3
Weight:	38,894kg (85,568lb)
Dimensions:	length 9.24m (30ft 4in); width 4.75m (15ft 7in); height 2.37m (7ft 9in)
Range:	550km (434 miles)
Armour:	classified
Armament:	one 125mm gun; one 12.7mm anti-aircraft machine gun; one 7.62mm coaxial machine gun
Powerplant:	one V-46 V-12 diesel engine developing 840hp (626kW)
Performance:	maximum road speed 80km/h (50mph); fording 1.4m (4ft 7in); vertical obstacle 0.85m (2ft 9in); trench 2.8m (9ft 2in)

T-80

The T-80 entered service with the Soviet Red Army in the mid-1980s. A development of the T-72 main battle tank. Like the T-72, the tank had an automatic loader for the main gun, thus allowing the crew to be kept to a minimum of three. The main gun was a standard fully stabilised 125mm weapon as fitted in the T-72, but was capable of firing a much greater range of ammunition, including depleted uranium rounds for extra armour-piercing capability. A laser rangefinder led to an improved fire-control system. Like all Soviet tanks, the T-80 was capable of making its own smoke screen and carried four dischargers on the hull for launching chaff or decoys to distract enemy missiles. Adjustable ground clearance provided extra cross-country mobility.

Country of origin:	USSR
Crew:	3
Weight:	48,363kg (106,400lb)
Dimensions:	length 9.9m (32ft 6in); width 3.4m (11ft 2in); height 2.2m (7ft 3in)
Range:	450km (281 miles)
Armour:	classified
Armament:	one 125mm gun; one coaxial 7.62mm machine gun; one 12.7mm anti-aircraft machine gun
Powerplant:	one multi-fuel gas turbine, developing 1000hp (745kW)
Performance:	maximum road speed 70km/h (43.75mph); fording 5m (16ft 5in); vertical obstacle 1m (3ft 4in); trench 2.85m (9ft 4in)

Arjun Mk 1

The Arjun is India's first indigenous main battle tank design. The Indian Army's Combat Vehicle Research and Development Establishment encountered numerous problems with the project, resulting in significant delays which held up the in-service date until 1994. One of the main problems was the lack of an indigenous powerplant, which forced the Indians to use a German MTU diesel. The Arjun's main armament is a locally designed stabilised 120mm rifled gun capable of firing a variety of ammunition types, such as high explosive, high explosive anti-tank and high explosive squash head. The tank has an advanced fire-control system integrated with a combined day/night thermal imaging gunner's assembly with built-in laser rangefinder. In addition, there is a full weather sensor package.

Country of origin:	India
Crew:	4
Weight:	58,000kg (127,600lb)
Dimensions:	length 9.8m (32ft 2in); width 3.17m (10ft 5in); height 2.44m (8ft)
Range:	400km (250 miles)
Armour:	classified
Armament:	one 120mm gun; one 7.62mm machine gun
Powerplant:	one MTU MB 838 Ka 501 water-cooled diesel developing 1400hp (1044kW)
Performance:	maximum road speed 72km/h (45mph); fording 1m (3ft 3in); vertical gradient 1.1m (3ft 7in); trench 3m (9ft 10in)

ENGESA EE-T1 Osorio

Designed to meet both home and export markets, the first prototype Osorio was completed in 1985. The layout is conventional with laser rangefinder, stabilisers to allow firing whilst on the move and thermal-imaging cameras, as well as a full nuclear, biological and chemical (NBC) defence system. The tank can be fitted with two different sizes of main gun. Variants include a bridgelayer, armoured recovery vehicle and an anti-aircraft gun vehicle. There is little innovation in the design of the Osorio compared to the latest designs being produced in Europe and the United States. However, it is attractive for smaller countries which lack the capacity to manufacture their own main battle tank, and for whom the European and American tanks are too expensive and complicated.

Country of origin:	Brazil
Crew:	4
Weight:	39,000kg (85,800lb)
Dimensions:	length 9.995m (32ft 9.5in); width 3.26m (10ft 8.3in); height 2.371m (7ft 9.3in)
Range:	550km (342 miles)
Armour:	classified
Armament:	one British 105mm/French 120mm gun; one 7.62mm machine gun
Powerplant:	one 12-cylinder diesel engine developing 1000hp (745kW)
Performance:	maximum road speed 70km/h (43.5mph); fording 1.20m (3ft 11in); vertical obstacle 1.15m (3ft 4in); trench 3.0m (9ft 10in)

AMX-40

Designed in the early 1980s, primarily for export, the GIAT-built AMX-40 was a significant improvement on its predecessor, the AMX-30, in the key areas of armour, mobility and firepower. The tank has a laser rangefinder, gun stabilisation equipment and a low-light television for night-fighting. One interesting feature is the ammunition stowage. Carried in the turret and surrounded by bulkheads, the ammunition compartment is designed so that if it is hit, the ammunition will explode upwards, away from the crew below. As it was intended for export, the French Army was forced to rely on the AMX-30 until the advent of the Leclerc. The AMX-40 carries the traditional number of crew for a main battle tank: four (commander, gunner, radio operator and driver).

Country of origin:	France
Crew:	4
Weight:	43,000kg (94,600lb)
Dimensions:	length 10.04m (32ft 11.3in); width 3.36m (11ft 0.3in); height 3.08m (10ft 1.3in)
Range:	600km (373 miles)
Armour:	classified
Armament:	one 120mm gun; one 20mm cannon in cupola; one 7.62mm machine gun
Powerplant:	one Poyaud 12-cylinder diesel engine developing 1100hp (820kW)
Performance:	maximum road speed 70km/h (44mph); fording 1.30m (4ft 3in); vertical obstacle 1.0m (6ft 7in); trench 3.20m (10ft 6in)

Leclerc

The Leclerc was designed to replace the French Army's fleet of AMX-30 tanks. Development began in 1983, and the first production Leclercs appeared in 1991. The Leclerc is an excellent vehicle. An automatic loading system for the main armament and remote-control machine guns allow the crew to be cut down to three. The tank can be fitted with extra fuel tanks to increase operational range, and standard equipment includes a fire-detection/suppression system, thermal-imaging and laser rangefinder for the main gun, and a land navigation system. The on-board electronic systems are fully integrated to allow automatic reconfiguration in case of battlefield failure or damage. As well as in French service, around 390 Leclercs have been exported to the United Arab Emirates.

Country of origin:	France
Crew:	3
Weight:	53,500kg (117,700lb)
Dimensions:	length 9.87m (30ft); width 3.71m (11ft 4in); height 2.46m (7ft 6in)
Range:	550km (345 miles)
Armour:	classified
Armament:	one 120mm gun, one 12.7mm machine gun, one 7.62mm machine gun, 3 x 9 smoke dischargers
Powerplant:	one SAEM UDU V8X 1500 T9 Hyperbar eight-cylinder diesel engine developing 1500hp; SESM ESM500 automatic transmission
Performance:	maximum road speed: 73km/h (45.6mph); fording 1m (3ft 3in); vertical obstacle 1.25m (4ft 1in); trench 3m (9ft 10in)

Close Combat Vehicle – Light

The CCV-L was designed as a private venture by the FNC Corporation, manufacturer of the M113 and Bradley Armoured Fighting Vehicles, and was destined for the US Army's Light Divisions. When the prototype appeared in 1985, it created interest because it only required a three-man crew, allowed for by an automatic loading system for the main armament. This gave a rate of fire of 12 round per minute. The CCV-L borrowed parts from various other vehicles, such as the M113 Armoured Personnel Carrier, in order to reduce development time. The CCV-L has a hull of all-welded aluminium construction with bolt-on steel to enhance ballistic protection. Additional armour can be applied to the outside of the tank if required, including explosive reactive armour.

Country of origin:	USA
Crew:	3
Weight:	19,414kg (42,710lb)
Dimensions:	length 9.37m (30ft 9in); width 2.69m (8ft 10in); height 2.36m (7ft 9in)
Range:	483km (300 miles)
Armour:	classified
Armament:	one 105mm gun
Powerplant:	one Detroit Diesel Model 6V-92 TA 6-cylinder diesel engine developing 552hp (412kW)
Performance:	maximum road speed 70km/h (43.5mph); fording 1.32m (4ft 4in); vertical obstacle 0.76m (2ft 6in); trench 2.13m (7ft)

TAM

For many years the Argentinian Army relied on World War II Sherman tanks to form the basis of its armoured forces. By the early 1970s, these were becoming difficult to maintain. Most foreign tanks of the period were too heavy for domestic conditions and thus a new tank was ordered from Thyssen Henschel of West Germany. Once developed, production moved to Buenos Aires and production began towards the end of the 1970s. The hull of the TAM was based on that of the MICV in use with the West German Army. The armour is comparatively poor against that of other main battle tanks, such as the Leopard 1 and the AMX-30, but is well-sloped to give as much protection as possible. The tank was not produced in time to have any impact on the 1982 Falklands conflict.

Country of origin:	Argentina
Crew:	4
Weight:	30,500kg (67,100lb)
Dimensions:	length, gun forward 8.23m (25ft 2in); width 3.12m (9ft 6in); height 2.42m (7ft 5in)
Range:	900km (560 miles)
Armour:	classified
Armament:	one 105mm gun; one coaxial 7.62mm machine gun; one 7.62mm anti-aircraft machine gun
Powerplant:	one V-6 turbo-charged diesel engine developing 720hp (537kW)
Performance:	maximum road speed: 75km/h (46.9mph); fording 1.5m (4ft 11in); vertical obstacle 1m (3ft 3in); trench 2.5m (8ft 2in)

Challenger 1

The Challenger 1 was introduced in 1982 as a replacement for the Chieftain. It reflected British thinking on tank design, being heavily armed and armoured. It was slower than contemporary Warsaw Pact vehicles, but made up for it with its composite Chobham armour, which was virtually impenetrable to enemy rounds, and the greater accuracy of its armament. In any case, NATO thinking regarding the war in central Europe with the forces of the Soviet Union and her allies, always placed the emphasis on defence and holding enemy forces until reinforcements arrived. Its armour and nimbleness, despite its lack of speed, allow for good survivability. As tanks become more complicated, this is important as the tanks are often easier to replace than their crews.

Country of origin:	UK
Crew:	4
Weight:	62,000kg (136,400lb)
Dimensions:	length, gun forward: 11.56m (35ft 4in); width 3.52m (10ft 8in); height 2.5m (7ft 5in)
Range:	400km (250 miles)
Armour:	classified
Armament:	one 120mm gun; two 7.62mm machine guns; two smoke dischargers
Powerplant:	one liquid-cooled diesel engine developing 1200hp (895kW)
Performance:	maximum road speed: 55km/h (35mph); fording 1m (3ft 4in); vertical obstacle 0.9m (2ft 10in); trench 2.8m (9ft 2in)

Challenger 2

The Challenger 2 is the current main battle tank of the British Army. The hull is similar to that of the Challenger 1, as is the powerpack, but the turret has been redesigned to fit updated armament, and the tank is in many ways a completely new tank. The first production versions appeared in mid-1994, boasting a carbon dioxide laser rangefinder, thermal-imaging and fully computerised fire-control systems, giving a high first-round hit probability. In addition, turret traverse is all electric and the gun is fully stabilised. It also has the capacity to be fitted with the Battlefield Information Control System in future years, to give even greater combat capability. A dozer can be fitted to the front of the hull. Nearly 400 were ordered by the British Army, with 18 being exported to Oman.

Country of origin:	UK
Crew:	4
Weight:	62,500kg (137,500lb)
Dimensions:	length 11.55m (35ft 4in); width 3.52m (10ft 8in); height 2.49m (7ft 5in)
Range:	400km (250 miles)
Armour:	classified
Armament:	one 120mm gun; two 7.62mm machine guns; two smoke rocket dischargers
Powerplant:	one liquid-cooled diesel engine developing 1200hp (895kW)
Performance:	maximum road speed: 57km/h (35.6mph); fording 1m (3ft 4in); vertical obstacle 0.9m (2ft 10in); trench 2.8m (9ft 2in)

Tanks

Type 59

The Type 59 was a Chinese version of the T-54 which had been supplied in numbers by the USSR in the early 1950s. Early models were very basic, with no gun stabilisation or infrared night vision equipment, though the latter was supplied to later models by the British company MEL. A laser rangefinder was also added later, but unusually this was mounted on the front of the turret, where it was vulnerable to shell splinters and small-arms fire. The tank can generate its own smoke screen by injecting diesel fuel into the exhaust pipe, and extra fuel can be mounted in drums on the rear hull. The Type 59 was exported in some quantity to Albania, the Congo, North Korea, Pakistan, Sudan and Vietnam, the latter proving an unwise choice given the war between China and Vietnam in 1979.

Country of origin:	China
Crew:	4
Weight:	36,000kg (79,200lb)
Dimensions:	length 9m (27ft 6in); width 3.27m (10ft); height 2.59m (7ft 8in)
Range:	600km (375 miles)
Armour:	39-203mm (1.5-8in)
Armament:	one 100mm gun; two 7.62mm machine guns; one 12.7mm machine gun
Powerplant:	one Model 12150L V-12 diesel engine developing 520hp (388kW)
Performance:	maximum road speed: 50km/h (31.3mph); fording 1.4m (4ft 7in); vertical obstacle 0.79m (2ft 7in); trench 2.7m (8ft 10in)

Type 69

The Type 69 was the replacement for the Type 59. First seen in public in 1982, during a parade in Beijing, the tank was very similar in appearance to the Type 59, but was fitted with a new 105/106mm gun, probably based on that of the Soviet T-62, examples of which were captured by the Chinese during border clashes with the USSR. There are a number of variants, including a self-propelled anti-aircraft gun, armoured bridgelayer and armoured recovery vehicle. The latter has a Type 69 chassis but the turret removed and replaced by a superstructure; there is also a dozer blade at the front and crane at the rear. Large quantities of the Type 69 were exported to Iraq in the early 1980s, with Saudi Arabia acting as intermediary, to make up for losses experienced during the war with Iraq.

Country of origin:	China
Crew:	4
Weight:	36,500kg (80,300lb)
Dimensions:	length 8.68m (26ft 6in); width 3.3m (10ft 1in); height 2.87m (8ft 10in)
Range:	375km (250 miles)
Armour:	100mm (3.94in)
Armament:	one 100mm gun; one 12.7mm machine gun; two 7.62mm machine guns; two smoke rocket dischargers
Powerplant:	one V-12 liquid-cooled diesel engine developing 580hp (432kW)
Performance:	maximum road speed: 50km/h (31.3mph); fording 1.4m (4ft 7in); vertical obstacle 0.8m (2ft 7in); trench 2.7m (8ft 10in)

Tanks

Type 80

The Chinese Type 80 main battle tank was a development of the T-69 series. It differs in design by having a brand new hull, as well as a larger main armament and a more modern computerised fire-control system, which includes a laser rangefinder, mounted either over the gunner's sights, or over the 105mm gun itself, depending on the version. The vehicle carries a snorkel which can be fitted to allow for deep fording. It has an in-built fire-detection/ suppression system and the capability of being easily uparmoured (by the addition of composite armour plates) to give increased battlefield survivability. Crew configuration is as follows: the driver sits at the front left with some of the ammunition, while the loader, commander and gunner sit in the turret.

Country of origin:	China
Crew:	4
Weight:	38,000kg (83,600lb)
Dimensions:	length 9.33m (28ft 6in); width 3.37m (10ft 4in); height 2.3m (7ft)
Range:	570km (356 miles)
Armour:	classified
Armament:	one 105mm gun; one 7.62mm coaxial machine gun; one 12.7mm coaxial machine gun
Powerplant:	one V-12 diesel engine developing 730hp (544kW); manual transmission
Performance:	maximum road speed: 60km/h (37.5mph); fording 1.4m (4ft 7in); vertical obstacle 0.8m (2ft 7in); trench 2.7m (8ft 10in)

Type 85

The Type 85 main battle tank entered production on a small scale in the late 1980s. The tank was based on the chassis of the Type 80, but, in something of an innovation for Chinese tanks, it was given an all-welded turret instead of the usual cast steel type, armour being increased all round. It also carried improved communications equipment. The increased main armament (125mm as opposed to the 105mm of the Type 80) is fed by an automatic loader, which allows the crew to be reduced to a minimum. However, space inside is reduced by the ammunition being made up of separate projectile and charge. The Type 85 is still in production and has been exported to Pakistan, where it is known as the Type 85-IIM. It is still inferior to American and European tanks.

Country of origin:	China
Crew:	3
Weight:	41,000kg (90,200lb)
Dimensions:	length 10.28m (31ft 5in); width: 3.45m (10ft 6in); height: 2.3m (7ft)
Range:	500km (312 miles)
Armour:	classified
Armament:	one 125mm gun; one 7.62mm coaxial machine gun; one 12.7mm anti-aircraft machine gun; two smoke grenade launchers
Powerplant:	one V-12 supercharged diesel engine developing 730hp (544kW)
Performance:	maximum road speed: 57.25km/h (35.8mph); fording 1.4m (4ft 7in); vertical obstacle 0.8m (2ft 7in); trench 2.7m (8ft 10in)

Type 74

The Type 74 main battle tank, a successor to the Type 61, entered production on a small scale in the late 1975, with the production rate never increasing above around 50 vehicles per year which meant a very high unit cost. The tank carries a laser rangefinder, computerised fire-control and nuclear, biological and chemical (NBC) defence system as standard. However, the Type 74 has an unusual cross-linked hydro-pneumatic suspension system, which allows it to raise or lower different parts of the chassis in order to cross difficult terrain or to engage targets outside of the gun's normal elevation/depression range. Internal layout is conventional, with a centre turret and rear powerplant. The Type 74 forms the basis of the Type 87 35mm self-propelled anti-aircraft gun tank.

Country of origin:	Japan
Crew:	3
Weight:	38,000kg (83,600lb)
Dimensions:	length 9.42m (28ft 8in); width 3.2m (9ft 10in); height 2.48m (7ft 7in)
Range:	300km (188 miles)
Armour:	classified
Armament:	one 105mm gun; one 7.62mm coaxial machine gun; one 12.7mm anti-aircraft machine gun; two smoke dischargers
Powerplant:	one 10ZF V-10 liquid-cooled diesel, developing 720hp (536kW)
Performance:	maximum road speed: 55km/h (34.4mph); fording; 1m (3ft 4in); vertical obstacle 1m (3ft 4in); trench 2.7m (8ft 10in)

Type 90

The Type 90 main battle tank was placed in development in the mid-1970s to meet the needs of the Japanese Ground Self-Defence Force. It entered production on a small scale in the 1992. Its slow production rate makes this the most expensive unit cost tank produced by any nation in the world. The vehicle carries a laser rangefinder, computerised fire control and NBC system as standard, as well as thermal imaging and night-driving capability. Like the Type 74, the vehicle has a cross-linked hydro-pneumatic suspension system, which allows it to raise or lower different parts of the chassis in order to cross difficult terrain or to engage targets outside of the gun's normal elevation/depression range. Variants include the Type 90 ARV with dozer blade and winch and the Type 91 AVLB bridgelayer.

Country of origin:	Japan
Crew:	3
Weight:	50,000kg (110,000lb)
Dimensions:	length 9.76m (29ft 10in); width: 3.4m (10ft 5in); height 2.34m (7ft 1in)
Range:	350km (219 miles)
Armour:	classified
Armament:	one 120mm gun; one 7.62mm coaxial machine gun; one 12.7mm anti-aircraft machine gun; two smoke dischargers
Powerplant:	one 10ZG V-10 fuel-injection diesel, developing 1500hp (1118kW)
Performance:	maximum road speed: 70km/h (43.8mph); fording 2m (6ft 6in); vertical obstacle 1m (3ft 4in); trench 2.7m (8ft 10in)

C1 Ariete

The C1 Ariete main battle tank was developed in response to a 1982 specification of the Italian Army for a replacement for its obsolete M47 Pattons. It has the typical slab-sided appearance of modern main battle tanks due to its special composite armour. The Ariete is conventional in layout, with the driver at the front right, a power-operated turret in the centre, gunner on the right, loader on the left and the powerplant at the rear of the vehicle. The main smoothbore armament has a thermal sleeve and fume extractor and uses the latest Galileo computerised fire-control system, the thermal vision night sight and laser rangefinder giving high single-shot kill probability, whether moving or stationary. An armoured recovery vehicle and AVLB based on the C1 chassis are expected to follow.

Country of origin:	Italy
Crew:	4
Weight:	54,000kg (118,800lb)
Dimensions:	length 9.67m (29ft 6in); width 3.6m (11ft); height: 2.5m (7ft 7in
Range:	600km (375 miles)
Armour:	classified
Armament:	one 120mm gun; one 7.62mm coaxial machine gun; one 7.62mm anti-aircraft machine gun; 2 x 4 smoke dischargers
Powerplant:	one IVECO FIAT MTCA V-12 turbocharged diesel engine developing 1250hp (932kW)
Performance:	maximum road speed: 66km/h (41.3mph); fording 1.2m (3ft 11in); vertical obstacle 2.1m (6ft 11in); trench 3m (9ft 10in)

Type 88

Also known as the K1, the Type 88 was developed by General Dynamics in the early 1980s in response to a South Korean requirement for a main battle tank which could be locally built. The main smoothbore armament has a thermal sleeve and fume extractor and uses a computerised fire-control system based on the M1 ballistic computer and an environmental sensor package. The vehicle has a nuclear, biological and chemical (NBC) system designed to give individual crew protection. Its successor, the K1A1, is already in development, armed with a larger gun and improved fire control system. An AVLB variant, based on the K1 chassis has been designed in the UK and 56 have already been ordered by the South Koreans. A new version of the Type 88 is under development, mounting a 120mm smoothbore gun.

Country of origin:	South Korea
Crew:	4
Weight:	52,000kg (114,400lb)
Dimensions:	length 9.67m (29ft 6in); width: 3.59m (10ft 11in); height: 2.25m (6ft 10in)
Range:	500km (313 miles)
Armour:	classified
Armament:	one 105mm gun; one 7.62mm coaxial machine gun; one 12.7mm anti-aircraft machine gun; 2 x 6 smoke dischargers
Powerplant:	one liquid-cooled turbocharged diesel, developing 1200hp (895kW)
Performance:	maximum road speed: 65km/h (40.6mph); fording 1.2m (3ft 11in); vertical obstacle 1m (3ft 4in)

Olifant Mk 1A

Like the Israelis with their Sho't programme, the South Africans took a basic Centurion tank and upgraded it to produce an indigenous main battle tank specifically suited to their needs, with improved firepower and mobility. The fire control system of the Olifant ('Elephant') remained that of the original Centurion, but the tank was fitted with a hand-held laser rangefinder for the commander and image-intensifier for the gunner. The Mk 1B version of the Olifant is much different, with a lengthened hull, new engine and transmission, and updated armour, as well as enhanced fire control systems. Variants include an armoured recovery vehicle and repair vehicle. The Olifant is undoubtedly the best indigenous tank design on the African continent.

Country of origin:	South Africa
Crew:	4
Weight:	56,000kg (123,200lb)
Dimensions:	length 9.83m (30ft); width: 3.38m (10ft 4in); height: 2.94m (8ft 11in)
Range:	500km (313 miles)
Armour:	17-118mm (0.66-4.6in)
Armament:	one 105mm gun; one 7.62mm coaxial machine gun; one 7.62mm anti-aircraft machine gun; 2 x 4 smoke dischargers
Powerplant:	one V-12 air-cooled turbocharged diesel, developing 750hp (559kW)
Performance:	maximum road speed: 45km/h (28.1mph); fording 1.45m (4ft 9in); vertical obstacle 0.9m (2ft 11in); trench 3.352m (11ft)

M551 Sheridan

The M551 was developed following a 1959 requirement for a air-portable tank to equip the US Army's airborne divisions. Between 1965 and 1970, 1700 vehicles were produced by General Motors and saw service in South Korea, Europe and Vietnam. It was in the latter that the M551's deficiencies were revealed when it proved highly susceptible to landmines, although its ability to fire canister ammunition was effective in beating off mass guerrilla attacks. As a result, it was withdrawn from most frontline units in the late 1970s, although many were modified by the National Training Center to resemble Soviet vehicles and used for training purposes. The main armament consisted of a 152mm weapon that fired a wire-guided Shilelagh missile.

Country of origin:	USA
Crew:	4
Weight:	15,830kg (34,826lb)
Dimensions:	length 6.299m (20ft 8in); width 2.819m (9ft 3in); height (overall) 2.946m (9ft 8in)
Range:	600km (310 miles)
Armour:	40-50mm (1.57-2in)
Armament:	one 152mm gun/missile launcher; one coaxial 7.62mm machine gun; one 12.7mm anti-aircraft machine gun
Powerplant:	one six-cylinder Detroit 6V-53T diesel, developing 300hp (224kW)
Performance:	maximum road speed 70km/h (43mph); fording amphibious; vertical obstacle 0.838m (2ft 9in); trench 2.54m (8ft 4in)

Light Tanks

Scorpion

The first prototype of the Alvis Scorpion, officially named Combat Vehicle Reconnaissance (Tracked), appeared in 1969, following a British Army requirement for a tracked reconnaissance vehicle to replace the Saladin armoured car. It entered service in 1972 and was exported to countries all over the world, particularly Belgium, where it was produced under licence. It saw action in the Falklands in 1982, where its flotation screens giving amphibious capability were particularly useful during the landings. The Scorpion proved its worth in both reconnaissance and in high-speed advances, and remains a key part of the British armoured forces. The Scorpion chassis has been used for a complete range of tracked vehicles, such as the Sultan, Spartan and Scimitar.

Country of origin:	UK
Crew:	3
Weight:	8073kg (17,760lb)
Dimensions:	length 4.794m (15ft 8.75in); width 2.235m (7ft 4in); height 2.102m (6ft 10.75in)
Range:	644km (400 miles)
Armour:	12.7mm (0.5in)
Armament:	one 76mm gun; one coaxial 7.62mm machine gun
Powerplant:	one Jaguar 4.2-litre petrol engine developing 190hp (142kW)
Performance:	maximum road speed 80km/h (50mph); fording 1.067m (3ft 6in); vertical obstacle 0.50m (1ft 8in); trench 2.057m (6ft 9in)

AMX-13

The AMX-13 was designed immediately after the end of World War II. Production began in 1952 and continued until the 1980s. Its design included an automatic loader in the turret bustle which included two revolver-type magazines, each holding six rounds of ammunition. The tank was widely exported, proving particularly popular with developing nations such as Chile, Djibouti and Nepal, as well as Israel, the Netherlands and Switzerland. One interesting feature is the oscillating turret in which the gun is fixed in the upper part, which in turn pivots on the lower part. The AMX-13 was extensively modified and used as the basis for a complete family of vehicles, from self-propelled guns and howitzers to engineer vehicles, recovery vehicles, bridgelayers and Infantry Fighting Vehicles.

Country of origin:	France
Crew:	3
Weight:	15,000kg (33,000lb)
Dimensions:	length 6.36m (20ft 10.3in); width 2.50m (8ft 2.5in); height 2.30m (7ft 6.5in)
Range:	400km (250 miles)
Armour:	10-40mm (0.4-1.57in)
Armament:	one 75mm gun; one 7.62mm machine gun
Powerplant:	one SOFAM eight-cylinder petrol engine developing 250hp (186kW)
Performance:	maximum road speed 60km/h (37mph); fording 0.60m (1ft 11.7in); vertical obstacle 0.65m (2ft 1.7in); trench 1.60m (5ft 3in)

Light Tanks

PT-76

The PT-76 was designed in the immediate period after World War II. For many years it was the standard reconnaissance vehicle of the Soviet Red Army, before being replaced by heavier T-62s, and was exported to more than 25 countries, seeing action in the 1967 Six-Day War, Vietnam and Angola. Intended as an amphibious tank, its armour was only sufficient to withstand small-arms fire, in order to keep the weight to a minimum. The tank was equipped with bilge pumps and water jets to allow it to move efficiently through water and could travel up to 65km (40 miles) in this fashion. The chassis was used for a number of other vehicles, including the BTR-50 Armoured Personnel Carrier and the FROG missile launcher. Though old, it is still in Russian service

Country of origin:	USSR
Crew:	3
Weight:	14,000kg (30,800lb)
Dimensions:	length 7.625m (25ft 0.25in); width 3.14m (10ft 3.7in); height 2.255m (7ft 4.75in)
Range:	260km (160 miles)
Armour:	5-17mm (0.19-0.66in)
Armament:	one 76mm gun; one coaxial 7.62mm machine gun; one 12.7mm anti-aircraft machine-gun
Powerplant:	one V-6 six-cylinder diesel engine developing 240hp (179kW)
Performance:	maximum road speed 44km/h (27mph); fording amphibious; vertical obstacle 1.10m (3ft 7.3in); trench 2.80m (9ft 2in)

Scimitar

The Scimitar is a variant of the Scorpion FV101 tracked reconnaissance vehicle, one of the CVR(T) family of light armoured vehicles developed for the British Army. Entering service in 1978, it was intended mainly for a fire support role. The powerful RARDEN cannon is able to penetrate all light armoured vehicles, and the side armour of most main battle tanks. Its own armour protection is minimal, though, being barely sufficient to resist small-arms fire. The Scimitar can be fitted with night-vision sights, laser rangefinder and computerised fire-control system. Unusually for a 1970s combat vehicle, it runs on petrol rather than diesel. Amphibious capability is provided by a collapsible flotation screen, and the vehicle is propelled in the water by its tracks.

Country of origin:	UK
Crew:	3
Weight:	7800kg (17,160lb)
Dimensions:	length 4.8m (15ft 9in); width 2.24m (7ft 4in); height 2.1m (6ft 11in)
Range:	644km (402 miles)
Armour:	12.7mm (0.5in)
Armament:	one 30mm Rarden gun; one 12.7m machine gun
Powerplant:	one Jaguar 4.2-litre petrol engine developing 190hp (142kW)
Performance:	maximum road speed 80km/h (50mph); fording 1.067m (3ft 6in); vertical obstacle 0.50m (1ft 8in); trench 2.057m (6ft 9in)

Wiesel

The Wiesel was developed to a requirement for an air-portable light armoured tracked vehicle for use by airborne troops. Prototypes were built by Porsche and deliveries began at the end of the 1980s – a total of 345 vehicles will be delivered to the German Army (210 will be armed with a wire-guided anti-tank weapon). There are two main versions, one armed with a conventional cannon (complete with 20 rounds of ready use ammunition), the other with a missile launcher. Its compact nature, necessary for air transport, makes it very difficult to detect the Wiesel on the battlefield. A whole host of variants are possible such as ambulance, anti-aircraft (equipped with Stinger surface-to-air missiles), armoured personnel carrier, command vehicle and recovery vehicle.

Country of origin:	Germany
Crew:	3
Weight:	2750kg (6050lb)
Dimensions:	length 3.265m (10ft 8.5in); width 1.82m (5ft 11.7in); height 1.875m (6ft 1.8in)
Range:	200km (124 miles)
Armour:	classified
Armament:	one 20mm cannon or a Hughes anti-tank missile launcher
Powerplant:	one five-cylinder turbocharged diesel engine developing 86hp (64kW)
Performance:	maximum road speed 80km/h (50mph); vertical obstacle 0.4m (1ft 4in); trench 1.20m (3ft 11in)

Stingray

The prototype of the Stingray was unveiled in 1984 by Cadillac Gage, who had foreseen the need for a light tank with good mobility and firepower which was simple to operate and maintain. Wherever possible, proven parts from other vehicles have been adapted to save development costs. The Stingray comes equipped with laser rangefinder, stabilisation devices for the gun, nuclear, biological and chemical (NBC) protection and has the firepower of a main battle tank. Its drawback is its light armour. However, given the power of modern high explosive anti-tank (HEAT) rounds, this may make little difference. The Stingray has performance and power at a much lower unit cost when compared to a main battle tank, and is thus the subject of great interest around the world.

Country of origin:	USA
Crew:	4
Weight:	19,051kg (41,912lb)
Dimensions:	length 9.35m (30ft 8in); width 2.71m (8ft 11in); height 2.54m (8ft 4in)
Range:	483km (300 miles)
Armour:	classified
Armament:	one 105mm rifled gun; one coaxial 7.62mm machine gun; one 7.62mm anti-aircraft machine gun
Powerplant:	one Diesel Model 8V-92 TA diesel engine developing 535hp (399kW)
Performance:	maximum road speed 69km/h (43mph); fording 1.22m (4ft); vertical obstacle 0.76m (2ft 6in); trench 1.69m (5ft 7in)

sIG 33

The sIG 33 was a self-propelled howitzer used to equip German infantry battalions of World War II. The first version appeared during the French Campaign of May 1940, and was simply the standard sIG 33 heavy infantry gun mounted on a PzKpfw I chassis and fitted with armoured shields to protect the crew. It was developed to provide armoured infantry with close fire support from a self-propelled armoured platform. The centre of gravity was rather high, though, and the chassis was overloaded. In consequence, the PzKpfw II chassis was converted for use in 1942, giving better armour protection, followed by the PzKpfw III. The vehicle served throughout the war and was still in production in 1944, with over 370 vehicles being made.

Country of origin:	Germany
Crew:	4
Weight:	11,505kg (25,300lb)
Dimensions:	length 4.835m (15ft 10.4in); width 2.15m (7ft 0.6in); height 2.40m (7ft 10.5in)
Range:	185km (115 miles)
Armour:	6-13mm (0.23-0.5in)
Armament:	one 15cm sIG 33 howitzer
Powerplant:	one Praga six-cylinder petrol engine developing 150hp (111.9kW)
Performance:	maximum road speed 35km/h (21.75mph); fording 0.914m (3ft); vertical obstacle 0.42m (1ft 5in); trench 1.75m (5ft 9in)

Hummel

The Hummel ('Bumble Bee') was a hybrid of the PzKpfw III and IV hulls, with a lightly armoured open superstructure, which formed the heavy artillery element of German panzer and panzergrenadier divisions from 1942 onwards. The Hummel first saw action at the Battle of Kursk in July 1943. They were useful and popular weapons and were used on all fronts, having plenty of room for the crew of five and the mobility to keep up with the panzer divisions. Well over 600 had been produced by late 1944, and 150 were converted into ammunition carriers as lorries proved inadequate for the task. Other variants included the Oskette, a wider-tracked version produced for winter fighting on the Russian Front. It was usual for 18 rounds of ammunition to be carried in the vehicle.

Country of origin:	Germany
Crew:	5
Weight:	23,927kg (52,640lb)
Dimensions:	length 7.17m (23ft 6.3in); width 2.87m (9ft 5in); height 2.81m (9ft 2.6in)
Range:	215km (134 miles)
Armour:	up to 50mm (1.97in)
Armament:	one 15cm sIG 33 howitzer or one 88mm anti-tank gun
Powerplant:	one Maybach V-12 petrol engine developing 265hp (197.6kW)
Performance:	maximum road speed 42km/h (26.1mph); fording 0.99m (3ft 3in); vertical obstacle 0.6m (2ft); trench 2.20m (7ft 3in)

StuG III Ausf F

The StuG III Ausf F was developed from 1941, by personal order of Adolf Hitler himself, to regain superiority over the Soviet KV-1 and T-34 tanks on the Eastern Front. The armour of the Ausf A-E series was upgraded and a new long StuK40 L/48 7.5cm gun was fitted in place of the original short 7.5cm version, which significantly improved the vehicle's anti-tank capability. The basic hull and superstructure remained the same, other than the addition of an exhaust fan to remove gun fumes. The gun mantlet was also redesigned to allow for the recoil mechanism of the larger gun. The Ausf F proved highly effective against the Soviet KV-1s and T-34s and the vehicle remained in service throughout the war –its low silhouette giving it an added advantage in tank-versus-tank combats.

Country of origin:	Germany
Crew:	4
Weight:	21,800kg (47,960lb)
Dimensions:	length 6.31m (19ft 2in); width 2.92m (8ft 11in); height: 2.15m (6ft 7in)
Range:	140km (92 miles)
Armour:	11-50mm (0.4-2in)
Armament:	one 75mm Stuk40 L/48 gun; one 7.92mm machine gun
Powerplant:	one Maybach HL120TRM engine
Performance:	maximum road speed 40km/h (25mph); fording 0.8m (2ft 8in); vertical obstacle 0.6m (2ft); trench 2.59m (8ft 6in)

StuG III Ausf G

The StuG III Ausf G was the last StuG to enter production in World War II. Based predominantly on the chassis of the PzKpfw III, which was being phased out of tank service in favour of the much more lethal Panther, the Ausf G carried thicker armour than its predecessors, which was fortunate, as the Stug III was called upon more and more to fill the role of a tank, being cheaper and easier to build. However, its lack of mobility proved a liability as it was vulnerable to infantry with anti-tank projectiles. The addition of armoured 'skirts' (Schützen) went some way towards improving protection, but despite a valiant effort, the StuG IIIs were not really suited for the tank role in which they found themselves. Nevertheless, the Ausf G version was the best of the bunch, and performed well on the battlefield.

Country of origin:	Germany
Crew:	4
Weight:	24,100kg (53,020lb)
Dimensions:	length 6.77m (20ft 7in); width 2.95m (9ft); height 2.16m (6ft 7in)
Range:	155km (97 miles)
Armour:	16-80mm (0.62-3.14in)
Armament:	one 75mm Stuk40 L/48 gun; one 7.92mm machine gun
Powerplant:	one Maybach HL120TRM engine
Performance:	maximum road speed 40km/h (25mph); fording 0.8m (2ft 8in); vertical obstacle 0.6m (2ft); trench 2.59m (8ft 6in)

Self-Propelled Artillery

Type 4

The Japanese produced few heavy armoured vehicles, partly because they were deemed unnecessary based on experiences in China and Manchuria, and partly because their industrial capacity was inadequate for the task. The Type 4 was a self-propelled howitzer using the Type 97 medium tank as a base. The howitzer itself dated from 1905 and had been with withdrawn from service in 1942 but continued to be used in the self-propelled version. The Type 4 was poorly armoured and a had a slow rate of fire, mainly because of the breech mechanism employed. The Japanese were unable to produce them on a mass scale, being deployed in ones and twos, mainly for island defence. They were hopelessly outnumbered against American artillery in the Pacific battles in World War II.

Country of origin:	Japan
Crew:	4 or 5
Weight:	13,300kg (29,260lb)
Dimensions:	length 5.537m (18ft 2in); width 2.286m (7ft 6in); height to top of shield 1.549m (5ft 1in)
Range:	250km (156miles)
Armour:	25mm (0.98in)
Armament:	one Type 38 150mm howitzer
Powerplant:	one V-12 diesel engine developing 170hp (126.8kW)
Performance:	maximum road speed 38km/h (23.6mph); fording 1.0m (3ft 3in); vertical obstacle 0.812m (2ft 8in); trench 2.0m (6ft 7in)

SU-76

The battles of 1941 showed the Soviet light tanks to be virtually useless. It was thus decided to combine the T-70 already in production with the excellent ZIS-3 and ZIS-76 guns to create a highly mobile anti-tank weapon. A wartime expedient, there were few comforts for the crew and it was known to troops as 'The Bitch'. The first SU-76s appeared in late 1942 and by mid-1943 they were deployed in appreciable numbers. Better German armour had by this time reduced the effectiveness of the ZIS gun and thus the vehicle's role was changed from anti-tank to infantry support. By 1945, many SU-76s were converted into ammunition carriers or recovery vehicles. After the war, many were transferred to China and North Korea, seeing service during the Korean War.

Country of origin:	USSR
Crew:	4
Weight:	10,600kg (23,320lb)
Dimensions:	length 4.88m (16ft 0.1in); width 2.73m (8ft 11.5in); height 2.17m (7ft 1.4in)
Range:	450km (280 miles)
Armour:	up to 25mm (0.98in)
Armament:	one ZIS-3 76mm gun
Powerplant:	two GAZ six-cylinder petrol engines each developing 70hp (52.2kW)
Performance:	maximum road speed 45km/h (28mph); fording 0.89m (2ft 11in); vertical obstacle 0.70m (2ft 3.6in); trench 3.12m (10ft 2.8in)

Self-Propelled Artillery

ISU-152

The ISU-152 was the first of the Soviet heavy self-propelled artillery carriages of World War II, entering service in 1943, just in time to take part in the Battle of Kursk in July. Built on a KV-2 heavy tank chassis, it was intended for a dual role as an anti-tank weapon and heavy assault gun. The vehicle was in the vanguard of the Soviet advances of 1944 and 1945, and the vehicles were amongst the first to enter Berlin at the end of the war. The ISU-152's major drawback was a lack of internal stowage space for ammunition, and each vehicle thus required constant supply by ammunition carriers, which was hazardous and affected tactical mobility. Nevertheless, the ISU-152 remained in service after the war, being used during the crushing of the 1956 Hungarian uprising.

Country of origin:	USSR
Crew:	5
Weight:	45,500kg (100,100lb)
Dimensions:	length overall 9.80m (32ft 1.8in) and hull 6.805m (22ft 3.9in); width 3.56m (11ft 8.2in); height 2.52m (8ft 3.2in)
Range:	180km (112 miles)
Armour:	35-100mm (1.38-3.94in)
Armament:	one 152mm howitzer; one 12.7mm anti-aircraft machine gun
Powerplant:	one V-12 diesel engine developing 520hp (387.8kW)
Performance:	maximum road speed 37km/h (23mph); fording 1.3m (4ft 3.2in); vertical obstacle 1.20m (3ft 8in); trench 2.59m (8ft 6in)

Sexton

In 1941, the British were searching for a suitable armoured vehicle to mount the standard British 25-pounder gun. The Canadians were producing the Ram tank, soon to be replaced by American M3s, and these were altered to accommodate the 25-pounder, becoming known as the Sexton. Used mainly as a field artillery weapon to support armoured divisions, the Sexton saw action in Northwest Europe in 1944 and 1945. By the time production ceased shortly after the war, a total of 2150 had been built. The main variant was a purpose-built command tank with the weapon removed and extra radios added. A reliable, rugged and effective weapon, the Sexton continued in service until the 1950s with the British Army, and until very recently with some other armies.

Country of origin:	Canada
Crew:	6
Weight:	25,300kg (55,660lb)
Dimensions:	length 6.12m (20ft 1in); width 2.72m (8ft 11in); height 2.44m (8ft 0in)
Range:	290km (180 miles)
Armour:	up to 32mm (1.25in)
Armament:	one 25-pounder howitzer; two .303in Bren Guns; one 0.5in Browning machine gun
Powerplant:	one nine-cylinder radial piston engine developing 400hp (298.3kW)
Performance:	maximum road speed 40.2km/h (25mph); fording 1.01m (3ft 4in); vertical obstacle 0.61m (2ft); trench 1.91m (6ft 3in)

M7 Priest

Nicknamed the 'Priest' by British crews because of its pulpit-shaped machine-gun turret at the front, the M7 grew from US experience with howitzers mounted on half-tracked vehicles. A fully tracked carriage was required, and the M3 tank was modified to fill the role. The British received many under the Lend-Lease scheme and deployed them first at the 2nd Battle of El Alamein in 1942. Some measure of their popularity is suggested by the British order for 5500 to be delivered within one year of their first use. The drawback was that the howitzer was not standard British issue, and thus required separate supplies of ammunition. Mobile and reliable, the M7 fought to the end of the war and remained in service in the role of armoured personnel carrier – it was also widely exported.

Country of origin:	USA
Crew:	5
Weight:	22,500kg (49,500lb)
Dimensions:	length 6.02m (19ft 9in); width 2.88m (9ft 5.25in); height 2.54m (8ft 4in)
Range:	201km (125 miles)
Armour:	up to 25.4mm (1in)
Armament:	one 105mm howitzer; one 12.7mm machine gun
Powerplant:	one Continental nine-cylinder radial piston engine developing 375hp (279.6kW)
Performance:	maximum road speed 41.8km/h (26mph); fording 1.219m (4ft); vertical obstacle 0.61m (2ft); trench 1.91m (6ft 3in)

M40

The M40 entered development in December 1943 and was based on the M4 tank chassis and used the 155mm 'Long Tom' gun. A heavy spade was attached to the rear which could be dug into the ground to help absorb recoil after firing. The first production vehicles appeared in January 1945, and arrived just as World War II in Europe was ending. It continued in service, with a total of 311 being built, and saw its main action in the Korean War (1950-53), where it proved an excellent weapon, and in Indochina with the French Army. The M40 appeared at a time when nuclear warfare was making its debut, and thus it was used extensively for post-war trials designed to provide protection against fallout for the crew, forming the blueprint for modern self-propelled vehicles.

Country of origin:	USA
Crew:	8
Weight:	36,400kg (80,080lb)
Dimensions:	length 9.04m (29ft 8in); width 3.15m (10ft 4in); height 2.84m (9ft 4in)
Range:	161km (100 miles)
Armour:	up to 12.7mm (0.5in)
Armament:	one 155mm gun
Powerplant:	one Continental nine-cylinder radial piston engine developing 395hp (294.6kW)
Performance:	maximum road speed 38.6km/h (24mph); fording 1.067m (3ft 6in); vertical obstacle 0.61m (2ft); trench 2.26m (7ft 5in)

Self-Propelled Artillery

Bishop

The Bishop was designed to relieve the 25-pounder batteries in North Africa of their role as anti-tank weapons, in which role they were taking a pounding from the Germans. A 25mm gun was therefore mounted on the chassis of a Valentine tank – it was not a success. The new vehicle had a high, slab-sided turret which made an excellent target for enemy gunners. The gun was mounted in a fixed turret with limited elevation. By the time they were introduced, the 25-pounder was no longer being used in an anti-tank role, so the Bishops were diverted for artillery use. The Bishop was the first British effort at a self-propelled gun and was useful in showing the potential of the type and what to avoid in future designs. When the M7 Priest arrived, the Bishop soon fell out of use.

Country of origin:	UK
Crew:	4
Weight:	7879kg (17,333lb)
Dimensions:	length 5.64m (18ft 6in); width 2.77m (9ft 1in); height 3.05m (10ft)
Range:	177km (110 miles)
Armour:	8-60mm (0.315-2.36in)
Armament:	one 25-pounder gun
Powerplant:	one AEC six-cylinder diesel engine developing 131hp (97.7kW)
Performance:	maximum road speed 24km/h (15mph); fording 0.91m (3ft); vertical obstacle 0.83m (2ft 9in): trench 2.28m (7ft 6in)

Mk F3 155mm

In the 1960s, the French Army replaced their American M41 howitzers with an indigenous design, based on the AMX-13 tank chassis and known as the Mk F3. It was equipped with two rear spades which were reversed into the ground to give added stability. The F3 fired a standard 155mm high-explosive projectile, other types of ammunition being rocket-assisted, smoke and illumination. There was no nuclear, chemical and biological protection (NBC), though. It remained in production until the 1980s, being exported to a number of South American and Middle East countries. One drawback of the vehicle, apart from the lack of protection for the crew, was that it could only carry two people, the rest of the crew having to follow behind in support vehicles.

Country of origin:	France
Crew:	2
Weight:	17,410kg (38,304lb)
Dimensions:	length 6.22m (20ft 5in); width 2.72m (8ft 11in); height 2.085m (6ft 10in)
Range:	300km (185 miles)
Armour:	20mm (0.78in)
Armament:	one 155mm gun
Powerplant:	one SOFAM 8Gxb eight-cylinder petrol engine developing 250hp (186kW)
Performance:	maximum road speed 60km/h (37mph); vertical obstacle 0.6m (2ft); trench 1.5m (4ft 11in)

Self-Propelled Artillery

GCT 155mm

The GCT 155mm was the designated successor to the Mk F3 in the French Army. Production began in 1977. Saudi Arabia received deliveries first, before the French Army, but it finally entered service in the 1980s and was deployed in regiments of 18 guns each. By 1995 some 400 had been built for the home and export markets. The main improvements over the Mk F3 were an automatic loading system, giving a rate of fire of eight rounds a minute, and protection for the increased on-board crew of four, as well as night vision, nuclear, biological and chemical (NBC) protection and the ability to fire a range of projectiles, including a round carrying multiple anti-tank mines. The GCT 155mm saw active service during the Iran-Iraq War, Iraq having received 85 of the vehicles.

Country of origin:	France
Crew:	4
Weight:	41,949kg (92,288lb)
Dimensions:	length 10.25m (33ft 7.5in); width 3.15m (10ft 4in); height 3.25m (10ft 8in)
Range:	450km (280 miles)
Armour:	20mm (0.78in)
Armament:	one 155mm gun; one 7.62mm/12.7mm anti-aircraft machine gun
Powerplant:	one Hispano-Suiza HS 110 12-cylinder water-cooled multi-fuel engine developing 720hp (537kW)
Performance:	maximum road speed 60km/h (37mph); vertical obstacle 0.93m (3ft 0.7in); trench 1.90m (6ft 3in)

M109

The M109 was developed following a 1952 requirement for a self-propelled howitzer to replace the M44. The first production vehicles were completed in 1962 and survived numerous adaptations and upgrades to become the most widely used howitzer in the world, seeing action in Vietnam, in the Arab-Israeli Wars and the Iran-Iraq War, and being exported to nearly 30 countries worldwide. It has an amphibious capability and fires a variety of projectiles including tactical nuclear shells. To date some 4000 are in use around the world, and the M109 has undergone numerous upgrades, including a new gun mount, new turret with longer barrel ordnance, automatic fire control, upgraded armour and improved armour. It will continue to serve well into the next century.

Country of origin:	USA
Crew:	6
Weight:	23,723kg (52,192lb)
Dimensions:	length 6.612m (21ft 8.25in); width 3.295m (10ft 9.75in); height 3.289m (10ft 9.5in)
Range:	390km (240 miles)
Armour:	classified
Armament:	one 155mm howitzer; one 12.7mm anti-aircraft machine gun
Powerplant:	one Detroit Diesel Model 8V-71T diesel engine developing 405hp (302kW)
Performance:	maximum road speed 56km/h (35mph); fording 1.07m (3ft 6in); vertical obstacle 0.533m (1ft 9in); trench 1.828m (6ft)

M107

The M107 was designed in the 1950s along with the M110 203mm self-propelled howitzer, which has the same chassis and gun mount. The first production models rolled off the factory line in 1962, and eventually a total of 524 M107s were built by the time production ceased in 1980. Though it is no longer in frontline service with the United States and the United Kingdom, it is still in first-line use with the forces of Greece, Iran, Israel, South Korea and Turkey. The M107 has a total crew of 13, but only the commander, driver and three gunners are carried on the vehicle itself, which has no crew protection. The rest are transported in a truck, along with the rounds, charges and fuses. The 175mm gun has a range of 32km (20 miles), firing a high-explosive round.

Country of origin:	USA
Crew:	5
Weight:	28,168kg (61,970lb)
Dimensions:	length 11.256m (36ft 7.75in); width 3.149m (10ft 4in); height 3.679m (12ft)
Range:	725km (450 miles)
Armour:	classified
Armament:	one 175mm gun
Powerplant:	one Detroit Diesel Model 8V-71T diesel engine developing 405hp (302kW)
Performance:	maximum road speed 56km/h (35mph); fording 1.06m (3ft 6in); vertical obstacle 1.016m (3ft 4in); trench 2.326m (7ft 9in)

Palmaria

The Palmaria was developed by OTO Melara specifically for the export market and included Libya as its first purchaser. The prototype appeared in 1981, based heavily on the OF-40 main battle tank already in service with Dubai, and the first production vehicles were completed a year later. One unusual feature is the auxiliary power unit for the turret, thus conserving fuel for the main engine. It comes equipped with an automatic loading system and a wide range of munitions including rocket-assisted projectiles, although these pay the penalty of lower explosive content. The vehicle has an automatic loader, giving it a rate of fire of one round every 15 seconds. There are no variants as such, though its chassis has been fitted with twin 25mm guns in an anti-aircraft configuration

Country of origin:	Italy
Crew:	5
Weight:	46,632kg (102,590lb)
Dimensions:	length 11.474m (37ft 7.75in); width 2.35m (7ft 8.5in); height 2.874m (9ft 5.25in)
Range:	400km (250 miles)
Armour:	classified
Armament:	one 155mm howitzer; one 7.62mm machine gun
Powerplant:	one eight-cylinder diesel engine developing 750hp (559kW)
Performance:	maximum road speed 60km/h (37mph); fording 1.2m (3ft 11in); vertical obstacle 1m (3ft 3in); trench 3m (9ft 10in)

Self-Propelled Artillery

Abbot

Post-war British designs for self-propelled guns focused on the excellent Centurion tank chassis with 25-pounder or 140mm guns. However, NATO required a standard 105 or 155mm gun. As a result, Vickers developed the 105mm Abbot self-propelled gun during the 1950s for deployment with the British Army of the Rhine. Fully armoured, the Abbot served with the Royal Artillery until being replaced by the American M109 in the 1980s. Like most British post-war armoured fighting vehicle designs, the Abbot was reliable, rugged and a potent force on the battlefield. One variant was the Value Engineered Abbot, produced for the Indian Army without extras such as flotation screen, night vision and nuclear, biological and chemical (NBC) protection.

Country of origin:	UK
Crew:	4
Weight:	16,494kg (36,288lb)
Dimensions:	length 5.84m (19ft 2in); width 2.641m (8ft 8in); height 2.489m (8ft 2in)
Range:	390km (240 miles)
Armour:	6-12mm (0.23-0.47in)
Armament:	one 155mm gun; one 7.62mm anti-aircraft machine gun; three smoke dischargers
Powerplant:	one Rolls-Royce six-cylinder diesel engine developing 240hp (179kW)
Performance:	maximum road speed 47.5km/h (30mph); fording 1.2m (3ft 11in); vertical obstacle 0.609m (2ft); trench 2.057m (6ft 9in)

Bandkanon

Bofors produced the prototype of the Bandkanon 1A in 1960, but with extensive trials and modifications being carried out, the first production models did not appear until 1966. It had the distinction of being the first fully automatic self-propelled gun to enter service with any army. Ammunition is kept in a 14-round clip carried externally at the rear of the hull. Once the first round is loaded manually, remaining rounds are loaded automatically. However, it was not produced in quantity (production ceased after only two years) mainly because its size and lack of mobility hindered its performance on the battlefield and made it very difficult to conceal. It has undergone some improvements, such as the addition of a Rolls Royce diesel engine and a new fire-control system.

Country of origin:	Sweden
Crew:	5
Weight:	53,000kg (116,600lb)
Dimensions:	length 11.00m (36ft 1in); width 3.37m (11ft 0.7in); height 3.85m (12ft 7.5in)
Range:	230km (143 miles)
Armour:	10-20mm (0.4-0.8in)
Armament:	one 155mm gun; one 7.62mm anti-aircraft machine gun
Powerplant:	one Rolls-Royce diesel engine developing 240hp (179kW) and Boeing gas turbine, developing 300hp (224kW)
Performance:	maximum road speed 28km/h (17.4mph); fording 1m (3ft 3in); vertical obstacle 0.95m (3ft 1.5in); trench 2.00m (6ft 6.75in)

DANA

The DANA was the first wheeled self-propelled howitzer to enter service in modern times. Wheeled vehicles have the advantage of being cheaper to build and easier to maintain, with greater strategic mobility. First seen in 1980, the DANA was built by Skoda and was based on the 8 x 8 Tatra 815 truck, the best off-road truck in existence at the time. Tyre pressure can be regulated to allow good mobility over rough terrain, and steering is power-assisted on the front four wheels. It carries three hydraulic stabilisers to be lowered into the ground before firing, and carries a crane on the roof to assist with loading the ammunition. Rate of fire is three rounds per minute for a period of 30 minutes, and the vehicle is in service in Libya, Poland, Russia, the Czech Republic and Slovakia.

Country of origin:	Czechoslovakia
Crew:	4 to 5
Weight:	23,000kg (50,600lb)
Dimensions:	length 10.5m (34ft 5in); width 2.8m (9ft 2in); height 2.6m (8ft 6in)
Range:	600km (375 miles)
Armour:	12.7mm (0.5in)
Armament:	one 152mm gun; one 12.7mm machine gun
Powerplant:	one V-12 diesel engine developing 345hp (257kW)
Performance:	maximum road speed 80km/h (49.71mph); fording 1.4m (4ft 7in); vertical obstacle 1.5m (4ft 11in); trench 1.4m (4ft 7in)

M1973

Known as the 2S3 Akatsiya in the former Soviet Union (the designation M1973 is a US Army term), 18 vehicles were deployed as support for each tank division and motorised rifle division in the Red Army. The chassis was a shortened version of that used for the SA-4 surface-to-air missile system and the GMZ armoured minelayer, both of which were used in the USSR for many years. Fitted with nuclear, biological and chemical (NBC) protection and with a tactical nuclear capability, the vehicle was not equipped for amphibious operations. During operation it was normal for two of the crew to stand at the rear of vehicle and act as ammunition handlers, feeding projectiles via two hatches in the hull rear. The M1973 proved a popular vehicle amongst Soviet client states and was exported to Iraq and Libya.

Country of origin:	USSR
Crew:	6
Weight:	24,945kg (54,880lb)
Dimensions:	length 8.40m (27ft 6.7in); width 3.20m (10ft 6in); height 2.80m (9ft 2.25in)
Range:	300km (186 miles)
Armour:	15-20mm (0.59-0.78in)
Armament:	one 152mm gun; one 7.62mm anti-aircraft machine gun
Powerplant:	one V-12 diesel engine developing 520hp (388kW)
Performance:	maximum road speed 55km/h (34mph); fording 1.5m (4ft 11in); vertical obstacle 1.10m (3ft 7in); trench 2.50m (8ft 2.5in)

Self-Propelled Artillery
M1974

After World War II the USSR concentrated development on towed artillery pieces, in contrast to NATO's drift towards self-propelled guns. It was not until 1974 that the first Soviet self-propelled howitzer made an appearance in public, hence its Western designation. Known as the Gvozdika in the USSR, the vehicle was deployed in large numbers (36 per tank division, 72 per motorised rifle division). Differing from the M1973 in being fully amphibious, the chassis has been used for a number of armoured command and chemical warfare reconnaissance vehicles, as well as a mine-clearing vehicle. It can also be fitted with wider tracks to allow it to operate in snow or swamp conditions. The M1974 was widely exported to Soviet client states as well as Angola, Algeria and Iraq.

Country of origin:	USSR
Crew:	4
Weight:	15,700kg (34,540lb)
Dimensions:	length 7.30m (23ft 11.5in); width 2.85m (9ft 4in); height 2.40m (7ft 10.5in)
Range:	500km (310 miles)
Armour:	15-20mm (0.59-0.78in)
Armament:	one 122mm gun; one 7.62mm anti-aircraft machine gun
Powerplant:	one YaMZ-238V V-8 water-cooled diesel engine developing 240hp (179kW)
Performance:	maximum road speed 60km/h (37mph); fording amphibious; vertical obstacle 1.10m (3ft 7in); trench 3.00m (9ft 10in)

ASU-57

The ASU-57 was developed in the 1950s specifically for use by Soviet airborne divisions (54 vehicles per division) and was designed to be parachuted with the troops, using pallets fitted with retro-rocket systems to soften impact on landing. The gun was a development of the World War II ZIS-2, while its engine was taken from the Pobeda civilian car. Despite its drawbacks – a hull made of welded aluminium which affords little protection for the crew, a rather underpowered engine and weaponry – the ASU-57 remained in service for around 20 years before being replaced by the ASU-85. For airborne troops such vehicles are invaluable, giving lightly armed soldiers, who are invariably isolated behind enemy lines, mobile artillery support on the battlefield.

Country of origin:	USSR
Crew:	3
Weight:	3300kg (7260lb)
Dimensions:	length 4.995m (16ft 4.7in); width 2.086m (6ft 10in); height 1.18m (3ft 10.5in)
Range:	250km (155 miles)
Armour:	6mm (0.23in)
Armament:	one 57mm CH-51M gun; one 7.62mm anti-aircraft machine gun
Powerplant:	one M-20E four-cylinder petrol engine developing 55hp (41kW)
Performance:	maximum road speed 45km/h (28mph); vertical obstacle 0.5m (20in); trench 1.4m (4ft 7in)

Self-Propelled Artillery

M56

After World War II, the US Army issued a requirement for a highly mobile anti-tank gun which could be dropped with the first wave of airborne troops and have a firepower similar to that of a tank. Cadillac began production of the M56 (also known as the Scorpion) in 1953 and ceased production in 1959. The M56 was deployed with the 82nd and 101st Airborne Divisions and saw action in the Vietnam War (although not on a large scale), mainly in a fire-support role. In addition, small numbers were exported to Spain and Morocco. The main drawbacks were a lack of armour and the massive recoil, which often moved the vehicle several feet and obscured the target with dust. In the 1960s, the vehicle was replaced by the M551, another flawed armoured fighting vehicle design.

Country of origin:	USA
Crew:	4
Weight:	7000kg (15,400lb)
Dimensions:	length 5.841m (19ft 2in); width 2.577m (8ft 5.5in); height 2.067m (6ft 9.3in)
Range:	225km (140 miles)
Armour:	classified
Armament:	one 90mm gun
Powerplant:	one Continental six-cylinder petrol engine developing 200hp (149kW)
Performance:	maximum road speed 45km/h (28mph); vertical obstacle 0.762m (2ft 6in); trench 1.524m (5ft)

LARS II

The Light Artillery Rocket System (LARS) was developed in the mid-1960s and was accepted into West German service in 1969. Known as the Artillerie Raketenwerfer 110SF, the LARS was upgraded to the LARS II and mounted on the MAN 4 x 4 chassis. With 36 launcher tubes, the full complement could be launched in only 17.5 seconds and could be reloaded in around 15 minutes with a variety of different rounds, including parachute-retarded anti-tank mines. The launcher was supported by a resupply vehicle containing 144 rockets. 209 launchers were in service with the West German Army, one battery per division, until replaced by the MLRS in the late 1980s. No doubt the design and thinking behind the LARS was influenced by Soviet rocket launchers on the Eastern Front in World War II.

Country of origin:	Germany
Crew:	3
Weight:	17,480kg (38,537lb)
Dimensions:	length 8.28m (27ft 2in); width 2.5m (8ft 2in); height 2.99m (9ft 10in)
Range:	480km (300 miles)
Armour:	none
Armament:	36 110mm rocket tubes
Powerplant:	one V-8 liquid-cooled diesel engine developing 320hp (238kW)
Performance:	maximum road speed 100km/h (62.5mph); fording 1.4m (94ft 7in); vertical obstacle 0.6m (1ft 11in); trench1.6m (5ft 3in)

Multiple Rocket Launchers

BM-21

The BM-21 entered service in the early 1960s and became the standard multiple rocket-launcher of Warsaw Pact armies, as well as most Soviet client states. Variants were produced in China, India, Egypt and Romania. The 40-round launcher was mounted on a URAL-375 6 x 6 truck (later a on a ZIL-131 in a modified 36-round form). For airborne troops, a smaller 12-round version was developed to be mounted on a 4 x 4 truck. Most BM-21 variants have been used in action, particularly in Afghanistan. In addition, customised versions were used by the PLO in battles around Beirut from 1982 onwards. The BM-21 is symbolic of Russian multiple rocket launchers, being crude and simple to operate. Nevertheless, when used in batteries it could deliver devastating firepower.

Country of origin:	USSR
Crew:	6
Weight:	11,500kg (25,300lb)
Dimensions:	length 7.35m (24ft 1in); width 2.69m (8ft 9in); height 2.85m (9ft 4in)
Range:	405km (253 miles)
Armour:	none
Armament:	40 122mm rocket-launcher tubes
Powerplant:	one V-8 water-cooled petrol engine developing 180hp (134kW)
Performance:	maximum road speed 75km/h (46.8mph); fording 1.5m (4ft 11in); vertical obstacle 0.65m (2ft 1in); trench 0.875m (2ft 10in)

BM-24

The BM-24 was the BM-21's predecessor, introduced into service during the early 1950s. Originally mounted on a ZIL-151 6 x 6 truck, the system was later transferred to a ZIL-157. The system consisted of two rows of six tubular frame rails. Two stabiliser jacks were fitted which had to be lowered before firing. The BM-24 saw widespread use with Arab armies against the Israelis, the latter being so impressed with the system that they pressed the large numbers of captured launchers into service and designed a new rocket for it, with shorter range but a more effective warhead. This version saw service in the 1973 Yom Kippur War and in Lebanon in 1982. Rocket types include high-explosive, smoke and chemical, with a typical range being 11km (6.84 miles).

Country of origin:	USSR
Crew:	6
Weight:	9200kg (20,240lb)
Dimensions:	length 6.7m (21ft 11in); width 2.3m (7ft 6in); height 2.91m (9ft 6in)
Range:	430km (269 miles)
Armour:	none
Armament:	12 240mm rocket-launcher tubes
Powerplant:	one six-cylinder water-cooled petrol engine developing 109hp (81kW)
Performance:	maximum road speed 65km/h (40.6mph); fording 0.85m (2ft 9in); vertical obstacle 0.46m (1ft 6in); trench 0.69m (2ft 3in)

Multiple Rocket Launchers

BM-27

The BM-27 entered service with the Soviet Army in the mid-1970s. With similar operational characteristics to contemporary American multiple rocket-launchers, the vehicle was designed to provide fire-support to frontline troops using chemical, high explosive and incendiary munitions. The system comprises one layer of four tubes on top of two layers of six tubes. The whole system is mounted on a ZIL-135 8 x 8 truck chassis. Four stabiliser jacks are lowered to provide support when firing. Support vehicles can reload the launcher within five minutes. A few BM-27s were transferred to Syria, where they saw action against Israeli troops in 1982. The BM-27 is much more sophisticated than earlier Russian rocket launchers, and can fire projectiles to a range of 40km (24.85 miles).

Country of origin:	USSR
Crew:	6
Weight:	22,750kg (49,940lb)
Dimensions:	length 9.3m (30ft 6in); width 2.8m (9ft 2in); height 3.2m (10ft 6in)
Range:	500km (312 miles)
Armour:	none
Armament:	16 220mm rocket-launcher tubes
Powerplant:	one V-8 water-cooled diesel engine developing 260hp (194kW)
Performance:	maximum road speed 65km/h (40.65mph); fording 1m (3ft 4in); vertical obstacle 1.1m (3ft 7in); trench 2.8m (9ft 2in)

Astros II

The Astros II is a conventional truck-based multiple rocket launcher built by Tectran in Brazil. The 10-tonnes (9.9-tons) 6 x 6 cross-country vehicle is equipped with armoured shutters to protect the crew cabin. In service with the Brazilian Army and exported in large numbers to Iraq during the Iran-Iraq War, the Astros system uses a common launcher, command and fire-control vehicle to deliver three different types of rocket, the SS-30, SS-40 and SS-60. The rockets range in weight from 68kg to 595kg (149.6lb to 1309lb), all of which are unguided. An ammunition resupply vehicle is always attached to the Astros system. Though less sophisticated than the MLRS, for example, the Astros does provide an excellent rocket launcher system for Third World and developing states.

Country of origin:	Brazil
Crew:	3
Weight:	10,000kg (22,000lb)
Dimensions:	length 7m (22ft 11in); width 2.9m (9ft 6in); height 2.6m (8ft 6in)
Range:	480km (300 miles)
Armour:	classified
Armament:	one battery of four, 16 or 32 rocket-launcher tubes
Powerplant:	one six-cylinder water-cooled diesel engine developing 212hp (158kW)
Performance:	maximum road speed 65km/h (40.62mph); fording 1.1m (3ft 7in); vertical obstacle 1m (3ft 4in); trench 2.29m (7ft 6in)

Multiple Rocket Launchers

MLRS

The Vought Multiple Launch Rocket System (MLRS) had its origins in a 1976 feasibility study into what was known as a General Support Rocket System. Following trials the Vought system was chosen and entered service with the US Army in 1982. These Self-Propelled Launcher Loaders on the chassis of the M2 Infantry Fighting Vehicle carry two pods of six rounds each. These rounds might consist of fragmentation bomblets, anti-tank mines, chemical warheads or mine-dispensing munitions. The Vought MLRS was licensed to the UK, France, Italy, West Germany and the Netherlands for production. It saw action during the 1991 Gulf War, when Allied MLRS batteries tore large holes in Iraqi defence lines prior to the ground offensive to free Kuwait.

Country of origin:	USA
Crew:	3
Weight:	25,191kg (55,420lb)
Dimensions:	length 6.8m (22ft 4in); width 2.92m (9ft 7in); height 2.6m (8ft 6in)
Range:	483km (302 miles)
Armour:	classified
Armament:	two rocket pod containers, each holding six rockets
Powerplant:	one Cummings VTA-903 turbo-charged eight-cylinder diesel engine developing 500hp 373kW)
Performance:	maximum road speed 64km/h (40mph); fording 1.1m (3ft 7in); vertical obstacle 1m (3ft 4in); trench 2.29m (7ft 6in)

Valkiri

South Africa began development of an indigenous multiple rocket launcher in 1977 as a counter to the various Soviet systems in service with neighbouring African countries. The Valkiri entered service in 1981, deployed in batteries of eight, to be used against guerrilla camps, troop concentrations and soft-skinned vehicle convoys. Mounted on a 4 x 4 SAMIL truck chassis, the full 24-round complement could be fired in 24 seconds, with a 10-minute reloading time. Highly mobile and with minimal launch signature, the Valkiri proved an ideal weapon for cross-border raids and counter-insurgency work, especially as the system could be easily camouflaged to resemble a standard truck. Each of the rockets the system fired had a maximum range of 22km (13.67 miles).

Country of origin:	South Africa
Crew:	2
Weight:	6440kg (14,168lb)
Dimensions:	length 5.41m (17ft 9in); width 1.985m (6ft 6in), height 3.2m (10ft 6in)
Range:	650km (406 miles)
Armour:	none
Armament:	24 127mm rocket-launcher tubes
Powerplant:	one six-cylinder diesel engine developing 120hp (89kW)
Performance:	maximum road speed 80km/h (50mph); fording 0.5m (1ft 7in); vertical obstacle 0.6m (1ft 11in); trench 0.6m (1ft 11in)

Walid

The Egyptian Army has relied in the main on copies of Soviet-produced multiple rocket launcher systems, reflecting the heavy Russian influence in the country in the 1950s and 1960s. However, since Egypt has moved closer to the West, a number of indigenous programmes have been initiated, in particular the Sakr-18 and Sakr-30 Multiple Rocket Launchers, as well as a specialised system for laying down smoke screens. Based on the Walid 4 x 4 armoured personnel carrier, a full salvo of D-3000 rockets is able to produce a smoke screen 1000m (3280ft) long, lasting for up to 15 minutes, sufficient to cover most activities on the battlefield. The same system can be mounted onto a T-62 tank. The rockets are carried in a ready-to-launch position (there is also a six-round version).

Country of origin:	Egypt
Crew:	2
Weight:	unknown
Dimensions:	length 6.12m (20ft); width 2.57m (8ft 5in); height 2.3m (7ft 6in)
Range:	800km (500 miles)
Armour:	8mm (0.31in)
Armament:	12 80mm rocket-launcher tubes
Powerplant:	one diesel engine developing 168hp (125kW)
Performance:	maximum road speed 86km/h (54mph); fording 0.8m (2ft 7in); vertical obstacle 0.5m (1ft 7in)

Type 70

The Type 63 was developed in the late 1950s. It consisted of three rows of four barrels. For firing the wheels were removed and the launcher was supported by two legs at the front, with a spade attached at the rear to absorb recoil. It could be fired independently, or mounted on a 4 x 4 truck chassis, this version being known as the Type 81. A smaller version was developed for use by airborne forces, which could be broken down for transport by men or horses. The Type 63 has seen extensive combat service around the world, being used by the Mujahideen in Afghanistan, by the North Vietnamese in Vietnam, by the Iranians in the Iran-Iraq War and by the PLO against the Israelis. The Type 70 rocket launcher, shown above and specified below, uses components of the YW 531C armoured personnel carrier.

Country of origin:	China
Crew:	2
Weight:	12,600kg (27,720lb)
Dimensions:	5.4m (17ft 9in); width 3m (9ft 9in); height 2.58m (8ft 6in)
Range:	500km (312 miles)
Armour:	10mm (0.39in)
Armament:	12 107mm rocket-launcher tubes
Powerplant:	one V-8 diesel engine developing 320hp (238kW)
Performance:	maximum road speed 65km/h (38mph); fording amphibious; vertical obstacle 0.6m (1ft 11in); trench 2m (6ft 6in)

Marder II

By 1941, the PzKpfw II was becoming obsolete. However, the production line was still in operation, so in order not to waste resources, the decision was taken to convert the chassis to a tank destroyer to tackle the large numbers of Soviet tanks on the Eastern Front. The standard Pak 40 anti-tank gun was mounted on the PzKpfw II's chassis. The combination of firepower and mobility worked well and the Marder II as it was known remained in production until 1944, with 1217 being made. The Marder II saw action in all theatres, particularly on the Eastern front, where some were later equipped with infrared systems for night-fighting. The Marder II proved an effective and versatile weapon and was the most widely used German self-propelled gun of World War II.

Country of origin:	Germany
Crew:	3 or 4
Weight:	11,000kg (24,200lb)
Dimensions:	length 6.36m (20ft 10.4in); width 2.28m (7ft 5.8in); height 2.20m (7ft 2.6in)
Range:	190km (118 miles)
Armour:	10mm (0.39in)
Armament:	one 7.5cm Pak 40/2 gun; one 7.92mm MG34 machine gun
Powerplant:	one Maybach HL 62 petrol engine developing 140hp (104.4kW)
Performance:	maximum road speed 40km/h (24.8mph); fording 0.9m (2ft 11in); vertical obstacle 0.42m (1ft 4in); trench 1.8m (5ft 11in)

Hetzer

Most tank destroyer conversions of existing tank chassis were rather cumbersome and lacked finesse in design. In contrast, the various Sturmgeschütz artillery vehicles had proved very effective tank killers, so it was decided to produce a light tank destroyer along the lines of a Sturmgeschütz. Based on the PzKpfw 38(t) chassis, the new Hetzer was put into production in 1943. Small, well-protected, with good mobility and able to knock out all but the heaviest tanks, the Hetzer was a tremendous success. By the time the factories were overrun in May 1944, 1577 had been built, including flame-thrower and recovery versions. The Czech Army took over production of the Hetzer after World War II and exports were still in service with the Swiss in the 1970s.

Country of origin:	Germany
Crew:	4
Weight:	14,500kg (31,900lb)
Dimensions:	length 6.20m (20ft 4.1in); width 2.50m (8ft 2.4in); height 2.10m (6ft 10.7in)
Range:	250km (155 miles)
Armour:	10-60mm (0.39-2.36in)
Armament:	one 7.5cm Pak 39 gun; one 7.92mm MG34 machine gun
Powerplant:	one Praga AC/2800 petrol engine developing 150-160hp (111.9-119.3kW)
Performance:	maximum road speed 39km/h (24.2mph); fording 0.9m (2ft 11in); vertical obstacle 0.65m (2ft 1in); trench 1.3m (4ft 3.2in)

Jagpanzer IV

Experience during 1942 suggested that the Sturmgeschütz vehicles would have to be upgunned if their role as tank destroyers was to continue. The armament of the Panther was selected, and while modifications were made to the Sturmgeschütz III to allow for this upgrade, the Panther gun was fitted to the chassis of the PzKpfw IV. Known as the Jagdpanzer IV, the first production models appeared in 1943. With a low silhouette and well-protected hull, the Jagdpanzer IV soon proved popular with crews, especially as the armament proved sufficient to knock out almost any enemy tank encountered. Under Hitler's instructions, some were later fitted with the more powerful L/70 gun, but the extra weight resulted in less mobility. A total of 1139 were produced between December 1943 and March 1945.

Country of origin:	Germany
Crew:	4
Weight:	25,800kg (56,933lb)
Dimensions:	length 8.58m (28ft 1.8in); width 2.93m (9ft 7.4in); height 1.96m (6ft 5.2in)
Range:	214km (133 miles)
Armour:	11-80mm (0.43-3.14in)
Armament:	one 7.5cm Pak 39 gun; two 7.92mm MG34 machine guns
Powerplant:	one Maybach HL 120 petrol engine developing 265hp (197.6kW)
Performance:	maximum road speed 35km/h (22mph); fording 1.2m (3ft 11in); vertical obstacle 0.6m (23.6in); trench 2.3m (7ft 6.6in);

Nashorn

In an effort to get sizeable numbers of tank destroyers into service on the Eastern Front, the Germans embarked on a series of hurried improvisations. A special weapon-carrier vehicle based on the PzKpfw IV chassis was adapted to take the 8.8cm Pak 43 gun. The first of these so-called Nashorns entered service in 1943. The Nashorn was a high vehicle which was difficult to conceal, a problem increased by poor armour with only the driver being fully protected. It was therefore used as a long-range weapon, in contrast to most other tank destroyers. Some 433 were built before production ceased in 1944. The powerful gun made the Nashorn a potent battlefield weapon, but it was too bulky for its prescribed role and only the lack of anything better kept it in production in Germany.

Country of origin:	Germany
Crew:	5
Weight:	24,400kg (53,680lb)
Dimensions:	length 8.44m (27ft 8.3in); width 2.86m (9ft 4.6in); height 2.65m (8ft 3.3in)
Range:	210km (130.5 miles)
Armour:	10-30mm (0.39-1.18in)
Armament:	one 8.8cm Pak 43 gun; one 7.92mm MG34 machine gun
Powerplant:	one Maybach HL 120 petrol engine developing 265hp (197.6kW)
Performance:	maximum road speed 40km/h (24.8mph); fording 0.8m (2ft 7.5in); vertical obstacle 0.6m (23.6in); trench 2.3m (7ft 6.6in)

Elefant

The Elefant stemmed from the Porsche design for the PzKpfw VI Tiger. Henschel was awarded the contract for the new tank, but it was decided to use the Porsche design as a tank destroyer. Hitler demanded that the new vehicle be ready for the 1943 offensive on the Russian Front, so development was rather hurried. As a result many broke down in their first action at the Battle of Kursk, and the lack of proper armour and ponderous mobility made them easy targets for Soviet gunners in the battle. In addition, the lack of machine guns meant that there was no defence against Soviet troops disabling them with explosive charges in close-quarter combat. The survivors were withdrawn to Italy, where unreliability and lack of spares ensured their continued ineffectiveness.

Country of origin:	Germany
Crew:	6
Weight:	65,000kg (143,000lb)
Dimensions:	length 8.128m (26ft 8in); width 3.378m (11ft 1in); height 2.997m (9ft 10in)
Range:	153km (95 miles)
Armour:	50-200mm (1.97-7.87in)
Armament:	one 8.8cm Pak 43/2 gun
Powerplant:	two Maybach HL 120 TRM V-12 petrol engines each developing 530hp (395.2kW)
Performance:	maximum road speed 20.1km/h (12.5mph); fording 1.0m (3ft 4in); vertical obstacle 0.8m (31.5in); trench 2.65m (8ft 8.3in)

Jagdpanther

The Jagdpanther was one of the first purpose-built tank destroyers, as opposed to a hasty tank-conversion. Using the Panther chassis, the prototype was demonstrated to Hitler in October 1943, who named it the Jagdpanther himself. The vehicle was superb. Fast, well-armoured and mounting a powerful gun, the Jagdpanther became one of the most famous of all World War II vehicles, able to knock out almost any tank it encountered. A machine gun and anti-magnetic mine paint helped with close-quarter defence. On all European fronts, the Jagdpanther became feared. Fortunately for the Allies, planned production levels were never reached, and by the time the factories were overrun in April 1945, only 382 had been completed, mainly due to the disruption caused by Allied bombing raids.

Country of origin:	Germany
Crew:	5
Weight:	46,000kg (101,200lb)
Dimensions:	length 9.90m (32ft 5.8in); width 3.27m (10ft 8.7in); height 2.715m (8ft 10.9in)
Range:	160km (99.4 miles)
Armour:	80-120mm (3.15-4.72in)
Armament:	one 8.8cm Pak 43/3 gun; one 7.92mm MG34 machine gun
Powerplant:	one Maybach HL 230 petrol engine developing 600-700hp (447.4-522kW)
Performance:	maximum road speed 55km/h (34.2mph); fording 1.7m (5ft 7in); vertical obstacle 0.9m (35in); trench 1.9m (6ft 3in)

Tank Destroyers

L.40

The Italians were ahead of tactical thinking in one aspect of armoured vehicle production, when they developed one of the first tank destroyers in the late 1930s. This thinking proved useful when it was realised that their light tanks were of little combat value in North Africa in 1941. The chassis of the Semovente M 40 was fitted with a Böhler 47mm gun, one of the hardest hitting anti-tank weapons of· its day. Around 280 of the tank destroyer vehicles were produced, and they fared adequately against Allied armour from 1942 onwards. Pressed into service by the Germans after the Italian surrender in 1943, the vehicle was unsuited for much of the Italian terrain and saw little action. Many had their armament removed and were converted into mobile command posts.

Country of origin:	Italy
Crew:	2
Weight:	6500kg (14,300lb)
Dimensions:	length 4.00m (13ft 1.5in); width 1.92m (6ft 3.6in); height 1.63m (5ft 4.2in)
Range:	200km (124 miles)
Armour:	6-42mm (0.23-1.65in)
Armament:	one Böhler 47mm gun or 8mm Breda modelo 38 machine gun
Powerplant:	one SPA 18D four-cylinder petrol engine developing 68hp (50.7kW)
Performance:	maximum road speed 42.3km/h (26.3mph); fording 0.8m (2ft 7in); vertical obstacle 0.8m (2ft 7in); trench 1.7m (5ft 7in);

M.41

The M 41 was the only heavy tank destroyer produced by Italy during World War II. Using the chassis of the M 14/41 tank, designers mounted a powerful anti-aircraft gun on the vehicle. Designed to operate at long range, the M 41 was not considered to require armour protection. The first production vehicles appeared in 1941, but only 48 were ever built, mainly because Italy's industrial plant was limited, but also because the gun was required for regular anti-aircraft duties. The M 41 proved effective in the open spaces of North Africa, but after being seized by the Germans after the Italian surrender proved to have little value in the mountainous terrain of Italy, where few tanks could operate. Most were therefore used as long-range artillery.

Country of origin:	Italy
Crew:	2 (on gun)
Weight:	17,000kg (37,400lb)
Dimensions:	length 5.205m (17ft 0.9in); width 2.20m (7ft 2.6in); height 2.15m (7ft 0.6in)
Range:	200km (124 miles)
Armour:	none
Armament:	one 90mm cannon
Powerplant:	one SPA 15-TM-41 eight-cylinder petrol engine developing 145hp (108.1kW)
Performance:	maximum road speed 35.5km/h (22mph); fording 1.0m (3ft 3in); vertical obstacle 0.9m (35.4in); trench 2.1m (6ft 10.7in)

Tank Destroyers
M10

During the period immediately before its entry into World War II, the US Army developed a concept to defeat fast-moving armoured formations using powerfully armed tank destroyers deployed *en masse*. The M10 was a product of this concept. Based on the M4 Sherman tank chassis and using the M7 gun, developed from an anti-aircraft weapon, the M10 was lightly armed as it was not intended for close-quarter combat. Production ran from September to December 1942, with nearly 5000 being produced. The concept of separate tank destroyer battalions was soon proved ineffective, and thus most M10s were used more as assault forces. The M10 continued in service until the end of the war, but its large and bulky nature and the diminishing effect of its gun reduced its usefulness.

Country of origin:	USA
Crew:	5
Weight:	29,937kg (65,861lb)
Dimensions:	length 6.83m (22ft 5in); width 3.05m (10ft 0in); height 2.57m (8ft 5in)
Range:	322km (200 miles)
Armour:	12-37mm (0.47-1.46in)
Armament:	one 76.2mm M7 gun; one 12.7mm Browning machine gun
Powerplant:	two General Motors six-cylinder diesel engines each developing 375hp (276.6kW)
Performance:	maximum road speed 51km/h (32mph); fording 0.91m (3ft); vertical obstacle 0.46m (18in); trench 2.26m (7ft 5in)

M18

Whereas most tank destroyers of World War II were converted tanks, the M18 Hellcat was designed for the role from the outset. Development began in 1942 and the first production models appeared in 1943, over 2500 being produced before October 1944. The M18 proved to be one of the best US tank destroyers of the war. Much smaller than the M10, it carried a more powerful gun and was considerably faster, in fact being the fastest tracked vehicle of the war, a good power-to-weight ratio providing excellent agility and acceleration. More importantly, it was able to hold its own on the battlefield. Despite their success, the decline of enthusiasm for specialist tank destroyer units led to the M18 being used more as assault guns and artillery towards the end of the war.

Country of origin:	USA
Crew:	5
Weight:	17,036kg (37,557lb)
Dimensions:	length 6.65m (21ft 10in); width 2.87m (9ft 5in); height 2.58m (8ft 5.5in)
Range:	169km (105 miles)
Armour:	9-25mm (0.35-0.98in)
Armament:	one 76.2mm M1A1 gun; one 12.7mm machine gun
Powerplant:	one Continental R-975 C1 radial petrol engine developing 340hp (253.5kW)
Performance:	maximum road speed 88.5km/h (55mph); fording 1.22m (4ft); vertical obstacle 0.91m (3ft); trench 1.88m (6ft 2in)

Archer

The Archer stemmed from a British decision to increase anti-tank gun calibres from 57mm to 76.2mm. The new guns were too heavy for tanks then in existence. An interim solution was found by adapting the Valentine tank chassis for use as a tank destroyer. The first production Archer, as the new vehicle was known, appeared in March 1943, but it was October 1944 before the Archer saw any action. Initial worries about the rear-facing gun proved groundless. The low silhouette was ideal for ambushes, and the rear-facing gun meant that the vehicle could be driven away quickly without having to turn round, thus avoiding retaliation. In total 655 were produced by the end of World War II, and the Archer continued in service with the British until the mid-1950s.

Country of origin:	UK
Crew:	4
Weight:	16,257kg (35,765lb)
Dimensions:	length 6.68m (21ft 11in); width 2.76m (9ft 0.5in); height 2.25m (7ft 4.5in)
Range:	225km (140 miles)
Armour:	8-60mm (0.31-2.36in)
Armament:	one 17-pounder gun; one 0.303in Bren gun
Powerplant:	one General Motors 6-71 six-cylinder diesel engine developing 192hp (143.2kW)
Performance:	maximum road speed 32.2km/h (20mph); fording 0.91m (3ft); vertical obstacle 0.84m (2ft 9in); trench 2.36m (7ft 9in)

Hornet Malkara

The Hornet Malkara was developed in the 1950s to provide a long-range anti-tank capability. The vehicle was essentially a modified Humber one-tonne (0.98 tons) 4 x 4 truck chassis with a Malkara missile launcher mounted on the back. It was designed specifically to be dropped by parachute. The operator fired the missile from the cab and controlled it by means of a joystick attached to a wire unreeling from the missile sights, along which were sent electronic signals. The missile carried the largest warhead ever fitted to an anti-tank guided weapon even in modern times, and could destroy any tank in service at that time. It continued in service until being replaced by the Ferret Mk 5 in the 1970s. Although crude, it was an indicator of the way anti-tank weapons would develop towards the end of the century.

Country of origin:	UK
Crew:	3
Weight:	5700kg (12,540lb)
Dimensions:	length 5.05m (16ft 7in); width 2.22m (7ft 3.5in); height 2.34m (7ft 8in)
Range:	402km (250 miles)
Armour:	8-16mm (0.31-0.62in)
Armament:	two Malkara anti-tank missiles
Powerplant:	one Rolls-Royce B60 Mk 5A six-cylinder petrol engine developing 120hp (89kW)
Performance:	maximum road speed 64km/h (40mph); trench not applicable

Austin-Putilov

The Austin-Putilov was a British design, though mostly produced and used in Russia. The Russians took the basic chassis (all that could be supplied by the over-stretched British production lines) and modified it considerably to cope with the harsh Russian conditions, including later replacing the rear wheels with tracks and adding additional armour and rear steering. Both in terms of numbers and performance, the Austin-Putilov was the most important armoured car the Russians possessed during World War I. Many also saw action in the internal fighting surrounding the October revolution and afterwards in the Russian Civil War. After 1918 some saw service with the Polish Army, with a number being sold to Japan. It was an extremely rugged vehicle.

Country of origin:	UK/Russia
Crew:	5
Weight:	5200kg (11,440lb)
Dimensions:	length 4.88m (16ft 0in); width 1.95m (6ft 4.75in); height 2.40m (7ft 10.5in)
Range:	200km (125 miles)
Armour:	8mm (0.315in)
Armament:	two Maxim machine guns
Powerplant:	one 50hp (37.3kW) Austin petrol engine
Performance:	maximum speed 50km/h (31mph)

Rolls-Royce

In 1914, the Royal Naval Air Service noted how the Belgians were using armoured cars to carry out raids on the advancing German Army. They decided to convert some of the Rolls-Royce Silver Ghost cars in their possession. The conversion was a success, and the Admiralty gave permission for an official armoured car based on the Silver Ghost chassis. With strengthened suspension and added armour, the Rolls-Royce saw service all over the world from March 1915, notably in Africa and the Arabian peninsula, where they proved to have excellent cross-country mobility. They were most at home in terrain where they could roam far and wide. They continued in service until being replaced in British Army service in 1922, although some were used in India well into World War II.

Country of origin:	UK
Crew:	3 or 4
Weight:	3400kg (7480lb)
Dimensions:	length 5.03m (16ft 6in); width 1.91m (6ft 3in); height 2.55m (8ft 4.5in)
Range:	240km (150 miles)
Armour:	9mm (0.35in)
Armament:	Vickers 0.303in machine gun
Powerplant:	one 40/50hp (30/37.3kW) Rolls-Royce petrol engine
Performance:	maximum road speed 95km/h (60mph)

Armored Cars

Lanchester

Originally designed to support air bases and retrieve downed pilots, the Lanchester was the most numerous armoured car in service after the Rolls-Royce by the end of 1914. A year later they were formed into armoured car squadrons. The engine of the original car was retained, but the hull was much modified. The army took control of operations at the end of 1915 and decided to use the Rolls-Royce as the standard armoured car, Lanchesters being phased out of service. However, many were sent with navy crews to the Russians, with whom they served with some distinction in terrain as varied as Persia, Romania and Galicia. Reliable and fast, they spearheaded armoured columns and were used for reconnaissance before being shipped back to the UK.

Country of origin:	UK
Crew:	4
Weight:	4700kg (10,340lb)
Dimensions:	length 4.88m (16ft); width 1.93m (6ft 4in); height 2.286m (7ft 6in)
Range:	290km (180 miles)
Armour:	unknown
Armament:	one Vickers 0.303in machine gun
Powerplant:	one 60hp (45kW) Lanchester petrol engine
Performance:	maximum speed 80km/h (50mph)

Autoblindo Mitragliatrice Lancia Ansaldo IZ

Based on the Lancia IZ truck, the IZ armoured car was quite an advanced design for its day. With a turret-mounted machine gun and later a further small turret on top with an additional machine gun, the vehicle had considerable firepower. Steel rails protruded over the bonnet for cutting wire (a feature that reflected the experience of World War I for European armies). Little used by the Italians in the mountainous fighting against the Austro-Hungarian Army, many were sent to North Africa for policing duties. Total production by 1918 was around 120, and after World War I some were sent to Albania where they formed the sole armoured force of that country for many years. Some were even used by the Italians in the Spanish Civil War, though by this time they were very outdated.

Country of origin:	Italy
Crew:	6
Weight:	3700kg (8140lb)
Dimensions:	length 5.40m (17ft 8.66in); width 1.824m (6ft 0in); height with single turret 2.40m (7ft 10.5in)
Range:	300km (186 miles)
Armour:	9mm (0.35in)
Armament:	two machine guns
Powerplant:	one 35/40hp (26/30kW) petrol engine
Performance:	maximum speed 60km/h (37mph)

Autoblindé Peugeot

Based on a commercial model, the first Peugeot armoured car was a rather hasty improvisation which appeared in 1914. Improvements followed quickly in terms of armament and firepower. With the development of trench warfare following the first year of World War I, there was a limited role for the Peugeot, since being confined to roads they could do little more than patrol rear areas. They were used to contain the German breakthrough of March 1918, being more suited to this type of fluid warfare, but their role was mainly overshadowed by the newly emerging tanks. The few Peugeots still in service at the end of World War I were handed over to the Polish Army, where they remained in service for some years, seeing action against the Russians.

Country of origin:	France
Crew:	4 or 5
Weight:	4900kg (10,780lb)
Dimensions:	length 4.8m (15ft 9in); width 1.80m (5ft 11in); height 2.80m (9ft 2.25in)
Range:	140km (87 miles)
Armour:	unknown
Armament:	one 37mm gun
Powerplant:	one 40hp (30kW) Peugeot petrol engine
Performance:	maximum speed 40km/h (25mph)

SdKfz 231

Although the SdKfz 231 was originally developed at the Kazan test centre in the Soviet Union, the vehicle was a German design intended for German use. A 6 x 4 Daimler-Benz truck chassis was used as the basis, and an armoured hull and turret added. Production ran from 1932-35, by which time around 1000 had been built. The hull was too heavy for the chassis, though, which resulted in poor cross-country performance. However, they were used on roads to good effect during the occupation of Czechoslovakia and the campaigns in Poland and France in 1939-40, their appearance alone having a good propaganda value. Their greatest achievement was to provide an invaluable training vehicle for the German Army's development during the 1930s.

Country of origin:	Germany
Crew:	4
Weight:	5700kg (12,540lb)
Dimensions:	length overall 5.57m (18ft 6.75in); width 1.82m (5ft 11.5in); height 2.25m (7ft 4.5in)
Range:	250km (150 miles)
Armour:	8mm (0.31in)
Armament:	one 20mm KwK 38 cannon; one coaxial 7.62mm machine gun
Powerplant:	one Daimler-Benz, Bussing-NAG or Magirus water-cooled petrol engine developing between 60 and 80hp (45 and 60kW)
Performance:	maximum road speed 65km/h (40mph); fording 0.6m (2ft)

Armored Cars
SdKfz 234

The SdKfz 234 was produced by Büssing-NAG in response to a 1940 German Army requirement for an 8 x 8 armoured car suitable for operations in hot climates. More streamlined than the earlier 231 series and with thicker armour, the 234's excellent performance ensured its place as probably the best vehicle of its type to see service in World War II with any army. The most famous model was the 234/2 Puma, which used the turret intended for the Leopard light tank. This gave sufficient firepower to deal with most enemy reconnaissance armour encountered. The quality of the vehicle may be judged by the fact that, despite its high cost of manufacture, the vehicle was the only reconnaissance vehicle kept in production by the starved German war industry in 1945.

Country of origin:	Germany
Crew:	4
Weight:	11,740kg (25,828lb)
Dimensions:	length 6.80m (22ft 3.66in); width 2.33m (7ft 6.5in); height 2.38m (7ft 9.5in)
Range:	1000km (625 miles)
Armour:	5-15mm (0.19-0.59in)
Armament:	one 20mm KwK 30/50mm KwK 39/1 cannon; one coaxial 7.92mm machine gun
Powerplant:	one Tatra Model 103 diesel engine developing 210hp (157kW)
Performance:	maximum road speed 85km/h (53mph); fording 1.2m (3ft 10.75in); vertical obstacle 0.5m (1ft 7.75in); trench 1.35m (4ft 5in)

SdKfz 222

When the Nazis began to rearm the German Army in the mid-1930s, a request was made for a series of light armoured cars based on a standard chassis. The demanding requirements could not be met by adapting commercial models, so a new design was produced. The first production SdKfz 222 appeared in 1938, and thereafter became the standard armoured reconnaissance car of the Wehrmacht. A reliable and popular vehicle, the SdKfz 222 served the army well during the Blitzkrieg against Poland and France in 1939-40, and later in North Africa. However, its restricted range, made evident in the latter theatre, proved problematic during the invasion of the Soviet Union in 1941. That said, it remained in German service in western Europe until the end of World War II.

Country of origin:	Germany
Crew:	3
Weight:	4800kg (10,560lb)
Dimensions:	length 4.80m (14ft 8.5in); width 1.95m (6ft 4.75in); height 2.00m (6ft 6.75in) with grenade screen
Range:	300km (187 miles)
Armour:	14.5-30mm (0.6-1.2in)
Armament:	one 20mm KwK 30 cannon; one 7.92 MG34 machine gun
Powerplant:	one Horch/Auto-Union V8-108 water-cooled petrol engine developing 81hp (60kW)
Performance:	maximum road speed 80km/h (50mph); fording 0.6m (24in)

Light Armoured Car M8

The M8 was developed following American observation of operational trends in Europe in 1940-41. A design by Ford was accepted for service, and production of the M8 began in March 1943, continuing until the last month of World War II, by which time over 11,000 had been built. Despite British worries over its thin armour (it was known to British forces rather unkindly as the Greyhound), the M8 was a superb vehicle and widely used. A low silhouette made concealment easy and the vehicle had excellent cross-country mobility, plus the firepower to deal with any similar enemy vehicle (the 37mm gun was a tank armament at the beginning of the war). The M8 became the most important American armoured car, not just because of its excellent qualities, but because it was produced in enormous quantities.

Country of origin:	USA
Crew:	4
Weight:	7940kg (17,468lb)
Dimensions:	length 5.00m (16ft 5in); width 2.54m (8ft 4in); height 2.248m (7ft 4.5in)
Range:	563km (350 miles)
Armour:	8mm (0.31in)
Armament:	one 37mm gun; one 7.62 coaxial machine gun; one 12.7mm anti-aircraft machine gun
Powerplant:	one Hercules JDX six-cylinder petrol engine developing 110hp (82kW)
Performance:	maximum road speed 89km/h (55mph); fording 0.61m (24in); vertical obstacle 0.3m (12in)

T17E1 Staghound

The Staghound was developed in response to a US Army requirement for a Light Armoured Car in the early years of World War II. However, by the time the vehicle was ready for production, the American requirement had changed and so all production models were shipped to British and Commonwealth forces. The vehicle was fast, manoeuvrable and easy to operate and maintain, faring well in its initial combat in Italy in 1943, where small and nimble vehicles were at a premium. The Mk II was fitted with a tank howitzer and the Mk III with the turret from a Crusader tank. Other variants included a mine-clearer and command car. A well-liked vehicle, the Staghound continued in service with the British for several years after the end of World War II.

Country of origin:	USA
Crew:	5
Weight:	13,920kg (30,624lb)
Dimensions:	length 5.486m (18ft 0in); width 2.69m (8ft 10in); height 2.36m (7ft 9in)
Range:	724km (450 miles)
Armour:	8mm (0.31in)
Armament:	one 37mm gun; three 7.62mm machine guns
Powerplant:	two GMC six-cylinder petrol engines each developing 97hp (72kW)
Performance:	maximum speed 89km/h (55mph); fording 0.8m (2ft 8in); vertical obstacle 0.533m (1ft 9in)

Armored Cars

Marmon Herrington

In 1938, the South African government ordered the development of an armoured car, based on foreign components but to be assembled in South Africa. The chassis and engine were made by Ford, the transmission by Marmon Herrington in the USA and the armament was imported from the UK. At the time it was first produced, the Marmon Herrington was the only armoured car available to British and South African forces in any numbers, and it saw extensive service in the Western Desert in the campaign against Rommel's *Afrika Korps*. Well-liked and sturdy, the vehicle was surprisingly effective despite light armour and armament, being relatively easy to maintain under operational conditions. The vehicles were much modified to suit local conditions, and were fitted in the field with many different weapons.

Country of origin:	South Africa
Crew:	4
Weight:	6000kg (13,200lb)
Dimensions:	length 4.88m (16ft); width 1.93m (6ft 4in); height 2.286m (7ft 6in)
Range:	322kg (200 miles)
Armour:	12mm (0.47in)
Armament:	one Vickers 7.7mm machine gun; one Boys 0.55in anti-tank rifle; one Bren Gun
Powerplant:	one Ford V-8 petrol engine
Performance:	maximum speed 80.5km/h (50mph)

Humber Mk I

Numerically, the Humber was the most important British armoured car of World War II, a total of 5400 being produced. Based on a pre-war wheeled light tank design by Guy, the Humber was initially fitted only with machine guns, which meant it was outgunned by the opposition. It was later upgunned and was used in North Africa from 1941 onwards, and wherever British troops were in action thereafter. Variants included a special radio carrier, known as Rear Link vehicle, which was fitted with a dummy gun, and an anti-aircraft version fitted with a special machine gun mounting. The vehicle gave excellent service, and was still being used by some armies in the Far East in the early 1960s. Like most British-produced armoured vehicles, the Humber was rugged, reliable and operationally sound.

Country of origin:	UK
Crew:	3 (4 in Mk III)
Weight:	6850kg (15,070lb)
Dimensions:	length 4.572m (15ft); width 2.184m (7ft 2in); height 2.34m (7ft 10in)
Range:	402km (250 miles)
Armour:	14.5-30mm (0.6-1.2in)
Armament:	one 15mm gun; one 7.92mm Besa machine gun
Powerplant:	one Rootes six-cylinder water-cooled petrol engine developing 90hp (77kW)
Performance:	maximum speed 72km/h (45mph); fording 0.6m (2ft); vertical obstacle 0.533m (1ft 9in); trench 1.22m (4ft)

Daimler Mk I

The Daimler armoured car was based on the same design as the Daimler scout car. Outwardly similar, it weighed almost twice as much and had a two-man turret. Work began in August 1939, but initial problems meant that the first production vehicles did not appear until April 1941. A total of 2694 were built. The turret was the same as that designed for the Tetrarch light airborne tank. The vehicle was equipped with hydraulic disc brakes, one of the earliest vehicles to be fitted with the system. First employed in North Africa, the vehicle established itself as an excellent addition to reconnaissance units, despite its limited combat capability, giving good all-round performance and reliability. The Daimler continued to serve for many years after the end of World War II.

Country of origin:	UK
Crew:	3
Weight:	7500kg (16,500lb)
Dimensions:	length 3.96m (13ft); width 2.44m (8ft); height 2.235m (7ft 4in)
Range:	330km (205 miles)
Armour:	14.5-30mm (0.6-1.2in)
Armament:	one 2-pounder gun; one Besa 7.92mm coaxial machine gun
Powerplant:	one Daimler six-cylinder petrol engine developing 95hp (71kW)
Performance:	maximum speed 80.5km/h (50mph); fording 0.6m (2ft); vertical obstacle 0.533m (1ft 9in); trench 1.22m (4ft)

Daimler Scout Car

When the British Army was forming its first armoured divisions in the late 1930s, a requirement was issued for a 4 x 4 scout car for reconnaissance purposes. The Daimler Scout Car was the result. Entering production just prior to the start of World War II, it was still being made at the end of the war and was to prove one of the most successful reconnaissance vehicles in use by any army in the war. Its inconspicuous nature and excellent mobility compensated for lack of armour and armament, deficiencies that are not necessarily fatal to vehicles that move fast on the battlefield and do not stand and engage in firefights with enemy armour. The folding roof was removed on later models, as experience showed it was rarely used operationally and gave minimal cover in any case.

Country of origin:	UK
Crew:	2
Weight:	3000kg (6600lb)
Dimensions:	length 3.226m (10ft 5in); width 1.715m (5ft 7.5in); height 1.50m (4ft 11in)
Range:	322km (200 miles)
Armour:	14.5-30mm (0.6-1.2in)
Armament:	one 0.303in Bren machine gun
Powerplant:	one Daimler six-cylinder petrol engine developing 55hp (41kW)
Performance:	maximum speed 88.5km/h (55mph); fording 0.6m (2ft); vertical obstacle 0.533m (1ft 9in); trench 1.22m (4ft)

Autoblinda 41

The Autoblinda had its origins in a dual requirement by the Italians for an armoured car for the cavalry divisions and a high-performance car for use in policing Italy's numerous African colonies. The Autoblinda 40 was produced to meet both these needs. The Autoblinda 41 was fitted with the turret of the L 6/40 light tank, complete with its 20mm cannon. This was a more effective combination, and thus production centred on this version. The vehicle could be adapted for desert use, with special sand tyres, and could also be adapted to run on railway tracks, being extensively used in this capacity for anti-partisan duties in the Balkans. One of the most numerous Italian armoured cars of World War II, the vehicle also saw action in the Western Desert and Tunisia.

Country of origin:	Italy
Crew:	4
Weight:	7500kg (16,500lb)
Dimensions:	length 5.20m (17ft 1.5in); width 1.92m (6ft 4.5in); height 2.48m (7ft 11.5in)
Range:	400km (248 miles)
Armour:	6-40mm (0.23-1.57in)
Armament:	one 20mm Breda cannon; two 8mm machine guns
Powerplant:	one SAP Abm 1 six-cylinder water-cooled inline petrol engine developing 80hp (60kW)
Performance:	maximum road speed 78km/h (49mph); fording 0.7m (28in); vertical obstacle 0.3m (12in); trench 0.4m (1ft 4in)

BA-10

The BA-10 was built on the chassis of the GAZ-AAA commercial truck (which was modified and reinforced to cope with the extra weight) and first appeared in 1932. It was a bulky, functional piece of equipment whose World War I ancestry was evident from its outmoded appearance. Despite its weight, the BA-10 proved well-suited to the terrain and distances of the Soviet Union, and its main armament was as good as many tanks. The Germans captured large numbers of the vehicle after the invasion of Russian in June 1941 and used them for anti-partisan duties both in the USSR and in the Balkans, a role in which it excelled. Those that remained in Soviet hands were replaced in frontline service after 1942 and stripped down, to be used as armoured personnel carriers.

Country of origin:	USSR
Crew:	4
Weight:	7500kg (16,500lb)
Dimensions:	length 4.70m (15ft 5in); width 2.09m (6ft 10.5in); height 2.42m (7ft 11.25in)
Range:	320km (199 miles)
Armour:	up to 25mm (0.98in)
Armament:	one 37mm/45mm gun; one 7.62mm machine gun
Powerplant:	one GAZ-M 14-cylinder water-cooled petrol engine developing 85hp (63kW)
Performance:	maximum speed 87km/h (54mph); fording 0.6m (1ft 11in); vertical obstacle 0.38m (1ft 3in); 0.5m (1ft 7in)

Daimler Ferret Mk 2/3

Following a 1946 British requirement for a scout car, the first prototype of the Ferret was built by Daimler in 1949. Thereafter the ferret remained in production until 1971, by which time nearly 4500 vehicles had been built for over 30 countries. The Mk I version was armed simply with a machine gun mounted on its open top. By the time the vehicle had reached the Mk V stage, the vehicle had acquired a turret and the ability to mount the Swingfire anti-tank missile. It also carried smoke dischargers. Metal channels were often carried on the front of the hull to facilitate movement across ditches or sandy terrain. The Ferret was still in use with the British Army in the 1980s, and had been widely used around the world for internal security roles.

Country of origin:	UK
Crew:	2
Weight:	4400kg (9680lb)
Dimensions:	length 3.835m (12ft 10in); width 1.905m (6ft 3in); height 1.879m (6ft 2in)
Range:	306km (191 miles)
Armour:	8-16mm (0.31-0.63in)
Armament:	one 7.62mm machine gun
Powerplant:	one Rolls-Royce six-cylinder petrol engine developing 129hp (96kW)
Performance:	maximum road speed 93km/h (58mph); fording 0.914m (3ft); vertical obstacle 0.406m (1ft 4in); trench 1.22m (4ft)

Saladin

The chassis of the Saladin is similar to that of the Saracen armoured personnel carrier, which was developed at the same time. Because of the requirements of the British forces in Malaya during the 1950s, the Saracen was given precedence and it was not until 1958 that production of the Saladin began. By 1972, when production ceased, 1177 had been built and they had been widely exported, particularly to Africa and the Middle East. A few Saladins were still in service with the British in Cyprus in the 1980s. One interesting feature was that all six wheels were powered, with steering on the front four, so the vehicle could be driven even if one wheel was blown off. Alvis has modified some Saladins, replacing the petrol engine with a more fuel-efficient model.

Country of origin:	UK
Crew:	3
Weight:	11,500kg (25,300lb)
Dimensions:	length 5.284m (17ft 4in); width 2.54m (8ft 4in); height 2.93m (9ft 7.3in)
Range:	400km (250 miles)
Armour:	8-32mm (0.31-1.25in)
Armament:	one 76mm gun; one 7.62mm coaxial machine gun; one 7.62mm anti-aircraft machine gun
Powerplant:	one eight-cylinder petrol engine developing 170hp (127kW)
Performance:	maximum road speed 72km/h (45mph); fording 1.07m (3ft 6in); vertical obstacle 0.46m (1ft 6in); trench 1.52m (5ft 0in)

Armored Cars
AMX-10

In the 1950s, the French Army issued a requirement for a replacement for the standard Panhard EBR armoured car with a more powerful armament. The first prototype of the AMX-10 was completed in 1971, and the vehicle entered service in 1979. The two main drawbacks were cost (being more expensive to build than some main battle tanks) and level of sophistication, particularly important for a conscript army. The suspension could be adjusted for different types of terrain and the fire-control system was the most sophisticated installed in any vehicle of its class, with a laser rangefinder, computer and low-light TV system and complete amphibious capability. The internal layout is conventional, with driver at the front, a three-man turret and engine and transmission at the rear.

Country of origin:	France
Crew:	4
Weight:	15,400kg (33,880lb)
Dimensions:	length 9.15m (30ft 0.25in); width 2.95m (9ft 8in); height 2.68m (8ft 9.5in)
Range:	800km (500 miles)
Armour:	8-32mm (0.31-1.25in)
Armament:	one 105mm gun; one 7.62mm machine gun
Powerplant:	one Baudouin Model 6F 11 SRX eight-cylinder diesel developing 260hp (194kW)
Performance:	maximum road speed 85km/h (53mph); fording amphibious; vertical obstacle 0.70m (2ft 3.25in); trench 1.15m (3ft 9in)

Panhard ERC

The first Panhard ERC appeared in 1977, based on technology developed for a 1970 French Army requirement but not used. Production began in 1979 and the vehicle was quickly exported to Nigeria, Argentina and Iraq amongst others, with the French using it as part of their Rapid Intervention Force. The vehicle was fully amphibious, with six-wheel drive capability. One interesting feature was that the centre wheels could be raised or lowered to deal with different types of terrain. Other features included laser rangefinder, night vision equipment, nuclear, biological and chemical (NBC) defence systems and a land navigation system, essential for desert operations. The Panhard is fully amphibious, being propelled in the water by its wheels.

Country of origin:	France
Crew:	3
Weight:	7400kg (16,280lb)
Dimensions:	length 7.693m (25ft 2.75in); width 2.495m (8ft 2.25in); height 2.254m (7ft 4.75in)
Range:	800km (500 miles)
Armour:	10mm (0.39in)
Armament:	one 90mm gun; one 7.62mm coaxial machine gun
Powerplant:	one Peugeot V-6 petrol engine developing 166hp (116kW)
Performance:	maximum road speed 100km/h (62mph); fording amphibious; vertical obstacle 0.80m (2ft 7.5in); trench 1.10m (3ft 7.5in)

BRDM-2

The BRDM-2 entered service in the early 1960s, being seen in public for the first time in 1966. It was an improvement in every way over its predecessor, the BRDM-1, with better range, armour and armament (including an improved missile launcher), as well as heightened performance. The vehicle was equipped with two extra wheels which could be lowered to assist cross-country mobility, as well as a tyre-pressure regulation system. Standard equipment includes decontamination kit and winch. Variants include a chemical warfare reconnaissance vehicle and a turretless command vehicle. The chassis forms the basis for the SA-9 missile launcher. The BRDM-2 has been exported to almost 40 countries and has seen combat in Angola, Egypt, Syria, Vietnam and Iraq.

Country of origin:	UK
Crew:	4
Weight:	11,500kg (25,300lb)
Dimensions:	length 5.75m (18ft 10.3in); width 2.35m (7ft 8.5in); height 2.31m (7ft 7in)
Range:	750km (465 miles)
Armour:	2-14mm (0.08-0.55in)
Armament:	six 'Sagger' ATGWs; one 7.62mm coaxial machine gun; one 14.5mm KPV machine gun
Powerplant:	one V-8 petrol engine developing 140hp (104kW)
Performance:	maximum road speed 100km/h (62mph); fording amphibious; vertical obstacle 0.40m (1ft 3.75in); trench 1.25m (4ft 1in)

Spähpanzer 2 Luchs

Having previously relied on American or European imports, West Germany began to develop a range of indigenous armoured vehicles during the 1960s. From 1975, Thyssen Henschel began production of an 8 x 8 armoured reconnaissance vehicle – the Luchs – completing 408 before 1978. Too expensive for significant export success, the vehicle was well-armoured and came with a range of extras such as power steering to reduce driver fatigue, night vision, a nuclear, biological and chemical (NBC) system and pre-heating for the engine, essential for winter operations. Fully amphibious, the vehicle has an exceptional operational range. In the water it is powered by two propellers mounted at the rear of the vehicle. The turret has full power traverse through 360 degrees.

Country of origin:	West Germany
Crew:	4
Weight:	19,500kg (42,900lb)
Dimensions:	length 7.743m (25ft 4.75in); width 2.98m (9ft 9.3in); height (including anti-aircraft machine gun) 2.905m (9ft 6.3in)
Range:	800km (500 miles)
Armour:	classified
Armament:	one 20mm cannon; one 7.62 machine gun
Powerplant:	one Daimler-Benz OM 403 A 10-cylinder diesel engine developing 390hp (291kW)
Performance:	maximum road speed 90km/h (56mph); fording amphibious; vertical obstacle 0.60m (1ft 11.7in); trench 1.90m (6ft 3in)

Amphibious Vehicles

T-37

The origins of the T-37 are to be found in the 1931 purchase by the USSR of a number of British Carden-Loyd amphibious tanks. The Soviets were duly impressed but realised that the tank was unsuited to fulfil all their requirements. Their version of the British design eventually became the T-37. The first production models appeared in late 1933. A small vehicle with a crew of just two, their buoyancy stemmed from pontoons attached to either side of the hull. Designed mainly for reconnaissance, and with only light armour and armament, they nevertheless were used in a combat role following the German invasion in 1941, where they fared badly and were replaced as quickly as possible. A few were retained for use as light tractors.

Country of origin:	USSR
Crew:	2
Weight:	3200kg (7040lb)
Dimensions:	length 3.75m (12ft 3.6in); width 2.10m (6ft 10.7in); height 1.82m (5ft 11.7in)
Range:	185km (115 miles)
Armour:	3-9mm (0.1-0.4in)
Armament:	one 7.62mm machine gun
Powerplant:	one GAZ AA petrol engine developing 40hp (29.8kW)
Performance:	maximum speed 56.3km/h (35mph); fording amphibious; vertical obstacle 0.787m (2ft 7in); trench 1.879m (6ft 2in)

T-40

The T-40 was designed to replace the T-37, whose manifold deficiencies had become painfully apparent by 1938. To speed development, the design included as many automobile components as possible. Flotation tanks were fitted at the rear, giving the vehicle a rather bulky appearance. The T-40 was equipped with very thin armour and fared poorly as a result during the fighting in Finland in 1939. It was thus decided to dispense with the amphibious characteristics and use the vehicle as a land tank. This proved an impractical conversion and its use was minimal after that, seeing some service with armoured formations as a reconnaissance vehicle during 1941 against the Germans. Only around 225 T-40s were ever built, as light tanks were given low priority at that time.

Country of origin:	USSR
Crew:	2
Weight:	5900kg (12,980lb)
Dimensions:	length 4.11m (13ft 5.8in); width 2.33m (7ft 7.7in); height 1.95m (6ft 4.8in)
Range:	360km (224 miles)
Armour:	8-14mm (0.3-0.55in)
Armament:	one 12.7mm machine gun
Powerplant:	one GAZ-202 petrol engine developing 70hp (52.2kW)
Performance:	maximum speed 44km/h (27.3mph); fording amphibious; vertical obstacle 0.70m (2ft 3.6in); trench 3.12m (10ft 2.8in)

Terrapin Mk 1

The Terrapin was the British equivalent of the American DUKW, although never produced on the same scale. It did make a useful contribution, though, during the latter stages of the war, particularly during its first action, being used to open up the water approaches to Antwerp in 1944. The Terrapin had a number of defects, though. Its two engines each drove one side of the vehicle, thus if one engine broke down the Terrapin tended to swing round violently. The centrally located engines split the cargo compartment in two, preventing large loads such as guns or vehicles being carried. Rather slow and easily swamped in rough waters, the Terrapin was adequate but further development was abandoned due to the large numbers of American DUKWs available, an altogether machine.

Country of origin:	UK
Crew:	2
Weight:	12,015kg (26,411lb)
Dimensions:	length 7.01m (23ft); width 2.67m (8ft 9in); height 2.92m (9ft 7in)
Range:	240km (150 miles)
Armour:	8mm (0.31in)
Armament:	none
Powerplant:	two Ford V-8 petrol engines each developing 85hp (63.4kW)
Performance:	maximum land speed 24.14km/h (15mph); maximum water speed 8km/h (5mph); fording amphibious

DD Sherman

The Duplex Drive (DD) Sherman was born from a British concept, designed to allow tanks to float in water during amphibious operations. Development began in 1941, with a collapsible fabric screen and rubber air tubes being fitted to a boat-shaped platform welded onto a Sherman tank. The tank was powered in the water by two rear propellers. Once in shallow water, the screen could be collapsed and the tank was ready for conventional use. The vehicle was rather slow and could only be used in fairly calm waters. However, the Sherman's main gun proved very useful in supporting amphibious landings, in particular those on D-Day in June 1944, and the tank was a nasty surprise for the Germans, whose attempts to develop a similar concept had failed.

Country of origin:	USA
Crew:	5
Weight:	32,284kg (71,025lb)
Dimensions:	length 6.35m (20ft 10in); width 2.81m (9ft 3in); height 3.96m (13ft)
Range:	240km (149 miles)
Armour:	12-51mm (0.47-2in)
Armament:	one 75mm gun; two 0.3in machine guns
Powerplant:	one Ford GAA V-8 petrol engine developing 400 or 500hp (335.6 or 373kW)
Performance:	maximum water speed four knots; fording amphibious; vertical obstacle 0.61m (2ft 0in); trench 2.26m (7ft 5in)

Amphibious Vehicles

DUKW

Universally known as the 'Duck', the DUKW first appeared in 1942. In essence it was a derivative of the GMC 6 x 6 truck with a boat-shaped hull for buoyancy. The simple design made it easy to operate and maintain and over 21,000 were built before the end of World War II, seeing service with all Allied forces. Designed to carry supplies from ships to the beach, it could in fact travel much farther inland, carrying troops or even light artillery. A number of weapons-carrying versions were produced, including the Scorpion, which could be used as a rocket launcher. Despite limited load-carrying capability and temperamental performance in rough seas, the DUKW was a sturdy and reliable vehicle and has often been described as an Allied war-winner.

Country of origin:	USA
Crew:	2
Weight:	9097kg (20,013lb)
Dimensions:	length 9.75m (32ft 0in); width 2.51m (8ft 2.9in); height 2.69m (8ft 10in)
Range:	120km (75 miles)
Armour:	none
Armament:	basic version – none.
Powerplant:	one GMC Model 270 engine developing 91.5hp (68.2kW)
Performance:	maximum land speed 80km/h (50mph); maximum water speed 9.7km/h (6mph); fording amphibious

LVT 2

The LVT 2 was an improvement on the LVT 1, which was a civil design intended for use in the Florida swamps and not really suited for combat. The new vehicle used the engine and transmission of the M3 Light Tank. Initially the engine was mounted at the rear which restricted cargo space, but this was soon solved by moving the engine to the front in later versions. Steering and brake systems were also problematic for inexperienced crews. These vehicles were used widely in the early Pacific campaigns, from Guadalcanal onwards. They also saw action in northwest Europe during the latter stages of the war. Some versions had rocket-launchers, flame-throwers and light cannon, but their main role was to carry ashore the first wave of a landing force.

Country of origin:	USA
Crew:	3
Weight:	17,509kg (38,519lb)
Dimensions:	length 7.95m (26ft 1in); width 3.25m (10ft 8in); height 3.023m (9ft 11in)
Range:	road radius 241km (150 miles); water radius 120.7km (75 miles)
Armour:	12mm (0.47in)
Armament:	one 0.5in and two 0.3in machine-guns
Powerplant:	two Cadillac petrol engines developing a total of 220hp (164.1kW)
Performance:	maximum land speed 27.3km/h (17mph); maximum water speed 9.7km/h (6mph); fording amphibious

LVT (A)

The LVT (A) was an ordinary LVT adapted to mount an M3 light tank turret with a 37mm gun. The intention was that this vehicle should provide fire-support during the initial stages of an amphibious landing, giving a significant punch in the battles to establish a beachhead. It was common for LVT (A)s to fire their 37mm guns while still in the water, a waste considering the amount of naval gunfire which usually accompanied an amphibious landing. However, the 37mm gun proved to be too light for this task and so a 75mm howitzer was installed, mounted in the turret of the M8 Howitzer Motor Carriage. The LVT (A) was used extensively along with the rest of the LVT family during the island-hopping operations in the Pacific in World War II, as well as in parts of northwest Europe with British forces.

Country of origin:	USA
Crew:	2
Weight:	10,800kg (23,760lb)
Dimensions:	length 7.95m (26ft 1in); width 3.25m (10ft 8in); height 3.023m (9ft 11in)
Range:	road radius 241km (150 miles); water radius 120.7km (75 miles)
Armour:	up to 67mm (2.63in)
Armament:	one 37mm cannon (later 75mm howitzer); one 7.62mm machine gun
Powerplant:	two Cadillac petrol engines developing a total of 220hp (164.1kW)
Performance:	maximum land speed 27.3km/h (17mph); maximum water speed 9.7km/h (6mph); fording amphibious

LVT 4

The LVT 4 was an improved LVT 2 with the engine moved forward and a ramp added at the rear for easier loading and unloading, giving the LVT 4 the capability to carry cargo such as jeeps and artillery. This was the most prolific of the series with over 8000 produced, four times as many as the LVT 2. Like the LVT 2, the LVT 4 was developed from the pre-war Roebling tractor, used in the Florida Everglades. Propelled in the water by its tracks, one problem was that the flotation chambers gave the vehicle a·high silhouette and thus made it an easier target. The British Army received a number of LVTs, designating them as the Buffalo, and these were used for river-crossings in the final stages of the war in Europe, particularly the crossing of the River Rhine in March 1945.

Country of origin:	USA
Crew:	3
Weight:	17,509kg (38,519lb)
Dimensions:	length 7.95m (26ft 1in); width 3.25m (10ft 8in); height 3.023m (9ft 11in)
Range:	road radius 241km (150 miles); water radius 120.7km (75 miles)
Armour:	12mm (0.47in)
Armament:	one 0.5in and two 0.3in machine-guns
Powerplant:	two Cadillac petrol engines developing a total of 220hp (164.1kW)
Performance:	maximum land speed 27.3km/h (17mph); maximum water speed 9.7km/h (6mph); fording amphibious

Amphibious Vehicles
Type 2 Ka-Mi

Development of the Type 2 began in the 1930s, with efforts to turn the Type 95 Kyu-Go light tank into an amphibious vehicle by adding flotation tanks. The unwieldy results prompted the designers to fit pontoons to the tank to provide buoyancy, retaining the main components of the tank. The new Type 2, as it was designated, went into production in 1942. The most commonly used Japanese amphibious tank, it contained several innovations including radio and telephone intercom system for the crew, as well as an onboard mechanic. It was used mainly for infantry support and often as just a land-based pillbox for island defence by 1944. This diminished their tactical effectiveness, and too few were built by the Japanese war machine to give this impressive design the impact it deserved.

Country of origin:	Japan
Crew:	5
Weight:	with pontoons 11,301kg (24,862lb); without pontoons 9571kg (21,056lb)
Dimensions:	length with pontoons 7.417m (24ft 4in); length without pontoons 4.826m (15ft 10in); width 2.79m (9ft 1.8in); height 2.337m (7ft 8in)
Range:	land radius 199.5km (125 miles); water radius 149.6km (93 miles)
Armour:	6-12mm (0.23-0.47in)
Armament:	one 37mm anti-tank gun; two 7.7mm machine gun
Powerplant:	one six-cylinder air-cooled diesel engine developing 110hp (82kW)
Performance:	maximum land speed 37km/h (23mph); maximum water speed 9.65km/h (6mph); fording amphibious

Land-Wasser-Schlepper

In 1936 the German Army contracted Rheimetall to build a special tractor for amphibious operations, which could tow behind it a cargo trailer also capable of floating. The Land-Wasser-Schlepper was essentially a motor tug fitted with tracks, capable of carrying up to 20 passengers. Its ungainly appearance belied its effective performance. However, it was rather cumbersome on land and suffered from a lack of armour. Even though designed for the calm waters of inland Europe, the project was pursued with enthusiasm while the invasion of England looked possible. After this was cancelled, interest waned and the project was cancelled in turn. Nevertheless, a pre-production series of seven vehicles was produced and some of them went on to serve on the Eastern Front after 1941.

Country of origin:	Germany
Crew:	3 + 20
Weight:	13,000kg (28,600lb)
Dimensions:	length 8.60m (28ft 2.6in); width 3.16m (10ft 4.4in); height 3.13m (10ft 3.3in)
Range:	240km (149 miles)
Armour:	unknown
Armament:	none
Powerplant:	one Maybach HL 120 TRM V-12 engine developing 265hp (197.6kW)
Performance:	maximum road speed 40km/h (24.85mph); maximum water speed unloaded 12.5km/h (7.8mph); fording amphibious

Amphibious Vehicles

Type 6640A

As the largest manufacturer of wheeled vehicles in Italy, it was no surprise that Fiat was chosen to build an amphibious vehicle, following a requirement for the Italian Home Office for a civil protection and fire-fighting vehicle. The hull was constructed of aluminium for lightness and the vehicle could carry a maximum payload of 2.14 tonnes (two tons). A winch was provided at the rear for cargo loading. Once afloat, the vehicle could be powered either by its wheels or by a propeller, the rudder being coupled to the steering wheel. The Type 6640A bore a striking resemblance, as do many modern amphibious vehicles, to the American DUKW of World War II. Production ended in the early 1980s. Like most modern Italian amphibious vehicles, the Type 6640A was well built.

Country of origin:	Italy
Crew:	2
Weight:	6950kg (15,290lb)
Dimensions:	length 7.30m (23ft 11.4in); width 2.50m (8ft 2.4in); height 2.715m (8ft 10.9in)
Range:	750km (466 miles)
Armour:	4mm (0.16in)
Armament:	none
Powerplant:	one six-cylinder diesel engine developing 117hp (87kW)
Performance:	maximum road speed 90km/h (56mph); maximum water speed with propeller 11km/h (6.8mph) or with wheels 5km/h (3.1mph); fording amphibious; vertical obstacle 0.43m (1ft 5in); trench not applicable

PTS

The PTS entered service with the Soviet Red Army in the mid-1960s. On water, the PTS could carry up to 10 tonnes (9.8 tons) of equipment or 70 men, but the drawback was that the position of the exhaust pipes on top of the cargo compartment tended to allow fumes to blow back onto the troops behind – a potentially fatal flaw. The PTS was the first Soviet amphibious vehicle to have a fully enclosed crew compartment. A PKP boat-shaped trailer was specially developed for the PTS. A variant was used by Poland which mounted a rocket-propelled mine-clearing system in the rear. The PTS was used by most Warsaw Pact countries, Iraq, Syria and also Egypt, which used it to good effect during the Yom Kippur War, during the crossing of the Suez Canal.

Country of origin:	USSR
Crew:	2
Weight:	22,700kg (49,940lb)
Dimensions:	length 11.50m (37ft 8.8in); width 3.30m (10ft 10in); height 2.65m (8ft 8.3in)
Range:	300km (186miles)
Armour:	6-10mm (0.23-0.39in)
Armament:	none
Powerplant:	one V-54P diesel engine developing 359hp (261kW)
Performance:	maximum road speed 42km/h (26mph); maximum water speed 10.6km/h (6.5mph); fording amphibious; vertical obstacle 0.65m (2ft 1.6in); trench 2.5m (8ft 2.4in)

CAMANF

For many years, the Brazilian Marines relied on American DUKWs of World War II vintage for transportation from offshore boats to the beach. By the 1970s, these were becoming difficult to maintain. BVEI began work on a replacement in 1975, and the first production vehicles were delivered towards the end of the decade. The CAMANF is in essence a 6 x 6 F-7000 Ford chassis fitted with a watertight body. It is virtually identical to the DUKW with minor modifications, such as a stronger bow to cope with rougher water, to suit regional requirements. The payload is officially five tonnes (4.9 tons), but this is much reduced in rough waters. The Brazilians made the correct decision in selecting a tried and trusted design, and although the CAMANF is unexceptional, it is a reliable amphibian.

Country of origin:	Brazil
Crew:	3
Weight:	13,500kg (29,700lb)
Dimensions:	length 9.50m (31ft 2in); width 2.50m (8ft 2.4in); height 2.65m (8ft 8.3in)
Range:	430km (267miles)
Armour:	6-10mm (0.23-0.39in)
Armament:	one 12.7mm anti-aircraft machine gun
Powerplant:	one 190hp (142kW) Detroit-Diesel Model 40-54N diesel engine
Performance:	maximum road speed 72km/h (45mph); maximum water speed 14km/h (8.7mph); fording amphibious; vertical obstacle 0.40m (1ft 3.7in); trench not applicable

LVTP7

In 1971, FMC completed the first production model of the LVTP7 designed specifically for the US Marine Corps. With an aluminium hull and propelled either by twin-waterjets or its tracks, the vehicle was capable of carrying up to 25 fully equipped troops, forming an important element in US power projection capabilities. The vehicle could be loaded alongside ships through an opening in the roof hatch, although troops usually exited through the rear. The vehicle was widely exported, notably to Argentina where it took part in the Falklands invasion in 1982. It also saw service on peacekeeping duties in Lebanon. Variants included a command vehicle and recovery vessel, and some vehicles in US Marine Corps service have been fitted with Enhanced Applique Armour for extra protection.

Country of origin:	USA
Crew:	3 + 25
Weight:	22,837kg (50,241lb)
Dimensions:	length 7.943m (26ft 0.7in); width 3.27m (10ft 8.7in); height 3.263m (10ft 8.5in)
Range:	482km (300miles)
Armour:	45mm (1.8in)
Armament:	one 12.7mm machine gun; optional 40mm grenade launcher
Powerplant:	one Detroit-Diesel Model 8V-53T engine, developing 400hp (298kW)
Performance:	maximum road speed 64km/h (40mph); maximum water speed 13.5km/h (8.5mph); fording amphibious; vertical obstacle 0.914m (3ft 0in); trench 2.438m (8ft)

Amphibious Vehicles

LARC-5

The LARC-5 was developed to a US Army requirement for a vehicle capable of transporting cargo from ship to shore and then inland to supply bases. Around 950 were built between 1962 and 1968. The LARC-5 was a fairly basic vehicle with no proper suspension and power steering on the front wheels only. It could carry just under 4.5 tonnes (4.3 tons) of cargo or 20 fully equipped troops between the cabin at the front and the engine at the rear. It was exported to Australia, West Germany and Argentina, seeing action with the latter in the Falklands conflict. The influence of the World War II-vintage DUKW can clearly be seen – testimony to the excellence of the original vehicle. The good range of the LARC-5 is indicative of the more mobile nature of modern warfare when compared to World War II.

Country of origin:	USA
Crew:	1 + 2
Weight:	14,038kg (30,883lb)
Dimensions:	length 10.668m (35ft 0in); width 3.149m (10ft 4in); height 3.034m (9ft 11.4in)
Range:	402km (250miles)
Armour:	none
Armament:	none
Powerplant:	one V8 diesel engine developing 300hp (224kW)
Performance:	maximum road speed 48.2km/h (30mph); maximum water speed 16km/h (10mph); fording amphibious; vertical obstacle about 0.5m (1ft 7.7in); trench not applicable

EKW Bison

Developed originally as a civilian truck for use in underdeveloped regions, the EKW Bison 4 x 4 was first seen in public in 1982, having been adopted for military use. Fully amphibious, the Bison is equipped with side flotation bags and two propellers (which can be traversed through 360 degrees for maximum manoeuvrability), as well as automatically activated bilge pumps. For land use, the Bison has power-assisted steering and a tyre-pressure regulation system for rough terrain, a feature which Soviet designers have been particularly fond of since the end of World War II. The Bison has a fully enclosed forward control cab with the engine to the rear. The engine itself is coupled to a fully automatic transmision with six forward and one reverse gear.

Country of origin:	Germany
Crew:	2
Weight:	16,000kg (35,200lb)
Dimensions:	length 9.34m (30ft 7.7in); width 2.50m (8ft 2.4in); height to cab roof 2.964m (9ft 8.5in)
Range:	900km (559miles)
Armour:	none
Armament:	none
Powerplant:	one V8 air-cooled diesel engine developing 320hp (239kW)
Performance:	maximum road speed 80km/h (49.7mph); maximum water speed 12km/h (7.4mph); fording amphibious; vertical obstacle not available; trench not applicable

Tracked Infantry Vehicles

SdKfz 2

The SdKfz 2 was developed for use by German infantry and airborne units. It was designed to be an artillery tractor for very light weaponry. Known as the Kettenkrad, the first of these small tractors entered service in 1941. However, by this time German airborne troops were generally being used as regular infantry, so the vehicle's intended role was largely redundant. As a result, the SdKfz 2 was used mainly as a supply vehicle in difficult terrain, where other vehicles could not travel. Their impact was limited by their low cargo capacity and limited production numbers. By 1944, they were seen as an expensive luxury and production ceased. One interesting variant was a high-speed cable-laying vehicle for linking command posts and forward positions.

Country of origin:	Germany
Crew:	3
Weight:	1200kg (2640lb)
Dimensions:	length 2.74m (8ft 11.9in); width 1.00m (3ft 3.4in); height 1.01m (3ft 3.8in)
Range:	100km (62.5 miles)
Armour:	none
Armament:	none
Powerplant:	one Opel Olympia 38 petrol engine developing 36hp (26.8kW)
Performance:	maximum road speed 80km/h (49.7mph)

Maultier

German trucks proved totally unable of operating successfully during the first winter of the Russian campaign in 1941-1942. It was thus decided to produce a low-cost half-track to take over many of the trucks' duties. The Wehrmachtsschlepper could not be produced in sufficient numbers to fulfil this need so Opel and Daimler-Benz chassis were fixed to tracked assemblies from PzKpfw II tanks. The new Maultier as it was known was a reasonable success, although lacking the mobility of 'proper' halftracks. By late 1942, the Maultier was being pressed into service as a launch-vehicle for the Nebelwerfer rocket launcher, with over 3000 conversions being ordered by the German Army. In combat Maultiers were organised into Nebelwerfer brigades.

Country of origin:	Germany
Crew:	3
Weight:	7100kg (15,620lb)
Dimensions:	length 6.00m (19ft 8.2in); width 2.20m (7ft 2.6in); height 2.50m (8ft 6in)
Range:	130km (81.25 miles)
Armour:	8-10mm (0.31-0.39in)
Armament:	one 15cm Nebelwerfer (later versions); one 7.92mm machine gun
Powerplant:	one 3.6-litre six-cylinder petrol engine developing 91hp (68kW)
Performance:	maximum road speed 38km/h (30mph); fording 0.6m (2ft); vertical obstacle 2.0m (6ft 6.7in); trench 1m (3ft 3in)

Tracked Infantry Vehicles
SdKfz 250/10

The SdKfz 250 was developed following a mid-1930's requirement for a one-tonne (0.98 tons) halftrack to provide mobility for infantry and other units operating with panzer divisions. The first example appeared in 1939 and saw action for the first time in May 1940 during the invasion of France. Production continued until 1944, with later models having redesigned hulls to make manufacture easier and cut down on the amount of raw materials required, as the basic design was rather expensive. Variants included a communications vehicle and mobile observation post, as well as a number of specialised weapons carriers, mounting everything from anti-aircraft guns to anti-tank cannons. The vehicle remained in service until the end of the war proving to be a reliable and popular halftrack.

Country of origin:	Germany
Crew:	6
Weight:	5380kg (11,836lb)
Dimensions:	length 4.56m (14ft 11.5in); width 1.945m (6ft 4.6in); height 1.98m (6ft 6in)
Range:	299km (186 miles)
Armour:	6-14.5mm (0.23-0.6in)
Armament:	one 3.7cm Pak 35/36 anti-tank gun
Powerplant:	one six-cylinder petrol engine developing 100hp (74.6kW)
Performance:	maximum road speed 59.5km/h (37mph); fording 0.75m (29.5in); vertical obstacle 2.0m (6ft 6.7in)

SdKfz 11

The first versions of the SdKfz 11 appeared in 1934 and after a series of manufacturing changes, the vehicle entered full production in 1939. Primarily intended as an artillery tractor, it was used initially by 10.5cm howitzer batteries. The vehicle proved so successful that it was later used to tow a wide variety of guns at the expense of heavier purpose-built vehicles, eventually seeing most service with Nebelwerfer batteries to tow the rocket launchers. The vehicle was one of the few to remain in production right through the war, and a number of variants were produced, including two designed specifically for chemical warfare decontamination, but these were not produced in significant numbers as large-scale chemical warfare never occurred during World War II.

Country of origin:	Germany
Crew:	9
Weight:	7100kg (15,620lb)
Dimensions:	length 5.48m (17ft 11.7in); width 1.82m (5ft 11.7in); height 1.62m (5ft 3.8in)
Range:	122km (76 miles)
Armour:	8-14mm (0.31-0.55in)
Armament:	none
Powerplant:	one six-cylinder petrol engine developing 100hp (74.6kW)
Performance:	maximum road speed 53km/h (33mph); fording 0.75m (29.5in); vertical obstacle 2.0m (6ft 6.7in)

Tracked Infantry Vehicles
SdKfz 251/1

The SdKfz 251 had its origins in the same requirement as the SdKfz 250. However, the 251 series was a heavier vehicle. It entered service in 1939, intended as an armoured personnel carrier. The 250 was a useful vehicle, capable of keeping up with panzer formations. There were 22 special-purpose variants, including rocket-launcher (referred to as the 'infantry Stuka'), flame-thrower, anti-tank, communications vehicle, observation post and ambulance and infrared searchlight carrier. Early reliability problems did not prevent the vehicle being produced by the thousands, and it was a sturdy vehicle used on all fronts, becoming a virtual trademark of German panzer formations. The SdKfz 251/1 was the standard armoured personnel carrier for the panzergrenadier group.

Country of origin:	Germany
Crew:	12
Weight:	7810kg (17,182lb)
Dimensions:	length 5.80m (19ft 0.3in); width 2.10m (6ft 10.7in); height 1.75m (5ft 8.9in)
Range:	300km (186 miles)
Armour:	6-14.5mm (0.23-0.6in)
Armament:	two 7.92mm machine guns
Powerplant:	one Maybach six-cylinder petrol engine developing 100hp (74.6kW)
Performance:	maximum road speed 52.5km/h (32.5mph); fording 0.6m (2ft); vertical obstacle 2.0m (6ft 6.7in)

SdKfz 251/20

The SdKfz 251/20 was one of the seemingly endless variants of the basic 251 model. Known as the 'Uhu', it was produced towards the end of the World War II and was used mainly on the Eastern Front. Like all the other 251 models, it was designed to operate with, and as part of, the panzer divisions, needing to be speedy, tough and reliable. It carried an infrared searchlight and its primary purpose was to illuminate enemy targets and allow panzer units to attack at night. The fact that the German war machine was still churning out such specialised variants at the end of the war is testament to the durability and excellent qualities of the vehicle. The main searchlight had a 360-degree traverse and could be folded down when not in use. In total around 60 were built before the war ended.

Country of origin:	Germany
Crew:	4
Weight:	7824kg (17,248lb)
Dimensions:	length 5.80m (19ft 0.3in); width 2.10m (6ft 10.7in); height 1.75m (5ft 8.9in)
Range:	300km (186 miles)
Armour:	6-14.5mm (0.23-0.6in)
Armament:	none
Powerplant:	one Maybach six-cylinder petrol engine developing 100hp (74.6kW)
Performance:	maximum road speed 52.5km/h (32.5mph); fording 0.6m (2ft); vertical obstacle 2.0m (6ft 6.7in)

SdKfz 7

Development of the SdKfz 7 can be traced back to a 1934 requirement for an eight-tonne (7.87 tons) half-track. The vehicle first appeared in 1938 and was destined to be used mainly as the tractor for the 8.8cm flak guns. The vehicle could carry up to 12 men and a considerable quantity of supplies, as well as pulling up to 8000kg (17,600lb). Most were fitted with a winch, and the vehicle was widely admired as a useful vehicle, being also used as a weapons carrier, to particularly good effect with anti-aircraft weapons. They also saw service as observation and command posts for V2 rocket batteries. They were admired even by their enemies, with the British trying to make exact copies of captured vehicles and some vehicles being appropriated for use by the Allies after World War II.

Country of origin:	Germany
Crew:	12
Weight:	11,550kg (25,410lb)
Dimensions:	length 6.85m (20ft 3in); width 2.40m (7ft 10.5in); height 2.62m (8ft 7.1in)
Range:	250km (156 miles)
Armour:	8mm (0.31in)
Armament:	basic version – none.
Powerplant:	one Maybach HL 62 six-cylinder petrol engine developing 140hp (104.4kW)
Performance:	maximum road speed 50km/h (31mph); fording 0.5m (1ft 7in); vertical obstacle 2.0m (6ft 6.7in)

Schwerer Wehrmachtsschlepper

By 1941, the German Army was in need of a medium halftrack, but it had to be economical to produce as the German war machine was already stretched. The Schwerer Wehrmachtsschlepper, or army heavy tractor, was intended for use by infantry units as a general supply vehicle and personnel carrier. To keep costs down, luxuries like a closed cab and rubber-capped tracks were mainly dispensed with. Production was slow, partly due to the lack of priority accorded the vehicle and partly due to the attentions of RAF Bomber Command. However, production continued until the end of the World War II, with a few vehicles seeing service in the post-war Czech Army. Variants included a rocket launcher, anti-aircraft vehicle and a frontline supply vehicle fitted with an armoured cab.

Country of origin:	Germany
Crew:	2
Weight:	13,500kg (29,700lb)
Dimensions:	length 6.68m (21ft 11in); width 2.50m (8ft 2.4in); height 2.83m (9ft 3.4in)
Range:	300km (187 miles)
Armour:	8-15mm (0.31-0.59in)
Armament:	one 3.7cm gun; one 7.92mm machine gun
Powerplant:	one Maybach HL 42 six-cylinder petrol engine developing 100hp (74.6kW)
Performance:	maximum road speed 27km/h (16.8mph); fording 0.6m (2ft); vertical obstacle 2.0m (6ft 6.7in)

SdKfz 9

The SdKfz 9 was by far the largest of all World War II half-tracks. It originated as a result of a 1936 requirement for a heavy recovery vehicle to operate alongside panzer units. The vehicle was used both for recovery and for towing heavy artillery and bridging units. A weapons-carrying version was produced in 1943 mounting an 8.8cm anti-aircraft gun, where it saw action in Poland and France. The recovery version was fitted with a crane and stabilising legs to allow it to cope with heavy tanks. However, even with an earth spade at the back for extra traction, two SdKfz 9s were generally required to recover tanks such as the massive Tiger, and when the more capable Bergepanther arrived the SdKfz's role was diminished somewhat and therefore production ceased in 1944

Country of origin:	Germany
Crew:	9
Weight:	18,000kg (39,600lb)
Dimensions:	length 8.25m (27ft 0.8in); width 2.60m (8ft 6in); height 2.76m (9ft 0.7in)
Range:	260km (162 miles)
Armour:	8-14.5mm (0.31-0.57in)
Armament:	none, though sometimes one 8.8cm Flak gun
Powerplant:	one Maybach HL V-12 petrol engine developing 250hp (186.4kW)
Performance:	maximum road speed 50km/h (31mph); fording 0.6m (2ft); vertical obstacle 2.0m (6ft 6.7in)

M3

American half-track production began in earnest in 1941, and by the end of the war over 40,000 of all types had been produced. The M3 was widely used by all Allied forces, mainly as a personnel carrier, although also saw service as an ambulance, communications vehicle and artillery tractor. In fact, it was so prolific that it became something of a trademark of Allied forces, particularly after the D-Day landings of June 1944. After World War II, the M3 was gradually reduced to the role of recovery vehicle. However, vehicles supplied to the Soviet Union before 1945 continued to see service with some Warsaw Pact countries for many years. It also remained a frontline vehicle for the Israeli Defence Force until relatively recently, seeing service in all the Arab-Israeli wars.

Country of origin:	USA
Crew:	13
Weight:	9299kg (20,458lb)
Dimensions:	length 6.18m (20ft 3.5in); width 2.22m (7ft 3.5in); height 2.26m (7ft 5in)
Range:	282km (175 miles)
Armour:	8mm (0.31in)
Armament:	one 12.7mm machine gun; one 7.62mm machine gun
Powerplant:	one White 160AX six-cylinder petrol engine developing 147hp (109.6kW)
Performance:	maximum road speed 64.4km/h (40mph); fording 0.81m (2ft 8in)

Tracked Infantry Vehicles

P 107

The P 107 came in two basic variants: an artillery tractor for light field pieces and an engineer tractor. The latter had an open cargo body behind the cab and was used to tow trailers carrying combat engineer equipment. Following the fall of France to the Germans in 1940, the P 107 was pressed into Wehrmacht service, being used to tow field and anti-tank guns. Then the Germans stripped the vehicles of their superstructures and fitted armoured hulls in their place. Most of these conversions remained in France for training purposes and general duties, though they did see combat following the D-Day landings in June 1944. The Germans retained the mounted roller under the nose of the vehicle, which was used to assist the vehicle in and out of ditches.

Country of origin:	France
Crew:	5-7
Weight:	4050kg (8910lb)
Dimensions:	length 4.85m (15ft 10.9in); width 1.80m (5ft 10.9in); height 1.95m (6ft 4.8in)
Range:	400km (248.5 miles)
Armour:	none (original version)
Armament:	none
Powerplant:	one four-cylinder petrol engine developing 55hp (41.0kW)
Performance:	maximum road speed 45km/h (28mph)

Wurfgranate 41

Nebelwerfer units were originally formed to lay down smoke screens for tactical use. The launchers were later adapted to fire artillery rockets, whose droning sound led to the Allied nickname 'Moaning Minnie'. The 15cm-Nebelwerfer 41 was mounted on a 3.7cm anti-tank gun carriage, but in 1942 the launcher was fitted to the half-tracked SdKfz 4/1 Maultier. This was a more effective system, as rockets betrayed their location immediately on firing and thus tended to draw swift retaliation. The Panzerwerfer 42, as it was known, allowed rapid escape from the point of firing and thus greater survivability. In the main, the mobile launchers were used to give fire-support for armoured operations. Note that the specifications below relate to the 15cm Wurfgranate 41 rocket.

Country of origin:	Germany
Crew:	
Weight:	overall 31.8kg (70lb); propellant 6.35kg (14lb); filling 2.5kg (5.5lb)
Dimensions:	length 979mm (38.55in); diameter 158mm (6.22in)
Range:	7055m (23,145ft)
Armour:	–
Armament:	–
Powerplant:	–
Performance:	initial velocity 342m (1120ft) per second

Tracked Infantry Vehicles

Wurfkörper M F1 50

The Wurfkörper 28cm and 32cm rockets were amongst the first to be fitted to vehicles to provide mobile firepower. The vehicle most often used was the SdKfz 251, this combination being known as the Stuka-zu-fuss ('Foot Stuka') or Heulende Kuh ('Howling Cow'). The combination saw action through World War II. The system was rather temperamental, as the rockets were highly inaccurate and aiming was achieved by simply pointing the vehicle in the general direction of the target. As a result, they tended to be used *en masse* where possible. They were still devastating weapons whenever they did hit the target, the high-explosive warhead being particularly well regarded for street fighting and demolishing houses. The specifications below relate to the Wurfkörper M FI 50 rocket.

Country of origin:	Germany
Crew:	–
Weight:	overall 79kg (174lb); propellant 6.6kg (14.56lb); filling 39.8kg (87.7lb)
Dimensions:	length 1.289m (50.75in); body diameter 320mm (12.6in)
Range:	2028m (6651ft)
Armour:	–
Armament:	–
Powerplant:	–
Performance:	–

AMX-10P

Designed in the mid-1960s, the first French AMX-10s rolled off the production line in 1973. With an all-aluminium hull, the AMX-10 was fully amphibious, being propelled by two waterjets. It also carried a nuclear, biological and chemical (NBC) defence system and night-vision equipment. Inside, there was capacity for eight troops. The vehicle has spawned a range of variants, including an ambulance, a repair vehicle, an anti-tank vehicle with four guided weapons and a mortar tractor for towing a Brandt 120mm mortar. The AMX-10 has been exported to many countries including Greece, Qatar, Mexico, Saudi Arabia and Indonesia, the vehicles for the latter having improved amphibious capability as they are designed to leave landing craft offshore and float in under their own power.

Country of origin:	France
Crew:	3 + 8
Weight:	14,200kg (31,240lb)
Dimensions:	length 5.778m (18ft 11in); width 2.78m (9ft 1in); height 2.57m (8ft 5in)
Range:	600km (373 miles)
Armour:	classified
Armament:	one 20mm cannon; one 7.62mm coaxial machine gun
Powerplant:	one HS-115 V-8 water-cooled diesel, developing 280hp (209kW)
Performance:	maximum road speed 65km/h (40mph); fording amphibious; vertical obstacle 0.70m (2ft 4in); trench 1.60m (5ft 3in)

Tracked Infantry Vehicles

FV432

In 1962, the FV432 was the first fully tracked armoured personnel carrier to be accepted into service by the British Army since World War II. Between 1963 and 1971 a total of 3000 were built by GKN Sankey. Few were exported, as the similar American M113 was a much cheaper option. At one time known as the Trojan, the FV432's main purpose was to transport fighting men to the battlefield, carrying 10 troops, the vehicle was one of the first to be fitted with a nuclear, biological and chemical (NBC) defence system. Initially the vehicles were fitted with flotation screens to give an amphibious capability, but these were removed as they were prone to damage. Variants included a command vehicle, ambulance, mortar carrier and mine-layer, as well as an anti-tank version armed with Swingfire missiles.

Country of origin:	UK
Crew:	2 + 10
Weight:	15,280kg (33,616lb)
Dimensions:	length 5.251m (17ft 7in); width 2.80m (9ft 2in); height (with machine gun) 2.286m (7ft 6in)
Range:	483km (300 miles)
Armour:	12mm (0.47in)
Armament:	one 7.62mm machine gun
Powerplant:	one Rolls-Royce K60 six-cylinder multi-fuel engine developing 240hp (170kW)
Performance:	maximum road speed 52.2km/h (32mph); fording 1.066m (3ft 6in); vertical obstacle 0.609m (2ft); trench 2.05m (6ft 9in)

Marder

The Marder Schützenpanzer was the first mechanised infantry combat vehicle to enter service in the West, and was one of a family of vehicles based on the chassis of the Swiss SPX12-3. Production began in 1970, and by 1975 some 3000 had been built. At the time, it was the most advanced of its type in the world. With excellent armour and high cross-country speed, it was able to operate with Leopard main battle tanks in combined operations. The troops inside were able to use their weapons from inside by means of a periscope and firing ports. A remote-controlled machine gun was provided for local defence. Later versions carried the Milan anti-tank guided missile. Variants include a surface-to-air missile (SAM) launcher and a radar carrier. Over 6000 rounds of ammunition are carried in the vehicle.

Country of origin:	West Germany
Crew:	4 + 6
Weight:	28,200kg (62,040lb)
Dimensions:	length 6.79m (22ft 3in); width 3.24m (10ft 8in); height 2.95m (9ft 8in)
Range:	520km (323 miles)
Armour:	classified
Armament:	one 20mm Rh 202 cannon; one coaxial 7.62mm machine gun
Powerplant:	one MTU MB 833 six-cylinder diesel, developing 600hp (447kW)
Performance:	maximum road speed 75km/h (46.6mph); fording 1.50m (4ft 11in); vertical obstacle 1.00m (3ft 3in); trench 2.50m (8ft 2in)

Tracked Infantry Vehicles

Pbv

Design on the Pbv 302 began in 1961 and full-scale production began in 1966. The Pbv was similar in layout to the American M113 and was one of the first vehicles of its type with a fully enclosed weapon station. The troop compartment is at the rear with room for 10 fully equipped soldiers. There are no firing ports, but soldiers are able to fire through the hatches on the top. The turret is manually operated, and the 20mm cannon can be fed from a belt holding 135 rounds of from 10-round box magazines. Fully amphibious, the Pbv is propelled through the water by its tracks. Variants include a command vehicle, observation vehicle and ambulance. Few were exported, mainly because of the strict controls placed on exports of military equipment by the Swedish government.

Country of origin:	Sweden
Crew:	2 + 10
Weight:	13,500kg (29,700lb)
Dimensions:	length 5.35m (17ft 7in); width 2.86m (9ft 5in); height 2.50m (8ft 2in)
Range:	300km (186 miles)
Armour:	classified
Armament:	one 20mm Hispano cannon
Powerplant:	one Volvo-Penta Model THD 100B 6-cylinder inline diesel engine developing 280hp (209kW)
Performance:	maximum road speed 66km/h (41mph); fording amphibious; vertical obstacle 0.61m (2ft); trench 1.80m (5ft 11in)

M113A2

The M113 was the result of a mid-1950s US requirement for a lightweight, amphibious and airportable armoured infantry vehicle. Production began in the early 1960s, since when 70,000 have been built and exported to nearly 50 countries, the vehicle being constantly updated to meet modern requirements. In particular, the early versions afforded the gunner no protection at all, this being addressed as a priority following combat experience, notably in Vietnam, the Middle East, North Africa and the Far East. With many variants, including mortar carrier, command vehicle, anti-aircraft and flame-thrower vehicles, the M113 will stay in service well into the 21st century and will probably be the most widely used armoured vehicle ever built.

Country of origin:	USA
Crew:	2 + 11
Weight:	11,341kg (24,950lb)
Dimensions:	length 2.686m (8ft 9in); width 2.54m (8ft 4in); height 2.52m (8ft 3in)
Range:	483km (300 miles)
Armour:	up to 44mm (1.73in)
Armament:	one 12.7mm machine gun; two 7.62mm machine guns
Powerplant:	one six-cylinder water-cooled diesel, developing 215bhp (160kW)
Performance:	maximum road speed 67.59km/h (42mph); maximum water speed 5.8km/h (3.6mph); fording amphibious; vertical obstacle 0.61m (2ft); trench 1.68m (5ft 6in)

M2 Bradley

The M2 Bradley was the US Army's first mechanised infantry combat vehicle. The first production models appeared in 1981, and they were soon being produced at the rate of 600 per year. The hull of the M2 is made of aluminium, with a layer of spaced laminate armour for added protection. The 25mm cannon has a stabiliser to allow for firing on the move. The troop compartment in the rear is fitted with firing ports and periscopes to allow the troops to fire from within the vehicle. Night vision and a nuclear, biological and chemical (NBC) defence system are standard. The Bradley plays a key role in the US Army's combined arms concept, but critics say it is too big, too expensive and too difficult to maintain and is insufficiently armoured to operate with main battle tanks on the battlefield.

Country of origin:	USA
Crew:	3 + 7
Weight:	22,666kg (49,865lb)
Dimensions:	length 6.453m (21ft 2in); width 3.20m (10ft 6in); height; 2.972m (9ft 0in)
Range:	483km (300 miles)
Armour:	classified
Armament:	one Hughes Helicopter 25mm Chain Gun; one 7.62mm coaxial machine gun; two anti-tank launchers.
Powerplant:	one Cummins eight-cylinder diesel, developing 500hp (373kW)
Performance:	maximum road speed 66km/h (41mph); fording amphibious; vertical obstacle 0.914m (3ft); trench 2.54m (8ft 4in)

AIFV

The shortcomings of the M113 prompted the US Army to order a new vehicle with better protection for the gunner and firing ports for the troops in the rear. The FMC Corporation realised that the resulting M2 would be too heavy and expensive for most countries, and thus developed the AIFV primarily for export. Better armed and armoured (with steel appliqué armour layers) than the M113, the vehicle is fully amphibious. The main gun is enclosed for better protection and the seven troops in the back all have firing ports. Night-vision and nuclear, biological and chemical (NBC) systems are available. The AIFV is a good compromise between the M113 and the M2 and has proved popular with Turkey, Belgium, the Philippines and the Netherlands all ordering significant quantities.

Country of origin:	USA
Crew:	3 + 7
Weight:	13,687kg (30,111lb)
Dimensions:	length 5.258m (17ft 3in); width 2.819m (9ft 3in); height (overall) 2.794m (9ft 2in)
Range:	490km (305 miles)
Armour:	classified
Armament:	one 25mm Oerlikon cannon; one 7.62 coaxial machine gun
Powerplant:	one Detroit-Diesel 6V-53T V-6 diesel engine developing 264hp (197kW)
Performance:	maximum road speed 61.2km/h (38mph); fording amphibious; vertical obstacle 0.635m (2ft 1in); trench 1.625m (5ft 4in)

Tracked Infantry Vehicles

BMD

The BMD was designed specifically for Soviet airborne forces to give increased firepower and mobility for troops behind enemy lines once on the ground. This was particularly important as the Soviets had only sufficient air transport to deliver one airborne division at a time. It entered service in 1970, and 330 were destined for each airborne division. Based on the BMP-1, the vehicle was fitted with an unusual hydraulic suspension-adjustment system to alter the level of ground clearance. Fully amphibious, the vehicle had night vision and a nuclear, chemical and biological (NBC) defence system, plus a smoke generating system. Variants included a mortar carrier and command vehicle. The BMD was used to spearhead the Soviet invasion of Afghanistan in 1979.

Country of origin:	USSR
Crew:	3 + 4
Weight:	6700kg (14,740lb)
Dimensions:	length 5.40m (17ft 9in); width 2.63m (9ft 8in); height 1.97m (6ft 6in)
Range:	320km (200 miles)
Armour:	15-23mm (0.59-0.9in)
Armament:	one 73mm gun; one coaxial 7.62mm machine gun; two front-mounted 7.62mm machine guns; one AT-3 'Sagger' ATGW
Powerplant:	one V-6 liquid-cooled diesel engine developing 240hp (179kW)
Performance:	maximum road speed 70km/h (43mph); fording amphibious; vertical obstacle 0.80m (2ft 8in); trench 1.60m (5ft 3in)

MT-LB

The MT-LB was developed to fulfil a variety of roles, such as towing artillery and anti-tank guns, moving cargo and acting as an armoured personnel carrier. Fully amphibious, being propelled in the water by its tracks, the MT-LB had room in the back for 11 troops. On snow-covered ground, the tracks could be removed and much wider ones added. In swampy ground, the MT-LB was used in place of the BMP mechanised infantry combat vehicle. Variants included an engineer combat vehicle, a command vehicle with specialised radar and a repair vehicle. The MT-LB was also used as the basis for the 2S1 self-propelled howitzer which entered service in the 1970s and was widely exported. It was exported to Bulgaria, Czechoslovakia, Finland, Hungary, Poland, Sweden and the former Yugoslavia.

Country of origin:	USSR
Crew:	2 + 11
Weight:	11,900kg (26,180lb)
Dimensions:	length 6.454m (21ft 2in); width 2.85m (9ft 4in); height 1.865m (6ft 5in)
Range:	500km (310 miles)
Armour:	3-10mm (0.1-0.39in)
Armament:	one 7.62mm machine gun
Powerplant:	one YaMZ 238 V-8 diesel engine developing 240hp (179kW)
Performance:	maximum road speed 61.5km/h (38mph); fording amphibious; vertical obstacle 0.70m (2ft 3in); trench 2.70m (8ft 10in)

Sultan

The Sultan is part of a group of vehicles based on the same aluminium hull which form part of the British Army's battle group formation. It is designed to provide the commander with an armoured platform to allow him to keep up with his forward elements. There is a compartment in the back with a desk, map boards and radios. Space is a real problem, although there is a tent which can be extended from the rear to give more room, but at the expense of mobility. Its cramped conditions while on the move (particularly while closed down during a nuclear, biological and chemical [NBC] exercises) make this a difficult vehicle to work in. Like many such armoured fighting vehicles currently in service around the world, its crew is prone to severe motion sickness.

Country of origin:	UK
Crew:	3
Weight:	8172kg (17,978lb)
Dimensions:	length 5.12m (16ft 9in); width 2.24m (7ft 4in); height 2.6m (8ft 6in)
Range:	483km (301 miles)
Armour:	classified
Armament:	one 7.62mm machine gun
Powerplant:	one 4.2-litre petrol engine developing 190hp (141kW)
Performance:	maximum road speed 80km/h (50mph); fording 1.067m (3ft 6in); vertical obstacle 0.5m (1ft 7in); trench 2.057m (6ft 9in)

Spartan

The Alvis Spartan is a member of the Scorpion family and entered service with the British Army in 1978. It has specialised roles, such as carrying Javelin surface-to-air missiles (SAMs) or Royal Engineer assault teams. It has a three-man crew and room in the back for four fully equipped troops, though the vehicle has no firing ports. Flotation screens can be fitted around the top of the hull, which, when erected, makes the Spartan fully amphibious (in the water it is propelled by its tracks). The newest production models incorporate a number of improvements, including an upgraded suspension system and a more fuel-efficient Perkins diesel engine. By the end of 1995, a total of 960 Spartan vehicles had been built. As shown above, it can be fitted with a Milan anti-tank weapon.

Country of origin:	UK
Crew:	3 + 4
Weight:	8172kg (17,978lb)
Dimensions:	length 5.125m (16ft 9in); width 2.24m (7ft 4in); height 2.26m (7ft 5in)
Range:	483km (301 miles)
Armour:	classified
Armament:	one 7.62mm machine gun; one Milan missile launcher
Powerplant:	one Jaguar six-cylinder petrol engine developing 190hp (142kW)
Performance:	maximum road speed 80km/h (50mph); fording 1.067m (3ft 6in); vertical obstacle 0.5m 1ft 7in); trench 2.057m (6ft 9in)

Warrior

The Warrior Mechanised Combat Vehicle entered development in 1972 and entered service with the British Army in 1987. The Warrior was part of a movement to change armoured personnel carriers from their role of merely transporting troops to and from the battlefield into a more capable infantry combat vehicle, this concept being inspired by the success of the Soviet BMP. Designed to supplement the FV432, the Warrior is heavier and much more heavily armoured. It is treated as a mobile fire base from which troops can fight, rather than a mere transport vehicle. Variants include a command vehicle, recovery vehicle, engineer and observation vehicle. It has been sold to Kuwait, whose Warriors have anti-tank launchers each side of the turret and air conditioning.

Country of origin:	UK
Crew:	3 + 7
Weight:	25,700kg (56,540lb)
Dimensions:	length 6.34m (20ft 10in); width 3.034m (10ft); height 2.79m (9ft 2in)
Range:	660km (412 miles)
Armour:	classified
Armament:	one 30mm Rarden cannon; one 7.62mm co-axial machine gun; four smoke dischargers
Powerplant:	one Perkins V-8 diesel engine developing 550hp (410kW)
Performance:	maximum road speed 75km/h (46.8mph); fording 1.3m (4ft 3in); vertical obstacle 0.75m (2ft 5in); trench 2.5m (8ft 2in)

BMP-2

First seen in public in 1982, the BMP-2 was designed to supplement rather than replace the BMP-1, having an almost identical chassis. Its low silhouette and long sloping front is useful in that it presents a small target. This is vital because its armour is extremely poor. One remarkable feature is that the rear doors are hollow and serve as fuel tanks, with obvious dangers for the troops inside. There are few concessions to comfort, the crew compartment being very crowded and uncomfortable, although the troops can fire their weapons from within. The two-man turret has the commander on the right and the gunner on the left, the 30mm cannon having a powered elevation for use against helicopters and slow-flying aircraft. The BMP-2 saw action in Afghanistan.

Country of origin:	USSR
Crew:	3 + 7
Weight:	14,600kg (32,120lb)
Dimensions:	length: 6.71m (22ft); width 3.15m (10ft 4in); height: 2m (6ft 7in)
Range:	600km (375 miles)
Armour:	classified
Armament:	one 30mm cannon; one At-5 anti-tank missile launcher; one 7.62mm coaxial machine gun
Powerplant:	one Model UTD-20 six-cylinder diesel engine developing 300hp (223kW)
Performance:	maximum road speed 65km/h (40.6mph); fording amphibious; vertical obstacle 0.7m (2ft 4in); trench 2.4m (8ft 2in)

VAB

In 1974 Renault was selected to build a wheeled armoured personnel carrier to complement the AMX-10 tracked vehicle being issued to infantry battalions. Produced in 4 x 4 and 6 x 6 versions, the vehicle is fully amphibious being propelled in water either by its wheels or by twin water jets. A nuclear, biological and chemical (NBC) defence system and night-vision capability are fitted as standard. Variants include an ambulance, internal security vehicle, command vehicle, anti-tank and mortar carrier. The vehicle has sold well abroad, in North Africa and the Middle East, in countries where France has a major influence, and in particular in Morocco, where it has been used in a counter-insurgency role against Polisario guerrillas. The VAB is a very rugged vehicle.

Country of origin:	France
Crew:	2 + 10
Weight:	13,000kg (28,660lb)
Dimensions:	length 5.98m (19ft 7.4in); width 2.49m (8ft 2in); height 2.063m (6ft 9in)
Range:	1000km (621 miles)
Armour:	classified
Armament:	one 7.62mm machine gun
Powerplant:	one MAN six-cylinder inline diesel engine developing 235hp (175kW)
Performance:	maximum road speed 92km/h (57mph); fording amphibious; vertical obstacle 0.6m (2ft); trench not applicable

Ratel 20

The Ratel was designed by the South Africans to replace the British Saracen, when it became clear that political considerations might place future supplies in jeopardy. The prototype appeared in 1976, with the first production vehicles arriving just a year later. Designed specifically for South African needs, the vehicle has an exceptional range (needed for large-scale anti-guerrilla operations in the vast expanses of Africa) with excellent mobility, armour and firepower. It has seen combat extensive service, being used for counter-insurgency raids in Namibia and Angola, and has been exported to Morocco for similar duties. Variants include the Ratel 60, which is equipped with a 60mm mortar, the Ratel 90, which mounts the 90mm gun, and the Ratel repair, which is optimised for field repairs.

Country of origin:	South Africa
Crew:	4 + 7
Weight:	19,000kg (41,800lb)
Dimensions:	length 7.212m (23ft 8.4in); width 2.516m (8ft 3in); height 2.915m (9ft 6.8in)
Range:	1000km (621 miles)
Armour:	20mm (0.78in)
Armament:	one 20mm cannon; two 7.62mm machine guns
Powerplant:	one D 3256 BTXF six-cylinder diesel engine developing 282hp (210kW)
Performance:	maximum road speed 105km/h (65mph); fording 1.2m (3ft 11.2in); vertical obstacle 0.35m (1ft 1.7in); trench 1.15m (3ft 9.3in)

Wheeled Infantry Vehicles
UR-416

The UR-416 was developed from the chassis of the civilian Unimog 4 x 4 which appeared in the 1950s. Work on the military version began in the early 1960s and production began in 1966. The UR-416 was a relatively inexpensive vehicle, easy to maintain and operate. Room was provided for eight troops in the rear compartment and there were firing ports to allow them to use their weapons from inside. Variants included a command vehicle, repair vehicle and an ambulance. The UR-416 has been widely exported, particularly to Africa and South America and is used by several European countries for such duties as airport security and riot control, the vehicles being fitted with public address systems, fire extinguishers and blades for removing obstacles when on anti-riot duties.

Country of origin:	West Germany
Crew:	2 + 8
Weight:	7600kg (16,720lb)
Dimensions:	length 5.21m (17ft 1in); width 2.30m (7ft 6.5in); height 2.225m (7ft 3.6in)
Range:	700km (435 miles)
Armour:	9mm (0.35in)
Armament:	one 7.62mm machine gun
Powerplant:	one Daimler-Benz OM 352 six-cylinder diesel engine developing 120hp (89kW)
Performance:	maximum road speed 85km/h (53mph); fording 1.4m (4ft 7in); vertical obstacle 0.55m (1ft 9.7in); trench not applicable

BTR-40

The BTR-40 entered service in 1951. Based on a GAZ-43 4 x 4 truck chassis, it was able to carry eight troops as part of the Soviet doctrine of armoured spearheads supported by mechanised infantry. The vehicle filled a variety of roles such as ambulance, reconnaissance and command vehicle, in addition to being an armoured personnel carrier. The BTR-40 lacked the tyre-pressure regulation system common to many post-World War II Soviet vehicles, nor did it have a nuclear, biological and chemical (NBC) defence system. There was a specialised chemical warfare variant, though, the BTR-40kh, which was used to mark clear lanes through contaminated areas. The BTR-40 was phased out of frontline Red Army service from the late 1950s onwards. It was exported extensively to Soviet client states.

Country of origin:	USSR
Crew:	2 + 8
Weight:	5300kg (11,660lb)
Dimensions:	length 5m (16ft 5in); width 1.9m (6ft 3in); height 1.75m (5ft 9in)
Range:	285km (178 miles)
Armour:	8mm (0.31in)
Armament:	one 7.62mm machine gun
Powerplant:	one GAZ-40 six-cylinder water-cooled petrol engine developing 80hp (60kW)
Performance:	maximum road speed 80km/h (50mph); fording 0.8m (2ft 8in); vertical obstacle 0.47m (1ft 6in); trench 0.7m (2ft 4in)

PSZH-IV

The PSZH-IV was a development of the FUG 4 x 4 amphibious scout car designed for the Hungarian Army in the early 1960s. Appearing in the mid-1960s (when it was thought by the West to be a reconnaissance vehicle), the vehicle was of all-welded steel construction and was a fully amphibious armoured personnel carrier, being propelled in water by two water jets and able to carry six troops (though their only means of exit and entry are via the small two-part door in each side of the hull). It was equipped with a tyre-pressure regulation system, nuclear, biological and chemical (NBC) defence system and infrared night-vision equipment. Variants included a command vehicle, ambulance and a NBC reconnaissance vehicle. It is in service with the armies of Bulgaria, Hungary, the Czech Republic and Iraq.

Country of origin:	Hungary
Crew:	3 + 6
Weight:	7500kg (16,500lb)
Dimensions:	length 5.70m (18ft 8.4in); width 2.50m (8ft 2.4in); height 2.30m (7ft 7in)
Range:	500km (311 miles)
Armour:	14mm (0.55in)
Armament:	one 14.5mm machine gun; one coaxial 7.62mm machine gun
Powerplant:	one Caspel four-cylinder diesel engine developing 100hp (74.57kW)
Performance:	maximum road speed 80km/h (50mph); fording amphibious; vertical obstacle 0.4m (1ft 3.7in); trench 0.6m (1ft 11.6in)

BTR-152V1

The BTR-152 was one of the first Soviet armoured personnel carriers, as Soviet forces had not used the type during World War II. First seen in public in 1951, the vehicle consisted of a ZIL-157 truck chassis with an armoured body. The main drawback of the early vehicle was the open-topped compartment, which left troops vulnerable to overhead shell bursts. In addition, its cross-country mobility was poor and it had no amphibious capability. Late vehicles have the central tyre pressure regulation system that allows the driver to adjust tyre pressure to suit the terrain being driven on. It was replaced in frontline service in the early 1960s by the BTR-60, but was exported widely to around 30 countries, seeing combat in the Middle East (with Syria, Egypt and Iraq in the Arab-Israeli wars), Africa and the Far East.

Country of origin:	USSR
Crew:	2 + 17
Weight:	8950kg (19,690lb)
Dimensions:	length 6.83m (22ft 4.9in); width 2.32m (7ft 7.3in); height 2.05m (6ft 8.7in)
Range:	780km (485 miles)
Armour:	4-13.5mm (0.15-0.53in)
Armament:	one 7.62mm machine gun
Powerplant:	one ZIL-123 six-cylinder petrol engine developing 110hp (82kW)
Performance:	maximum road speed 75km/h (47mph); fording 0.8m (2ft 7.5in); vertical obstacle 0.6m (1ft 11.6in); trench 0.69m (2ft 3.2in)

BTR-60PB

The BTR-60 was introduced into Red Army service in the late 1960s to replace the BTR-152. The early BTR-60s still had an open-topped compartment, but this was soon remedied. The vehicle was fully amphibious and was propelled in water by a single water jet. It carried 14 troops, who were able to fight from inside the vehicle by means of firing ports, but who had to enter and exit the vehicle through roof hatches, with the obvious exposure to danger that this carried. Exported to over 30 countries, the BTR-60 has seen action in many parts of the world, having an integral role in protecting Soviet convoys in Afghanistan during the Russian occupation of the country, and even taking on the Americans during the invasion of Grenada in 1983, although they were quickly knocked out.

Country of origin:	USSR
Crew:	2 + 14
Weight:	10,300kg (22,660lb)
Dimensions:	length 7.56m (24ft 9.6in); width 2.825m (9ft 3.2in); height 2.31m (7ft 6.9in)
Range:	500km (311 miles)
Armour:	7-9mm (0.27-0.35in)
Armament:	one 12.7mm machine gun; two 7.62mm machine guns
Powerplant:	two GAZ-49B six-cylinder petrol engines, each developing 90hp (67kW)
Performance:	maximum road speed 80km/h (50mph); fording amphibious; vertical obstacle 0.4m (1ft 3.7in); trench 2m (6ft 7in)

OT-64C(1)

The OT-64 was Czechoslovakia and Poland's answer to the Soviet BTR-60. The OT-64 entered service in 1964, with the advantage over its Soviet counterpart of having a fully enclosed compartment for troops and being diesel, rather than petrol-powered, which extended range and reduced the risk of fire. It was heavier, though, with a lower power-to-weight ratio. Fully amphibious with two propellers, entry was through the rear, and a winch, nuclear, biological and chemical (NBC) defence system and night vision capability were fitted as standard. There were command and recovery variants and some OT-64s were adapted for anti-aircraft and anti-tank capability, the latter being fitted with 'Sagger' anti-tank guided weapons. North African and Middle East countries were the main export customers.

Country of origin:	Czechoslovakia/Poland
Crew:	2 + 15
Weight:	14,500kg (31,900lb)
Dimensions:	length 7.44m (24ft 5in); width 2.55m (8ft 4.4in); height 2.06m (6ft 9in)
Range:	710km (441 miles)
Armour:	10mm (0.39in)
Armament:	one 7.62mm machine gun
Powerplant:	one Tatra V-8 diesel engine developing 180hp (134kW)
Performance:	maximum road speed 94.4km/h (59mph); fording amphibious; vertical obstacle 0.5m (1ft 7.7in); trench 2m (6ft 7in)

MOWAG

The MOWAG was designed by Kreuzlingen for easy conversion to a number of diverse roles, such as ambulance, command vehicle or armoured personnel carrier. The MOWAG entered production in 1964, and its small size (there was only room for three troops in the rear, plus the commander, machine gunner and driver) proved ideal for internal security duties, particularly when fitted with a blade for clearing obstacles, a public address system and wire mesh protection for the vision blocks and headlamps. The vehicle was also available with bullet-proof tyres (with metal disks attached to the outside of the tyre). Export customers included Greece, Argentina, Bolivia, Chile and Iraq, all of which no doubt saw the vehicle's value in internal suppression. Production is now complete.

Country of origin:	Switzerland
Crew:	3 + 3
Weight:	8200kg (18,040lb)
Dimensions:	length 5.31m (17ft 5in); width 2.2m (7ft 3in); height 1.88m (6ft 2in)
Range:	400km (248 miles)
Armour:	8mm (0.31in)
Armament:	one 12.7mm or 7.62mm machine gun
Powerplant:	one V-8 four-stroke water-cooled petrol engine developing 202hp (151kW)
Performance:	maximum road speed 80km/h (50mph); fording 1.1m (3ft 7in); vertical obstacle 0.4m (1ft 4in); trench not applicable

V-150 Commando

The V-150 Commando was the successor to the V-100 developed in the early 1960s. It first appeared in the early 1970s, containing a number of improvements on the V-100, its most significant being the installation of a diesel engine to provide a greater range and less risk of fire than with a petrol engine. The V-150 was easily adapted for a number of roles, ranging from armoured personnel carrier to riot control and recovery vehicle. A wide range of armaments could be fitted to give extra flexibility, from anti-aircraft cannon to mortars and anti-tank guided weapons. All versions are fully amphibious, propelled in the water by their wheels. In addition, a wide variety of armaments can be fitted. A popular export model, the V-150 has been sold to around 25 countries.

Country of origin:	USA
Crew:	3 + 2
Weight:	9888kg (21,753lb)
Dimensions:	length 5.689m (18ft 8in); width 2.26m (7ft 5in); height 1.981m (6ft 6in)
Range:	643km (400 miles)
Armour:	classified
Armament:	various, including one 25mm cannon; one 7.62mm machine gun
Powerplant:	one V-540 V-8 diesel engine developing 202hp (151kW)
Performance:	maximum road speed 88.5km/h (55mph); fording amphibious; vertical obstacle 0.609m (2ft 0in); trench not applicable

Wheeled Infantry Vehicles

M706

Cadillac Gage began design on a multi-purpose armoured vehicle at the beginning on the 1960s which, following successful trials, was put into production in 1964 as the V-100 Commando, powered by a Chrysler engine. The US Army later designated the vehicle as M706. The vehicle was primarily destined for export but the conflict in Vietnam in the 1960s soon required a vehicle to fill the dual patrol and escort roles. Significant numbers of M706s saw service with both South Vietnamese and US troops. In Vietnam it proved a versatile and effective counter-insurgency weapon, being ideal for rapid counterattack when attached to ambushed convoys. A scaled-up version, the V-200, was sold to Singapore, and 1971 the V-100 was replaced by the V-150.

Country of origin:	USA
Crew:	3 + 2
Weight:	9888kg (21,753lb)
Dimensions:	length 5.689m (18ft 8in); width 2.26m (7ft 5in); height 1.981m (6ft 6in)
Range:	643km (400 miles)
Armour:	classified
Armament:	two 7.62mm machine guns
Powerplant:	one V-8 diesel engine developing 202bhp (151kW)
Performance:	maximum road speed 88.5km/h (55mph); fording amphibious; vertical obstacle 0.609m (2ft 0in); trench not applicable

V-300 Commando

The V-300 was a 6 x 6 version of the Commando range. Built by Cadillac as a private venture to complement its 4 x 4 vehicles, the first production models were delivered in 1983 for export to Panama. The layout of the vehicle was different from that of the earlier V-150. Troops entered and exited the vehicle through rear doors only (the V-150 having side and rear doors), with additional hatches in the roof. A wide variety of armament could be fitted. Standard equipment includes a front-mounted winch with a capacity to lift 9072kg (19,958lb). Variants include a command post vehicle, ambulance (with a higher roof), a mortar carrier, anti-aircraft model and an anti-tank vehicle. Fully amphibious, the vehicle is propelled through the water by its wheels.

Country of origin:	USA
Crew:	3 + 9
Weight:	13,137kg (28,900lb)
Dimensions:	length 6.40m (21ft 0in); width 2.54m (8ft 4in); height 1.981m (6ft 6in)
Range:	700km (435 miles)
Armour:	classified
Armament:	one 25mm Hughes Helicopter Chain Gun; one 7.62mm coaxial machine gun
Powerplant:	one turbocharged diesel engine developing 235hp (175kW)
Performance:	maximum road speed 93km/h (58mph); fording amphibious; vertical obstacle 0.609m (2ft); trench not applicable

Commando Ranger

In 1979, Cadillac Gage was selected to meet the US Air Force's requirement for an armoured vehicle to provide security and protect its foreign air bases from attack by terrorists or other groups, and escort ordnance to and from bases. The Ranger entered service in 1980, based on a standard Chrysler truck chassis. The fully armoured compartment carried six men, who could fire from within the vehicle through firing ports, and this compartment was insulated and air-conditioned to reduce crew fatigue on lengthy patrols. Known to the USAF as the Peacekeeper, the vehicle was exported to Luxembourg and Indonesia. Optional equipment includes grenade launchers, spotlight and front-mounted winch. Variants included a command vehicle and an ambulance.

Country of origin:	USA
Crew:	2 + 6
Weight:	4536kg (9979lb)
Dimensions:	length 4.699m (15ft 5in); width 2.019 (6ft 7.5in); height 1.981m (6ft 6in)
Range:	556km (345 miles)
Armour:	7mm (0.27in)
Armament:	one or two 7.62mm machine guns
Powerplant:	one Dodge 360 CID V-8 petrol engine developing 180hp (134kW)
Performance:	maximum road speed 112.5km/h (70mph); fording 0.457 (1ft 6in); vertical obstacle 0.254m (10in); trench not applicable

Humber 'Pig'

Designed to supplement the Alvis Saracen, the Humber 'Pig' was based on the chassis of the Humber FV1600 truck chassis and entered service with the British Army in the 1950s. It was intended purely for transport to and from the battlefield rather than for any combat role. Carrying six men and equipped with firing ports, the Pig found itself being phased out with the arrival of the FV432 into service. However, the conflict in Northern Ireland rescued it from the scrapheap – the British needed a riot-control vehicle. It was given additional armour for the internal security role and equipped with barricade-removal equipment at the front. It remained in service in Northern Ireland until the 1980s. Variants included an ambulance and an anti-tank version equipped with Malkara missiles.

Country of origin:	UK
Crew:	2 + 6 (or 2 + 8)
Weight:	5790kg (12,738lb)
Dimensions:	length 4.926m (16ft 2in); width 2.044 (6ft 8.5in); height 2.12m (6ft 11.5in)
Range:	402km (250 miles)
Armour:	8mm (0.31in)
Armament:	2 x 4 smoke dischargers
Powerplant:	one Rolls-Royce B60 Mk 5A six-cylinder petrol engine developing 120hp (89kW)
Performance:	maximum road speed 64km/h (40mph); fording 0.5m (1ft 7in); vertical obstacle 0.23m (9in); trench not applicable

Wheeled Infantry Vehicles

Alvis Saracen

The Saracen was part of the FV600 family of armoured vehicles developed for the British Army after World War II. The Saracen, first produced in 1952, was given priority because of its suitability for use in the guerrilla situation then occurring in Malaya. The vehicle was the only real British armoured personnel carrier in service during the 1950s, but began to be phased out in the 1960s in favour of the FV432 tracked vehicle, with its better armour range and mobility. It remained in service in Northern Ireland, however, into the 1980s, as well as in parts of Africa and the Middle East. It shares many components with the Alvis 6 x 6 Saladin. Variants included an ambulance and command vehicle, but radar-carrying, self-propelled gun and mine-clearing versions never entered service.

Country of origin:	UK
Crew:	2 + 10
Weight:	8640kg (19,008lb)
Dimensions:	length 5.233m (17ft 2in); width 2.539 (8ft 4in); height 2.463m (8ft 1in)
Range:	400km (248 miles)
Armour:	16mm (0.62in)
Armament:	two 7.62mm machine guns
Powerplant:	one Rolls-Royce B80 Mk 6A eight-cylinder petrol engine developing 160hp (119kW)
Performance:	maximum road speed 72km/h (44.7mph); fording 1.07m (3ft 6in); vertical obstacle 0.46m (1ft 6in); trench 1.52m (5ft 0in)

Saxon

The Saxon was developed in the early 1970s in response to a British Army requirement for a wheeled armoured personnel carrier for the 1980s and 1990s. Based on the Bedford Mk4 4 x 4, the standard truck of the British Army, production began in 1976 and the first models were delivered to British battalions in 1984. The Saxon was one of the best armoured vehicles of its type when it was introduced. One unusual feature was that the mudguards were designed to blow off in the event that the vehicle hit a mine, thus allowing the blast to escape sideways rather than up into the vehicle. The Saxon could be fitted with a range of armaments and variants included a command vehicle, an anti-riot vehicle and an ambulance. Some Saxons have a one-man 7.62mm machine-gun turret fitted.

Country of origin:	UK
Crew:	2 + 8
Weight:	10,670kg (23,474lb)
Dimensions:	length 5.169m (16ft 11.5in); width 2.489 (8ft 2in); height 2.86m (9ft 4.6in)
Range:	510km (317 miles)
Armour:	classified
Armament:	one 7.62mm machine gun
Powerplant:	one Bedford 500 six-cylinder diesel engine developing 164hp (122kW)
Performance:	maximum road speed 96km/h (60mph); fording 1.12m (3ft 8in); vertical obstacle 0.41m (1ft 4in); trench not applicable

Wheeled Infantry Vehicles

EE-11

In 1970, ENGESA began work on an armoured 6 x 6 wheeled vehicle in response to a Brazilian armed forces requirement. Production of the Urutu armoured personnel vehicle began in 1974. The vehicle was fully amphibious, being fitted with a trim vane, bilge pumps and two propellers. The Urutu was fitted with tyre-pressure regulation system, night vision and nuclear, biological and chemical (NBC) defence system and could carry up to 12 troops in the rear (who exit via doors in each side and one in the rear). Firing ports were available to allow these troops to fight from within the vehicle. Variants included an ambulance, cargo-transport, command vehicle, anti-aircraft and anti-tank versions, the latter being fitted with Milan or HOT anti-tank guided weapons.

Country of origin:	Brazil
Crew:	1 + 12
Weight:	13,000kg (28,600lb)
Dimensions:	length 6.15m (20ft 2in); width 2.59 (8ft 6in); height 2.09m (6ft 10.3in)
Range:	850km (528 miles)
Armour:	classified
Armament:	one 12.7mm machine gun; one 7.62mm machine gun
Powerplant:	one Detroit Diesel 6V-53N six-cylinder diesel engine developing 212hp (158kW)
Performance:	maximum road speed 90km/h (56mph); fording amphibious; vertical obstacle 0.6m (1ft 11.6in); trench not applicable

SIBMAS

The SIBMAS 6 x 6 armoured personnel carrier started as a private venture in the mid-1970s by the Belgian company BN Constructions Ferroviaires et Métalliques, with the first vehicles being delivered in 1983 to the Royal Malaysian Army, who eventually bought nearly 200 as fire-support vehicles, armed with the 90mm Cockerill Mk III gun. As expected, the basic model is fully amphibious without preparation and is propelled in the water by its wheels or by two propellers. Night vision and nuclear, biological and chemical (NBC) systems can be fitted as well as a range of different armaments. There are three entry doors: one in each side and one at the rear. The troop compartment has firing ports. Variants include an ambulance, a command vehicle and a cargo vehicle.

Country of origin:	Belgium
Crew:	3 + 11
Weight:	16,500kg (36,300lb)
Dimensions:	length 7.32m (24ft 0in); width 2.50 (8ft 2.4in); height (hull) 2.24m (7ft 4.2in)
Range:	1000km (621 miles)
Armour:	classified
Armament:	one 90mm Cockerill Mk III gun; one coaxial 7.62mm machine gun; one anti-aircraft 7.62mm machine gun
Powerplant:	one six-cylinder turbocharged diesel developing 320hp (239kW)
Performance:	maximum road speed 100km/h (62mph); fording amphibious; vertical obstacle 0.6m (1ft 11.6in); trench 1.5m (4ft 11in)

AMX-30 Bridge

The prototype of the AMX-30 bridgelayer was built in the mid-1960s, but delays meant that the vehicle did not enter production until the mid-1970s. Based on the AMX-30 tank chassis, with an almost identical layout, the scissors bridge was laid hydraulically over the rear of the vehicle. It took around five minutes to erect and a similar time to recover the bridge. The bridge span was 20m (65ft 7in). A nuclear, biological and chemical (NBC) defence system and night-vision capability were installed as standard. The vehicle was designed to operate in tandem with the AMX-30 tank, and has no armament of its own, relying on accompanying vehicles for protection. The major disadvantage was that the bridge is erected vertically and thus can easily be seen by enemy forces.

Country of origin:	France
Crew:	3
Weight:	42,500kg (93,500lb)
Dimensions:	length (with bridge) 11.40m (37ft 4.8in); width (with bridge) 3.95m (12ft 11.5in); height (with bridge) 4.29m (14ft 0.9in)
Range:	600km (373 miles)
Armour:	80mm (3.14in)
Armament:	none
Powerplant:	one Hispano-Suiza HS-110 12-cylinder multi-fuel diesel engine developing 700hp (522.0kW)
Performance:	maximum road speed 50km/h (31.1mph); fording 1.0m (3ft 4in); vertical obstacle 0.93m (3ft 0.6in); trench 2.9m (9ft 6.2in)

AMX-30 Tractor

The AMX-30 EBG was based on the AMX-30 main battle tank chassis and designed to carry out a number of roles, including laying mines and clearing battlefield obstacles, by means of a hydraulically operated dozer blade mounted at the front of the vehicle. In addition, the teeth of the dozer blade can be used to dig up roads, thus making them impassable to enemy wheeled vehicles. At the rear is a winch for recovering damaged vehicles. Also, the vehicle has a powerful demolition-charge launcher for destroying bunkers and other fortifications. Standard equipment includes night vision, nuclear, biological and chemical (NBC) defence system and a deep-fording kit to provide some amphibious capability. The AMX-30 tractor is integral to the movement of French armoured forces on the battlefield.

Country of origin:	France
Crew:	3
Weight:	38,000kg (83,600lb)
Dimensions:	length 7.90m (25ft 11in); width 3.50m (11ft 5.8in); height 2.94m (9ft 7.7in)
Range:	500km (311 miles)
Armour:	80mm (3.14in)
Armament:	one 7.62mm machine gun; one 142mm demolition-charge launcher
Powerplant:	one Hispano-Suiza HS 110-2 12-cylinder multi-fuel engine developing 700hp (522.0kW)
Performance:	maximum road speed 65km/h (40.4mph); fording 2.50m (8ft 2.4in); vertical obstacle 0.9m (2ft 11.4in); trench 2.9m (9ft 6.2in)

M728

Following the development of the M60 main battle tank, a decision was taken to create a combat engineer vehicle based on the same chassis. The M728 was finally accepted for service in 1963 as the standard combat engineer vehicle for the US Army. The two vehicles were very similar. The M60's 105mm gun was replaced by a demolition-charge launcher and a hydraulically operated dozer blade added, together with a winch, which was mounted on an A-frame. The A-Frame was laid flat over the top of the vehicle when travelling. Night-vision equipment (as well as a searchlight) and a nuclear, biological and chemical (NBC) defence system were standard. The vehicle could be equipped for deep-fording. In addition to the US Army, the vehicle saw service with Singapore and Saudi Arabia.

Country of origin:	USA
Crew:	4
Weight:	53,200kg (117,040lb)
Dimensions:	length (travelling) 8.92m (29ft 3in); width (overall) 3.71m (12ft 2in); height (travelling) 3.20m (10ft 6in)
Range:	451km (280 miles)
Armour:	classified
Armament:	one 165mm demolition gun; one 7.62mm machine gun
Powerplant:	one Teledyne Continental AVDS-1790-2A 12-cylinder diesel engine developing 750bhp (559.3kW)
Performance:	maximum road speed 48.3km/h (30mph); fording 1.22m (4ft); vertical obstacle 0.76m (2ft 6in); trench 2.51m (8ft 3in)

Leopard 1

The Leopard 1 Armoured Engineer Vehicle was designed by Krupp specifically for the requirements of the West German Army. Based on the chassis of the Leopard 1 main battle tank and almost identical to the Leopard I Armoured Recovery Vehicle, production began in 1968. The vehicle has a dozer blade fitted to the front which can be widened if necessary and is fitted with 'scarifiers' for digging up road surfaces. It can also be equipped with an auger for digging holes. The vehicle is designed to fulfil many different roles, from preparing fire positions to removing battlefield obstacles and preparing river crossings. The Leopard 1 was designed for the defence of West Germany against a Warsaw Pact attack, hence the capability for digging up road surfaces and preparing fire positions.

Country of origin:	West Germany
Crew:	4
Weight:	40,800kg (89,760lb)
Dimensions:	length 8.98m (26ft 2.2in); width 3.75m (12ft 3.6in); height 2.69m (8ft 9.9in)
Range:	850km (528 miles)
Armour:	10-70mm (0.39-2.75in)
Armament:	one 7.62mm machine gun
Powerplant:	one MTU MB 838 Ca.M500 10-cylinder diesel engine developing 830hp (618.9kW)
Performance:	maximum road speed 65km/h (40.4mph); fording 2.10m (6ft 11in); vertical obstacle 1.15m (3ft 9.3in); trench 3m (9ft 10in)

Biber

The first production vehicles were completed by Krupp in 1975, based on the chassis of the Leopard 1 main battle tank. The hull of the Biber AVLB was virtually identical to that of the tank. However, with the AVLB the turret was replaced by a two-part aluminium bridge, capable of spanning a 20m (65ft 7in) gap. A support blade was fitted to the front, to be lowered before the bridge was laid, but this was also useful for levelling surfaces on either side of the gap. One of the main advantages of the Biber was that its bridge was laid horizontally rather than vertically, which made for much better concealment. The Biber carried four electrically operated smoke dischargers to provide extra cover for its operations, but otherwise relied on other armoured vehicles for protection.

Country of origin:	West Germany
Crew:	2
Weight:	with bridge 45,300kg (99,660lb)
Dimensions:	length (with bridge) 11.82m (38ft 9.4in); width (with bridge) 4.0m (13ft 1.5in); height (with bridge) 3.57m (11ft 8.6in)
Range:	550km (342 miles)
Armour:	70mm (2.75in)
Armament:	none
Powerplant:	one MTU MB 838 Ca.M500 10-cylinder multi-fuel engine developing 830hp (618.9kW)
Performance:	maximum road speed 62km/h (38.5mph); fording 1.2m (3ft 11in); vertical obstacle 0.7m (2ft 3.6in); trench 2.5m (8ft 2.4in)

TMM Bridge

The TMM truck-mounted treadway bridge consists of four spans, launched over the rear of a 6 x 6 Kr AZ-214 or Kr AZ 255B truck chassis. Each span is extended vertically and supported by cables until it reaches its final position, at which point trestle legs are swung into place. The truck then disconnects and drives off to pick up the next span. The basic unit has a span of around 40m (131ft 3in), but more spans can be added if necessary. The bridge takes 45-60 minutes to erect. One disadvantage of the system is that it relies on legs which must be kept level – if the depth of water cannot be ascertained, problems may arise. There is nothing sophisticated about the TMM system, but it is cheap, easy to operate and can be produced in mass numbers if need be.

Country of origin:	USSR
Crew:	3
Weight:	19,500kg (42,900lb)
Dimensions:	length (with bridge) 9.30m (30ft 6.1in); width (with bridge) 3.20m (10ft 6in); height (with bridge) 3.15m (10ft 4in)
Range:	530km (329 miles)
Armour:	none
Armament:	none
Powerplant:	one YaMZ M206B six-cylinder water-cooled diesel engine developing 205hp (152.9kW)
Performance:	maximum road speed 55km/h (34.2mph); fording 1.0m (3ft 3in); vertical obstacle 0.4m (1ft 4in); trench no capability

PMP Floating Bridge

The PMP bridge entered service with the USSR in the 1960s, and was soon in use in most Warsaw Pact armies. Originally mounted on the Kr AZ-214 truck chassis, it was later transferred to the Kr AZ-255. The truck was backed up to the shore and the bridge rolled off into the water where it unfolded automatically. The full set consisted of 32 river pontoons, four shore pontoons and 12 bridging boats, the whole structure spanning some 389m (1275ft). The pontoons could also be used to form a ferry to be pushed across by boats. The PMP was exported outside of the Warsaw Pact on a significant scale, notably being used by the Egyptian Army to cross the Suez Canal during the Yom Kippur War of 1973. Note that the specifications below relate to the river pontoon bridge.

Country of origin:	USSR
Crew:	3
Weight:	6676kg (14,687lb)
Dimensions:	length (open) 6.75m (22ft 1.75in); width (open) 7.10m (23ft 3.5in); depth (open) 0.915m (3ft 0in)
Range:	–
Armour:	none
Armament:	none
Powerplant:	–
Performance:	–

IMR

The IMR was introduced into service with the Red Army in the 1970s and was essentially a T-55 tank with the standard turret replaced by a crane and an armoured cupola. A pincer device was fitted for removing trees and a front-mounted dozer blade were standard. An unditching beam was also carried, to be fitted to the tracks in order to improve traction if the vehicle became stuck (an idea pioneered by the British in World War I). Like most vehicles based on the T-55 chassis, the IMR could lay its own smoke screen. The vehicle was very limited by Western standards, carrying no demolition charge or mine-laying equipment, but the Soviets had other vehicles to perform these tasks. The IMR saw service with most Warsaw Pact countries and the former Yugoslavia.

Country of origin:	USSR
Crew:	2
Weight:	34,000kg (74,800lb)
Dimensions:	length 10.60m (34ft 9.3in); width 3.48m (11ft 5in); height 2.48m (8ft 1.6in)
Range:	400km (249 miles)
Armour:	up to 203mm (8in)
Armament:	none
Powerplant:	one Model V-55 V-12 diesel engine developing 580hp (432.5kW)
Performance:	maximum road speed 48km/h (29.8mph); fording 1.4m (4ft 7in); vertical obstacle 0.8m (2ft 7.5in); trench 2.7m (8ft 10.3in)

Centurion AVRE

In the 1960s, the Centurion Mk V Assault Vehicle Royal Engineers (AVRE) replaced the World War II-vintage Churchill AVRE as the main combat engineer vehicle of the British Army. Based on the Centurion main battle tank, the AVRE carries a heavy demolition gun for blasting enemy fortifications and a dozer blade for removing obstacles. The vehicle is also capable of laying down tracks for wheeled vehicles to help them across muddy ground, and can carry a fascine-layer to cope with anti-tank ditches. Later models were fitted with mine-clearing ploughs at the front of the hull, which were used to rip up the ground and push any anti-tank mines to one side. In addition, the tank can tow a two-wheeled trailer carrying the Giant Viper mine-clearance system. A deep-fording system was developed but not used.

Country of origin:	UK
Crew:	5
Weight:	51,809kg (113,979lb)
Dimensions:	length 8.69m (28ft 6in); width 3.96m (13ft 0in); height 3m (9ft 10in)
Range:	177km (110 miles)
Armour:	17-118mm (0.66-4.6in)
Armament:	one 165mm demolition gun; one 7.62mm co-axial machine gun; one 7.62mm anti-aircraft machine gun
Powerplant:	one Rolls-Royce Meteor Mk IVB 12-cylinder petrol engine developing 650hp (484.7kW)
Performance:	maximum road speed 34.6km/h (21.5mph); fording 1.45m (4ft 9in); vertical obstacle 0.94m (3ft 1in); trench 3.35m (11ft 0in)

Combat Engineer Tractor

The Combat Engineer Tractor (CET) was designed by the British Army to fulfil the Royal Engineers' requirement for a vehicle combining elements of an armoured vehicle and an earthmover. Between 1978 and 1981, a total of 181 vehicles were built to undertake a variety of roles such as vehicle recovery, clearing obstacles and preparing river banks for vehicle crossings. Mounted on the roof is a rocket-propelled anchor which could be fired into the earth to enable the vehicle to winch itself out if it became stuck. The CET has full amphibious capability and when afloat is powered by twin water jets. The hull is made of all-welded aluminium armour, which is supplied by Alcan. The vehicle saw extensive service during the 1982 Falklands Conflict and was exported to India.

Country of origin:	UK
Crew:	2
Weight:	18,000kg (39,600lb)
Dimensions:	length 7.54m (24ft 9in); width 2.90m (9ft 6in); height 2.67m (8ft 9in)
Range:	322km (200 miles)
Armour:	classified
Armament:	one 7.62mm machine gun
Powerplant:	one Rolls-Royce C6TFR six-cylinder inline diesel engine developing 320hp (238.6kW)
Performance:	maximum road speed 56km/h (35mph); fording 1.83m (6ft 0in); vertical obstacle 0.61m (2ft); trench 2.06m (6ft 9in)

Chieftain AVRE

The Chieftain AVRE has replaced the Centurion Mk 5 AVRE, which was used by the British Army since the 1960s. It is similar to a standard Chieftain MK 5 main battle tank in terms of its chassis and engine. The main difference is that the gun turret is removed and replaced with an armoured 'penthouse', on top of which is situated the commander's cupola. The vehicle carries three large hampers for storing equipment and a dozer blade or mine plough is fitted at the front. In addition, the vehicle carries a crane capable of lifting 3.6 tonnes (3.5 tons). At the back there is a winch capable of pulling 10.1 tonnes (10 tons). Around 50 of these vehicles are currently in service with the British Army. The illustration above shows the AVRE optimised for maxi-pipe fascines and trackway.

Country of origin:	UK
Crew:	3
Weight:	51,809kg (113,979lb)
Dimensions:	length: 7.52m (24.8ft); width: 3.663m (11.8ft); height: 2.89m (9.4ft)
Range:	500km (300 miles)
Armour:	classified
Armament:	one 7.62mm machine gun; 2 x 6 smoke dischargers (front); 2 x 4 smoke dischargers (rear)
Powerplant:	one Leyland L60 (No.4 Mk 8) 12-cylinder diesel engine, developing 750hp (559kW)
Performance:	maximum road speed 48km/h (28.8mph); fording 1.067m (3ft 6in); vertical obstacle 0.9m (3ft); trench 3.15m (10ft 4in)

Gepard

The Gepard self-propelled anti-aircraft gun system was designed specifically to protect armoured formations. The system uses the hull of the Leopard 1 main battle tank to carry a welded-steel turret capable of powered traverse through 360 degrees and accommodating the weapon system. The two 35mm cannon are located externally to avoid the problem of gun gas in the fighting compartment. Each of the weapons has a cyclic rate of fire of 550 rounds per minute, though it is standard procedure to fire bursts of between 20 and 40 rounds. Ammunition types include high explosive and armour-piercing. The fire-control system is based on a computer supplied with target data by two radars: the acquisition unit and the tracking unit. Other features are optical sights and a land navigation system

Country of origin:	Germany
Crew:	4
Weight:	47,300kg (104,060lb)
Dimensions:	length: 7.68m (25ft 3in); width: 3.27m (10ft 9in); height: 3.01m (9ft 10in)
Range:	550km (342 miles)
Armour:	40mm (1.57in)
Armament:	two 35mm cannon; eight smoke dischargers
Powerplant:	One MTU MB 838 Ca M500 10-cylinder multi-fuel engine developing 830hp (619kW)
Performance:	maximum road speed 65km/h (40.5mph); fording 2.5m (8ft 2in); vertical obstacle 1.15m (3ft 9in); trench 3m (9ft 10in)

Anti-Aircraft Guns

Type 63

To meet their needs for a self-propelled anti-aircraft gun, the Chinese took the chassis of the Soviet T-34 tank (supplied to them in large numbers before relations were broken off between the two countries) and added an open-topped turret with twin anti-aircraft guns. The vehicle was severely limited in that it had no provision for radar control and had to be sighted and elevated manually, a major drawback when faced with fast, low-flying aircraft, particularly as the gun had to be loaded manually with five-round clips. The Type 63 was supplied to the Viet Cong during the Vietnam War in the 1960s, but otherwise was only used in numbers by the People's Liberation Army. Amazingly, given its mediocre qualities, it continued in use with Chinese force until the late 1980s.

Country of origin:	China
Crew:	6
Weight:	32,000kg (70,400lb)
Dimensions:	length 6.432m (21ft 1in); width 2.99m (9ft 10in); height 2.995m (9ft 10in)
Range:	300km (186 miles)
Armour:	18-45mm (0.7-1.8in)
Armament:	twin 37mm anti-aircraft cannon
Powerplant:	one V-12 water-cooled diesel engine developing 500hp (373kW)
Performance:	maximum road speed 55km/h (34mph); fording 1.32m (4ft 4in); vertical obstacle 0.73m (2ft 5in); trench 2.5m (8ft 2in)

242

ZSU-57-2

The ZSU-57-2 was the first Soviet self-propelled anti-aircraft gun to see service on a significant scale after World War II. The chassis was a lightened version of the T-54 main battle tank with thinner armour, the distinctive feature of the vehicle being the large, open-topped turret. This created a greater power-to-weight ratio than the T-54 and, coupled with extra fuel tanks, gave the gun good mobility and operating range. Practical firing rate was around 70 rounds per minute, with the empty cartridge cases being transported to a wire basket at the rear by a conveyor belt. The vehicle was exported widely to other Warsaw Pact countries, North Africa and the Middle East, seeing extensive action with Syrian forces during the fighting in Lebanon against the Israelis in 1982.

Country of origin:	USSR
Crew:	6
Weight:	28,100kg (61,820lb)
Dimensions:	length 8.48m (27ft 10in); width 3.27m (10ft 9in); height 2.75m (9ft)
Range:	420km (260 miles)
Armour:	15mm (0.59in)
Armament:	twin 57mm anti-aircraft cannon
Powerplant:	one Model V-54 V-12 diesel engine developing 520hp (388kW)
Performance:	maximum road speed 50km/h (31mph); fording 1.4m (4ft 7in); vertical obstacle 0.80m (2ft 7in); trench 2.70m (8ft 10in)

Anti-Aircraft Guns

ZSU-23-4

The ZSU-23-4 was developed in the 1960s as the replacement for the ZSU-57-2. Although having a shorter firing range, radar fire-control and an increased firing rate made the weapon much more effective. The chassis was similar to that of the SA-6 surface-to-air missile (SAM) system and used components of the PT-76 tank. Known to the Soviets as the 'Shilka', the vehicle can create an impassable wall of anti-aircraft fire over a 180-degree arc. Widely exported, the ZSU-23-4 was particularly effective in Egyptian hands during the Yom Kippur War of 1973, bringing down Israeli aircraft who were forced to fly low by the Egyptian missile defence system. It also saw extensive combat service with the North Vietnamese during the Vietnam War, bringing down numerous American aircraft.

Country of origin:	USSR
Crew:	4
Weight:	19,000kg (41,800lb)
Dimensions:	length 6.54m (21ft 5in); width 2.95m (9ft 8in); height (without radar) 2.25m (7ft 4in)
Range:	260km (162 miles)
Armour:	10-15mm (0.39-0.6in)
Armament:	four AZP-23 23mm anti-aircraft cannon
Powerplant:	one V-6R diesel engine developing 280hp (210kW)
Performance:	maximum road speed 44km/h (27mph); fording 1.4m (4ft 7in); vertical obstacle 1.10m (3ft 7in); trench 2.80m (9ft 2in)

M42

The M42 anti-aircraft system, commonly known as the 'Duster', was based on the M41 Bulldog tank and was one of a family of vehicles developed after the end of World War II. Between 1951 and 1956, around 3700 were built, mainly by Cadillac. The main drawback of the vehicle was its petrol engine, which restricted its operating range and its lack of a radar fire-control system, the gunner being forced to rely on optic sights. In addition, the open-topped turret afforded the crew little protection. However, it saw extensive service in Vietnam, albeit mainly in a ground-support rather than anti-aircraft role, and continued to serve with the National Guard into the 1980s. Its power-assisted twin 40mm turret was the same as that used on the M19 self-propelled anti-aircraft gun system used in World War II.

Country of origin:	USA
Crew:	6
Weight:	22,452kg (49,394lb)
Dimensions:	length 6.356m (20ft 10in); width 3.225m (10ft 7in); height 2.847m (9ft 4in)
Range:	161km (100 miles)
Armour:	12-38mm (0.47-1.5in)
Armament:	twin 40mm anti-aircraft guns; one 7.62mm machine gun
Powerplant:	one Continental AOS-895-3 six-cylinder air-cooled petrol engine developing 500hp (373kW)
Performance:	maximum road speed 72.4km/h (45mph); fording 1.3m (4ft 3in); vertical obstacle 1.711m (2ft 4in); trench 1.829m (6ft)

M163 Vulcan

In the early 1960s, Rock Island Arsenal developed a self-propelled air-defence system based on the M113 armoured personnel carrier chassis. GEC began production and the vehicle was soon being deployed to Vietnam, where it was widely used by both US and South Vietnamese troops in a ground-support role. An electrically operated turret was mounted on the M113 chassis and armed with a six-barrelled Gatling-type cannon. This had adjustable rates of fire depending on whether it was being used for ground attack or anti-aircraft defence, and was the same weapon used by F-16 fighter aircraft. In the direct-fire role the Vulcan has a rate of fire of 1180 rounds per minute. The vehicle was exported to Ecuador, Israel, Morocco, North Yemen, South Korea and Tunisia.

Country of origin:	USA
Crew:	4
Weight:	12,310kg (27,082lb)
Dimensions:	length 4.86m (15ft 11in); width 2.85m (9ft 4in); height 2.736m (9ft 11in)
Range:	83km (300 miles)
Armour:	38mm (1.5in)
Armament:	one 20mm six-barrelled M61 series cannon
Powerplant:	one Detroit 6V-53 six-cylinder diesel engine developing 215hp (160kW)
Performance:	maximum road speed 67km/h (42mph); fording amphibious; vertical obstacle 1.61m (2ft); trench 1.68m (5ft 6in)

Sergeant York

The Vulcan was noted for its short range and relative inaccuracy (though not poor rate of fire), so in 1978 the US Army issued a requirement for a self-propelled anti-aircraft gun based on the M48 main battle tank chassis to replace it. The first production M247 arrived in 1983, built by FAC. The vehicle has a comprehensive fire-control system including both surveillance and tracking radar. The M247 is capable of engaging both aircraft and helicopters, as well as tactical missiles (the latter capability being very important on the modern battlefield). The modified M48 chassis gives the vehicle the mobility and protection needed to operate with the M1 Abrams main battle tank and M2 Bradley infantry fighting vehicle, in turn providing viable anti-aircraft defence for both vehicles.

Country of origin:	USA
Crew:	3
Weight:	54,430kg (119,746lb)
Dimensions:	length 7.674m (25ft 2in); width 3.632m (11ft 11in); height (radar up) 4.611m (15ft 2in)
Range:	500km (311 miles)
Armour:	up to 120mm (4.72in)
Armament:	twin 40mm L/70 Bofors guns
Powerplant:	one Teledyne Continental AVDS-1790-2D diesel engine developing 750hp (559kW)
Performance:	maximum road speed 48km/h (30mph); fording 1.219m (4ft); vertical obstacle 1.914m (3ft); trench 2.591m (8ft 6in)

AMX-13 DCA

The AMX-13 DCA entered production in the late 1960s to meet French requirements for a self-propelled anti-aircraft gun. It is essentially an AMX-13 main battle tank chassis fitted with a cast-steel turret. The vehicle entered service with the French Army in 1969. A total of 60 were delivered before production ceased and up to the 1980s, the AMX-13 DCA was the only self-propelled anti-aircraft gun in use with French forces. To aid fire control, there is an Oeil Noir 1 radar scanner fitted to the back of the turret, which is retractable while on the move. The DCA turret was fitted to the improved AMX-30 chassis for export to Saudi Arabia in the late 1970s and 1980s. The AMX-13 DCA is an adequate air defence vehicle, though now rather long in the tooth.

Country of origin:	France
Crew:	3
Weight:	17,200kg (37,840lb)
Dimensions:	length 5.40m (17ft 11in); width 2.50m (8ft 2in); height (radar up) 3.80m (12ft 6in); height (radar down) 3.00m (9ft 10in)
Range:	300km (186 miles)
Armour:	25mm (0.98in)
Armament:	twin 30mm Hispano (now Oerlikon) cannon
Powerplant:	one SOFAM Model 8Gxb eight-cylinder water-cooled petrol engine developing 250hp (186kW)
Performance:	maximum road speed 60km/h (37mph); fording 0.6m (1ft 11in); vertical obstacle 0.65m (2ft 2in); trench 1.70m (5ft 7in)

Wildcat

Realising that the self-propelled gun based on the Leopard 1 chassis and the American Sergeant York M247 would be too expensive for many countries, Krauss-Maffei decided to build a new family of anti-aircraft guns for sale abroad to tap into the lucrative market for arms outside of Europe. It was decided to use the automotive components of the 6 x 6 Transportpanzer already in production for the West German Army. With a laser rangefinder, radar scanner and automatic target-tracking, the fully computerised fire-control system makes the Wildcat an effective weapon, either against aircraft or against ground targets. It is also relatively inexpensive to maintain and spares are easy to come by – two attributes which make it attractive to countries with tight defence budgets.

Country of origin:	West Germany
Crew:	3
Weight:	18,500kg (40,700lb)
Dimensions:	length 6.88m (22ft 7in); width 2.98m (9ft 9in); height (radar down) 2.74m (9ft)
Range:	600km (373 miles)
Armour:	classified
Armament:	twin 30mm Mauser Mk 30-F cannon
Powerplant:	one Mercedes-Benz turbocharged eight-cylinder diesel engine developing 320hp (239kW)
Performance:	maximum road speed 80km/h (50mph); fording amphibious; vertical obstacle 0.6m (1ft 11in); trench 1.1m (3ft 7in)

GDF-CO3

Produced by Oerlikon-Bührle, the GDF series was designed to be a highly mobile anti-aircraft defence system to protect rear-area targets such as factories and air bases. The chassis for the tracked version is derived from the M113 series of armoured vehicles; the wheeled version is based on the 4 x 4 HYKA cross-country vehicle. The GDF-CO3 has a day/night fire-control system with laser rangefinder, in addition to a Contraves search radar. The vehicle fires a range of ammunition, including armour-piercing discarding sabot-tracer rounds for use against ground targets. Its layout is unusual in that the crew compartment is at the front with the guns behind them. Nevertheless, as a mobile air-defence platform the vehicle is ideally suited to Switzerland's needs.

Country of origin:	Switzerland
Crew:	3
Weight:	18,000kg (39,600lb)
Dimensions:	length 6.70m (22ft 0in); width 2.813m (9ft 3in); height 4.00m (13ft 2in)
Range:	480km (297 miles)
Armour:	8mm (0.31in)
Armament:	twin 35mm KDF cannon
Powerplant:	one GMC 6V-53T 6-cylinder diesel engine developing 215hp (160kW)
Performance:	maximum road speed 45km/h (28mph); fording 0.6m (1ft 11in); vertical obstacle 0.609m (2ft 0in); trench 1.80m (5ft 11in)

M53/59

In the 1950s, Czechoslovakia developed and began production of the M53/59 self-propelled anti-aircraft gun. Based on the Praga V3S 6 x 6 truck chassis with an armoured cab, the vehicle was used in place of the Soviet ZSU-57-2. Essentially a clear-weather system, the vehicle carried neither infrared night vision equipment nor a nuclear, biological and chemical (NBC) defence system. Both armour-piercing incendiary ammunition for ground targets and high-explosive incendiary for aircraft were carried. Other than its reliance on clear-weather systems, the other main drawback was its poor cross-country mobility, which prevented effective operation with tracked vehicles. In addition to the Czech Army, the M53/59 saw service with both the former Yugoslavia and Libya.

Country of origin:	Czechoslovakia
Crew:	6
Weight:	10,300kg (22,660lb)
Dimensions:	length 6.92m (22ft 8in); width 2.35m (7ft 9in); height 2.585m (8ft 6in)
Range:	500km (311 miles)
Armour:	none (vehicle as a whole)
Armament:	twin 30mm cannon
Powerplant:	one Tatra T912-2 six-cylinder diesel engine developing 110hp (82kW)
Performance:	maximum road speed 60km/h (37mph); vertical obstacle 0.46m (1ft 6in); trench 0.69m (2ft 3in)

Light Vehicles

Stöwer 40

In 1934, the Germans began to create standardised vehicles for the Wehrmacht in preparation for the inevitable war in Europe. Up until then, cross-country vehicles had been based on commercial designs, with all their disadvantages with relation to military uses. The new method would involve taking into account not only technical but operational considerations when designing a vehicle. The Kfz 2 entered production in 1936, based on a number of different manufacturers' components, including Stöwer, BMW and Hanomag. A 4 x 4 design, it was often used as the basis for radio cars. The chassis was normal, except for additional bracing on the engine, suspension and transmission for strength. The Stöwer 40 had five forward and one reverse gears, and was a solid and reliable vehicle.

Country of origin:	Germany
Crew:	1
Weight:	1815kg (3993lb)
Dimensions:	length 3.58m (11ft 9in); width 1.57m (5ft 2in); height 1.78m (5ft 10in)
Range:	500km (311 miles)
Armour:	none
Armament:	none
Powerplant:	one Stower AW2 or R180W four-cylinder OHV petrol engine developing 50hp (37.3kW)
Performance:	maximum road speed 100km/h (62.5mph); fording 0.6m (1ft 11in)

VW Kübel

The Kübel was one of the most famous military cars of World War II, and became something of a trademark with German forces in the conflict. Development began in 1936, and following design changes to accommodate more requirements, when it was announced that it would be the standard personnel carrier of the army, production began in 1940. The two main design considerations were lightness and ease of manufacture. It was also very cheap to make. Reliable, mobile and simple to maintain, the vehicle met all the demands made on it. By the time production ceased in 1944, some 55,000 had been made. Variants included the Type 92 with an enclosed body. In the desert the vehicle performed poorly, but a way round this was found in the Tropenfest version, which was equipped with sand tyres.

Country of origin:	Germany
Crew:	1
Weight:	635kg (1397lb)
Dimensions:	length 3.73m (12ft 3in); width 1.60m (5ft 3in); height 1.35m (4ft 5in)
Range:	600km (375 miles)
Armour:	none
Armament:	none
Powerplant:	one Volkswagen 14-cylinder HIAR 998cc petrol engine developing 24hp (17.9kW), or from March 1943 one Volkswagen four-cylinder 1131cc petrol engine developing 25hp (18.6kW)
Performance:	maximum road speed 100km/h (62.5mph); fording 0.4m (1ft 4in)

Kraftfahrzeug (Kfz) 11

The Auto-Union/Horch Typ 830 was a commercial vehicle fitted with a military body as an initial method of motorising the armed forces prior to the introduction of the standard vehicles (contrary to popular opinion, the German Army was not fully mechanised when war broke out in 1939). Given larger tyres and V8 engine to improve cross-country capability, the vehicle was developed in the late 1920s and early 1930s. Mostly open-topped, it was used in the main for carrying infantry, towing light guns or as a communications vehicle. The Kfz 11 was a closed body version, designed for signal troops, the body being initially made of wood and later sheet metal. Production ended in 1937 with the arrival of standard personnel carriers, but the vehicle saw action in most theatres of World War II.

Country of origin:	Germany
Crew:	1
Weight:	990kg (2178lb)
Dimensions:	length 4.80m (15ft 9in); width 1.80m (5ft 11in); height 1.85m (6ft 1in)
Range:	136km (225 miles)
Armour:	none
Armament:	none
Powerplant:	one Horch V-8 2.98-litre petrol engine developing 70hp (52.2kW)
Performance:	maximum road speed 75km/h (46.85mph); fording 0.4m (1ft 4in)

Kraftfahrzeug (Kfz) 15

The main role of the Kfz 15 was as a communications vehicle. Powered by a V8 engine, the vehicle was based on a number of commercial chassis, including that of the Mercedes-Benz 340 chassis between 1938 and 1940. When the German Army was being rebuilt in the early 1930s, the theory was that that it should have specially built vehicles to carry out Blitzkrieg attacks. However, at first commercial car and light lorry chassis were used – with special bodies simply placed on top. The result was a whole series of poor military vehicles with low ground clearance. Thus the long wheelbase of this chassis tended to impair cross-country performance in spite of four-wheel drive. However, even after the introduction of the standard personnel carrier, many were used as staff cars and radio cars.

Country of origin:	Germany
Crew:	1
Weight:	2405kg (5291lb)
Dimensions:	length 4.44m (14ft 7in); width 1.68m (5ft 6in); height 1.73m (5ft 8in)
Range:	400km (250 miles)
Armour:	none
Armament:	none
Powerplant:	one Mercedes-Benz six-cylinder petrol engine developing 90hp (67.1kW)
Performance:	maximum road speed 88km/h (55mph); fording 0.6m (1ft 11in)

Daimler-Benz G5

The G series was developed to fill a Wehrmacht requirement for a personnel carrier with full cross-country capability. The first efforts by Daimler-Benz resulted in powerful vehicles with four-wheel drive and four-wheel steering, but their cross-country performance was poor. They were also too large and too expensive. Not chosen for production of the standard Einheit range of personnel carriers, Daimler-Benz continued to develop the G series. Between 1937 and 1941, 378 G5 vehicles were built, but few saw service with the Wehrmacht, although some were used as communications vehicles by high officials of the Nazi Party and the General Staff (an additional problem with many German light vehicles was that they were too complicated for reliability in rugged conditions, especially Russia).

Country of origin:	Germany
Crew:	1
Weight:	1630kg (3586lb)
Dimensions:	length 4.52m (14ft 10in); width 1.70m (5ft 7in); height 1.80m (5ft 11in)
Range:	480km (300 miles)
Armour:	none
Armament:	none
Powerplant:	one Mercedes-Benz six-cylinder petrol engine developing 90hp (67kW)
Performance:	maximum road speed 75km/h (46.8mph); fording 0.7m (2ft 4in)

Car, Heavy Utility, 4 x 2, Ford C 11 ADF

The Ford C 11 ADF was based on the commercial 1942 Ford Fordor Station Wagon. Produced mainly for the British (and fitted with right-hand drive for this purpose), but also used by the Canadian Army, the vehicle saw extensive service as a staff vehicle in the Western Desert and in Italy. The all-steel body had space for five passengers. The vehicle was fitted with strengthened bumpers, internal rifle racks, entrenching tools and radio-interference suppression equipment, as well as a full medical kit and map containers. In short it was adequately equipped to allow staff officers to operate it as a mobile command centre. It was also rugged enough to stand up to the adverse terrain of North Africa. Transmission consisted of three forward and one reverse gears.

Country of origin:	Canada
Crew:	1
Weight:	1814kg (3990lb)
Dimensions:	length 4.93m (16ft 2in); width 2.01m (6ft 7in); height 1.83m (6ft 0in)
Range:	500km (311 miles)
Armour:	none
Armament:	none
Powerplant:	one Ford mercury V-8 3.91-litre petrol engine developing 95hp (70.8kW)
Performance:	maximum road speed 90km/h (56mph); fording 0.4m (1ft 4in)

Light Vehicles

Dodge T215

Dodge was the sole provider of 0.5-tonnes (0.5-tons) trucks for the US Army. The order for 14,000 was made in mid-1940. Dodge altered the basic commercial chassis slightly for military use, giving it four-wheel drive. There was the option of an open cab (as with the command, reconnaissance, radio and weapons carrier versions) or fixed bodywork as with the ambulance). The Dodge was a sturdy vehicle manufactured in large numbers, many of which were shipped to the United Kingdom and USSR under the Lend-Lease scheme of World War II. Interestingly, the Russians were less than impressed with the tanks supplied by the British and Americans under the scheme, but they were very grateful when it came to the jeeps and lorries supplied, using them for many years after the end of the war.

Country of origin:	USA
Crew:	1
Weight:	2046kg (4501lb)
Dimensions:	length 4.67m (15ft 4in); width 1.93m (6ft 4in); height 2.13m (7ft 0in)
Range:	500km (311 miles)
Armour:	none
Armament:	none
Powerplant:	one Dodge T215 six-cylinder petrol engine developing 92hp (68.6kW)
Performance:	maximum road speed 70km/h (43.75mph); fording 0.6m (1ft 11in)

Dodge T214

Introduced in 1942, the Dodge T214 0.75-tonnes (0.75-tons) truck was the successor to the T215 and was slightly wider and lower with larger wheels and stronger suspensions. Referred to as 'Beeps' (a contraction of 'Big Jeeps'), the T214 had a range of body types for different roles: weapons carrier, winch-equipped, ambulance, radio vehicle, command reconnaissance vehicle and repair vehicle. The differences were mainly in the number of seats, map boards and type of canvas cover. The fact that many vehicles are still in use around the world today is a tribute to the sturdy design of these vehicles, which were characterised by an ability to take a lot of punishment and ease of maintenance. Transmission consisted of four forward and one reverse gears.

Country of origin:	USA
Crew:	1
Weight:	2449kg (5388lb)
Dimensions:	length 4.24m (13ft 11n); width 1.99m (6ft 6.5in); height 2.07m (6ft 9.5in)
Range:	450km (281 miles)
Armour:	none
Armament:	none
Powerplant:	one Dodge T214 six-cylinder petrol engine developing 92hp (68.6kW)
Performance:	maximum road speed 110km/h (68.75mph); fording 0.5m (1ft 7in)

Light Vehicles

Dodge WC53

The Dodge T214 WC53 Command and Reconnaissance Vehicle was used in a very similar way to the ubiquitous Jeep. The most common variant of the Dodge T214 series, it was used for reconnaissance as its name suggests and for liaising between different units. It also served as a staff vehicle for high-ranking officers. The vehicle was fitted with map boards and had a detachable canvas top and side-screens. A good all-round utility vehicle, reliable and mobile, it served in all theatres of the war. One of its greatest attributes was its Dodge six-cylinder petrol engine, which could withstand poor maintenance, hard treatment and a variety of adverse weather conditions. In addition, the chassis was able to take on most types of terrain, from the humid jungles of the Pacific to the snows of northern Europe.

Country of origin:	USA
Crew:	1
Weight:	2449kg (5387lb)
Dimensions:	length 4.24m (13ft 11in); width 1.99m (6ft 6.5in); height 2.07m (6ft 9.5in)
Range:	450km (281 miles)
Armour:	none
Armament:	none
Powerplant:	one Dodge T214 six-cylinder petrol engine developing 92hp (68.6kW)
Performance:	maximum road speed 110km/h (68.75mph); fording 0.5m (1ft 7in)

4 x 4 Jeep

In June 1940, the US Army issued a requirement for a 'go-anywhere' vehicle. After initial design changes, Ford and Willys both began production of the Jeep and between them manufactured nearly 650,000 vehicles. Intended for reconnaissance and liaison duties, the Jeep was so successful that it was soon adapted for other duties, including airborne landings and for use as rocket-launchers. They were adapted by the British SAS for long-range desert raids, mainly by being stripped of luxuries and heavily armed. Jeeps were used as ambulances and for laying telephone lines. If fitted with special flanged wheels, the Jeep could even travel along railway lines. Adapted for different climactic conditions, the Jeep served with distinction in all Allied theatres.

Country of origin:	USA
Crew:	1
Weight:	1247kg (2743lb)
Dimensions:	length 3.33m (11ft 0.25in); width 1.57m (5ft 2in); height 1.14m (3ft 9in)
Range:	363km (225 miles)
Armour:	none
Armament:	none (basic model)
Powerplant:	one Willys 441 or 442 'Go Devil' 4-cylinder petrol engine developing 60hp (44.7kW)
Performance:	maximum road speed 88.5km/h (55mph); fording 0.5m (1ft 7in)

Humber

The Humber Heavy Utility Car was the standard staff and command car of the British Army during World War II (the army was the only fully motorised force when war broke out in September 1939). It was also the only 4 x 4 British-built four-wheel drive utility car employed. Production of the 'Box' began in May 1941 and continued until 1945. Widely used, the vehicle remained in service until the late 1950s – testimony to the quality of its design. Its fixed steel bodywork carried six seats and a folding map table. In the desert, the fixed cab was sometimes replaced by a canvas cover. The Humber was unspectacular in design, but more importantly it did the job required of it, and in different theatres. Transmission consisted of four forward and one reverse gears.

Country of origin:	UK
Crew:	1
Weight:	2413kg (5308lb)
Dimensions:	length 4.29m (14ft 1in); width 1.88m (6ft 2in); height 1.96m (6ft 5in)
Range:	500km (311 miles)
Armour:	none
Armament:	none
Powerplant:	one Humber six-cylinder 1-L-W-F 4.08-litre petrol engine developing 85hp (63.4kW)
Performance:	maximum road speed 75km/h (46.8mph); fording 0.6m (1ft 11in)

Morris C8

The Morris C8 artillery tractor was one of the most successful of the range of vehicles produced by Morris for the British Army. Popularly known as the Quad, the vehicle was introduced in 1939. It was used to tow the 18- or 25-pounder gun and was equipped with a winch, which lift loads of up to 4000kg (8800lb). Inside there was room for the gun crew. The Morris C8 was a sturdy vehicle with good cross-country mobility and adequate stowage space for ammunition. Early models had a distinctive beetle shape, but from 1944 onwards the vehicle was fitted with an open top. A large number of C8s were lost during the British Expeditionary Force's withdrawal from Dunkirk in 1940, but the vehicle did go on to see service in North Africa. Transmission consisted of five forward and one reverse gears.

Country of origin:	UK
Crew:	1
Weight:	3402kg (7484lb)
Dimensions:	length 4.49m (14ft 8.75in); width 2.21m (7ft 3in); height 2.26m (7ft 5in)
Range:	480km (300 miles)
Armour:	none
Armament:	none
Powerplant:	one Morris four-cylinder 3.5-litre petrol engine developing 70hp (52.2kW)
Performance:	maximum road speed 80km/h (50mph); fording 0.4m (1ft 4in)

Bedford MWD

The prototype of the Bedford MWD appeared in 1937. It was based on a commercial 2-tonnes (2-tons) truck with a modified chassis to increase ground clearance. The British War Office ordered 2000 trucks in August 1939, the early deliveries being constructed specifically to carry the 2-pounder anti-tank gun. The vehicle had a flat, full-width bonnet, designed to incorporate an extra-large air filter as per War Office requirements. Originally the vehicle was fitted with a canvas hood and collapsible windscreen, but this was replaced in 1943 by an enclosed cab. Bedford produced over 200,000 of these vehicles by the end of the war, and the type remained in service with the British Army until the late 1950s. Transmission consisted of four forward and one reverse gears.

Country of origin:	UK
Crew:	1
Weight:	2132kg (4690lb)
Dimensions:	length 4.38m (14ft 4.5in); width 1.99m (6ft 6.5in); height 2.29m (7ft 6in) with GS tilt and 1.93m (6ft 4in) without GS tilt
Range:	430km (268 miles)
Armour:	none
Armament:	none
Powerplant:	one Bedford six-cylinder OHV 3.5-litre petrol engine developing 72hp (53.7kW)
Performance:	maximum road speed 95km/h (59.4mph); fording 0.7m (2ft 4in)

GAZ-67B

The GAZ-67B was designed as a cross-country vehicle for transporting both personnel and light equipment. First produced in 1943, its design was greatly influenced by the US Bantam Jeep, many of which had been supplied to the Soviet Union under the Lend-Lease programme (one of the early Russian attempts at reverse engineering). Its performance was not quite as good, though, particularly in terms of acceleration which was poor. However, its simple and very basic design did not detract from the essential strength of the vehicle, which had very good cross-country mobility. The vehicle went on to see extensive service in Korea and Indochina, and formed the backbone of Soviet airborne divisions. Production ceased in 1953. Transmission consisted of four forward and one reverse gears.

Country of origin:	USSR
Crew:	1
Weight:	1220kg (2684lb)
Dimensions:	length 3.34m (10ft 11.33in); width 1.68m (5ft 6in); height 1.70m (5ft 7in)
Range:	750km (468 miles)
Armour:	none
Armament:	none
Powerplant:	one GAZ-A four-cylinder 3.28-litre petrol engine developing 54hp (40.3kW)
Performance:	maximum road speed 75km/h (46.8mph); fording 0.45m (1ft 6in)

Light Vehicles

Fiat 508

The major manufacturer of light vehicles for the Italian Army, Fiat had designed several military-type vehicles prior to World War II. The 508 CM was one such vehicle. The type was referred to as a colonial vehicle, specially designed for the rough terrain found in Italian-controlled territories in North Africa and adapted to avoid sinking in soft terrain. Produced in response to a requirement for a lightweight, inexpensive vehicle with good road speed and fair cross-country performance, the vehicle was based on the similar 'balilla' civilian model. The 508 CM was the most prolific military vehicle employed by the Italians, large numbers being built between 1939 and 1945. It was a capable vehicle, though uninspiring. Transmission was four forward and one reverse gears.

Country of origin:	Italy
Crew:	1
Weight:	1065kg (2343lb)
Dimensions:	length 3.35m (11ft 0in); width 1.37m (4ft 6in); height 1.57m (5ft 2in)
Range:	400km (250 miles)
Armour:	none
Armament:	none
Powerplant:	one Fiat 108C four-cylinder petrol engine developing 32hp (23.9kW)
Performance:	maximum road speed 80km/h (50mph); fording 0.45m (1ft 6in)

Type 95 Scout Car

The Type 95 Scout Car, known as the 'Black Medal', was developed after Japanese experiences in Manchuria had revealed the need for such a vehicle. Some 4800 were built by Kurogane and this was the only native vehicle of its type used by the Japanese Army before and during World War II, most others being of American origin or pattern. Built in closed cab, truck and convertible versions, this proved an ideal vehicle for operations in northern China and Manchuria as it coped well with low temperatures and its air-cooled engine was not reliant on the limited supplies of unpolluted water found in the region. Special tyres with heavy rubber treads were added to cope with difficult terrain.The Type 95's transmission was a selective sliding type giving three forward and one reverse gears

Country of origin:	Japan
Crew:	1
Weight:	1100kg (2420lb)
Dimensions:	length 3.38m (11ft 1in); width 1.52m (5ft 0in); height 1.68m (5ft 6in)
Range:	450km (281 miles)
Armour:	none
Armament:	none
Powerplant:	one two-cylinder four-stroke V-1-A-F petrol engine developing 33hp (24.6kW)
Performance:	maximum road speed 75km/h (46.8mph); fording 0.5m (1ft 7in)

Light Vehicles

M37

The M37 was the replacement vehicle for the World War II Dodge T214 'Beep'. Dodge built over 125,000 M37s between 1950 and 1970, both for the US Army and for export. The basic M37 was designed to carry cargo either by road or cross-country, and was similar in layout to a standard commercial pick-up truck. A winch was often mounted to assist with recovery operations, and the vehicle could be fitted with a deep-fording capability. Variants included an ambulance with fully enclosed body and a command vehicle, as well as more specialised vehicles, such as a telephone repair vehicle. A Japanese variant of the M37, built by Toyota, saw service with US forces during the Vietnam War. Rugged and reliable, the M37 served American forces well in the period immediately after World War II.

Country of origin:	USA
Crew:	1 + 2 (plus 6 or 8 in rear)
Weight:	3493kg (7684lb)
Dimensions:	length 4.81m (15ft 9in); width 1.784m (5ft 10in); height 2.279m (7ft 6in)
Range:	362km (225 miles)
Armour:	none
Armament:	none
Powerplant:	one Dodge T245 six-cylinder petrol engine developing 78hp (58kW)
Performance:	maximum road speed 88.5km/h (55mph); fording 1.066m (3ft 6in)

M151

The M151 was designed to a 1950 requirement for a 0.25-tonnes (0.25-tons) vehicle to replace the M38. Production began in 1960, and from then on the M151 became one of the most widely used vehicles in the world, seeing service in around 100 armies worldwide, as well as being extensively used by US forces in Vietnam as the standard light vehicle of the US Army. From the mid-1980s, all M151s were built solely for export, as the M151 was replaced in US service by the Hummer. The vehicle was used for reconnaissance and light transport duties. Among the many variants were an ambulance, a communications vehicle and several armed versions, carrying a 7.62mm machine gun, 12.7mm machine gun, recoilless rifle or the Hughes TOW anti-tank guided weapons system.

Country of origin:	USA
Crew:	1 + 1 (plus 2 in rear)
Weight:	1575kg (3465lb)
Dimensions:	length 3.352m (11ft); width 1.584m (5ft 2in); height 1.803m (5ft 11in)
Range:	483km (300 miles)
Armour:	none
Armament:	none (basic version); other versions a variety of weapons
Powerplant:	one four-cylinder petrol engine developing 72hp (53.69kW)
Performance:	maximum road speed 106km/h (66mph); fording 0.533m (1ft 9in)

Land Rover One-Tonne

The Land Rover One-Tonne was developed in the mid-1960s, when it was realised that the original Land Rover would not be capable of towing the heavier weapon systems of the future, as well as those earmarked to enter service in the immediate future. The first production models appeared in 1975. This version of the Land Rover was designed specifically for military use (rather than as a multi-purpose vehicle suitable for agricultural and industrial use) and thus far fewer were built than of its more famous ancestor. Typical roles for the vehicle included towing the 105mm Light Gun and Rapier surface-to-air missile (SAM) system. Variants included an ambulance, communications vehicle and electronic warfare vehicle. Like all Land Rover vehicles, this truck was rugged and reliable.

Country of origin:	UK
Crew:	1 + 1 (plus 8 in rear)
Weight:	3120kg (6864lb)
Dimensions:	length 4.127m (13ft 6in); width 1.842m (6ft 1in); height 2.138m (7ft)
Range:	560km (348 miles)
Armour:	none
Armament:	none
Powerplant:	one Rover V-8 petrol engine developing 128hp (95.5kW)
Performance:	maximum road speed 120km/h (74mph); fording 1.1m (3ft 7in)

SAS Land Rover

The British Special Air Service (SAS) has made good use of a long-wheelbase version of the Land Rover, specially adapted for the conditions faced in the types of low-intensity warfare in which the SAS has become expert. Painted pink for camouflage during desert operations (where its colour blends in with the desert haze), and known as Pink Panthers, the vehicles used a similar chassis to that of ordinary British Army Land Rovers. Widely used in the Persian Gulf, they were equipped with metal sand-crossing channels, smoke dischargers and machine guns. In addition, they carried specialist navigational equipment and external stowage racks, to give them the capability to carry out long-range desert reconnaissance missions behind enemy lines.

Country of origin:	UK
Crew:	1
Weight:	3050kg (6710lb)
Dimensions:	length 4.67m (15ft 4in); width 1.79m (5ft 11in); height 2.03m (6ft 8in)
Range:	748km (4655 miles)
Armour:	none
Armament:	two 7.62mm machine guns
Powerplant:	one V-8 water-cooled petrol engine developing 134hp (100kW)
Performance:	maximum road speed 105km/h (65.6mph); fording 0.5m (1ft 7in)

Land Rover 4 x 4

Since production started in 1948, the Land Rover has become one of the most famous light vehicles in service. Over one million had been produced by 1976. Designed by Rover to appeal to both domestic and export markets, the vehicle was initially targeted at agricultural and industrial customers. Constant design improvements demonstrated the potential of the vehicle, and in 1956 the British Army selected it to be the standard military vehicle in its class. Endlessly adaptable, from ambulance to artillery tractor to reconnaissance vehicle, the Land Rover has seen action all over the world with the British Army (which used specially armoured variants for patrols in Northern Ireland) and with numerous other armies. Transmission is manual with four forward and one reverse gears.

Country of origin:	UK
Crew:	1
Weight:	2120kg (4664lb)
Dimensions:	length 3.65m; width 1.68m; height 1.97m
Range:	560km (350 miles)
Armour:	none
Armament:	none
Powerplant:	one four-cylinder OHV diesel engine developing 51hp (30kW)
Performance:	maximum road speed 105km/h (65.6mph); fording 0.5m (1ft 7in)

GAZ-69

The GAZ-69 was the Soviet equivalent of the ubiquitous American Jeep. The vehicle entered production in 1952 and continued to be built well into the 1960s. As well as being used for reconnaissance and general liaison duties, the vehicle's chassis was used for a number of different applications. One of these was the GAZ-69 anti-tank vehicle, which acted as the launch platform for an AT-1 'Snapper' missile launcher, which saw action during the numerous Arab-Israeli wars. An amphibious vehicle was built, designed to reconnoitre river crossing points, and a mine-detecting version also appeared, with the sensory equipment carried on the roof and then swung over in front of the vehicle when required. The vehicle stopped automatically when the alarm sounded.

Country of origin:	USSR
Crew:	1 + 1 (plus 4 in rear)
Weight:	1525kg (3355lb)
Dimensions:	length 3.85m (12ft 8in); width 1.85m (5ft 2in); height 2.03m (6ft 8in)
Range:	530km (330 miles)
Armour:	none
Armament:	none
Powerplant:	one M-20 four-cylinder petrol engine developing 52hp (39kW)
Performance:	maximum road speed 90km/h (56mph); fording 0.55m (1ft 10in)

Light Vehicles

DAF
YA 126

The YA 126 was one of a complete range of vehicles produced by what is now the DAF Trucks company for the Dutch Army in the immediate period after World War II. Production began in 1952 and lasted until 1960. Capable of carrying up to eight troops in addition to other duties, many YA 126 vehicles were fitted with a winch for recovering other stuck vehicles or for self-recovery. One unusual feature was that spare wheels were mounted on each side of the vehicle, which could spin freely and thus aid the vehicle in overcoming obstacles. Variants included a mobile workshop, a fully enclosed ambulance and command/radio vehicle. This vehicle was the precursor of whole range of DAF trucks which were built to serve the Dutch Army, and which continue to serve in Holland.

Country of origin:	Holland
Crew:	1 + 1 (plus 8 in rear)
Weight:	3230kg (7106lb)
Dimensions:	length 4.55m (14ft 11in); width 2.10m (6ft 11in); height 2.20m (7ft 3in)
Range:	330km (205 miles)
Armour:	none
Armament:	none
Powerplant:	one Hercules JXC six-cylinder petrol engine developing 102hp (76kW)
Performance:	maximum road speed 84km/h (52mph); fording 0.76m (2ft 6in)

M998

The High Mobility Multi-Purpose Wheeled Vehicle (HMMWV) – 'Hummer' – prototype appeared in August 1980, and in March 1983 AM General was awarded a contract to build 54,973 vehicles, of which 39,000 were for the US Army. The vehicle has a four-man crew, who sit on either side of the drive chain, which allows for a low centre of gravity. The frame is strong enough to serve as a roll bar and support for various equipment kits. The Hummer can also mount of variety of weapons: such as the TOW anti-tank system, 7.62mm and 12.7mm machine guns, Mk 19 40mm grenade launchers and even batteries of Stinger surface-to-air missiles (SAMs). The vehicle has a fully synchronised transmission with 16 forward and eight reverse gears. The M998 has been exported to the Middle East and Asia.

Country of origin:	USA
Crew:	1 + 3
Weight:	3870kg (8375lb)
Dimensions:	length 4.457m (14ft 7in); width 2.15m (7ft); height 1.75m (5ft 8in)
Range:	563km (352 miles)
Armour:	none
Armament:	various, including machine guns, grenade launchers and surface-to-air missile (SAM) launchers
Powerplant:	one V-8 6.21 air-cooled diesel engine developing 135hp (101kW)
Performance:	maximum road range 105km/h (65.6mph); fording 0.76m (2ft 6in); vertical obstacle 0.56m (1ft 9in)

Chevrolet WA

When the British found themselves unable to supply their own needs for vehicles in World War II, they turned to Canada for help. The Canadians had been working since 1937 on a standard truck based around a Ford V8 chassis. This 'Canadian Military Pattern Chassis' was to form the basis of many light and medium trucks supplied to Allied forces. Produced by both Ford and Chevrolet, the 4 x 4 was the mainstay of Canadian production through the war years. The Chevrolets were produced with either wood or steel bodies and used in an enormous number of roles, from ambulances to mobile gun carriages. Many were adapted for use by special forces such as the Long Range Desert Group in North Africa. Over 900,000 of all types of the basic chassis were produced before 1945.

Country of origin:	Canada
Crew:	1
Weight:	3048kg (6705lb)
Dimensions:	6.579m (21ft 7in); width 2.49m (8ft 2in); height 3m (9ft 9in)
Range:	274km (170 miles)
Armour:	none
Armament:	two machine guns, various calibres
Powerplant:	one Ford V-8 petrol engine developing 95hp (71kW)
Performance:	maximum road speed 80km/h (50mph); fording 0.5m (1ft 7in)

Chevrolet C60L

The Chevrolet C60L was one of the most numerous trucks built by the Canadians during World War II for supply to the British and other Commonwealth forces. This three-tonne (three-ton) 4 x 4 was a tremendously reliable vehicle, of sturdy yet simple design which allowed for rapid production. An enormous number of different models were produced including fuel tankers, ambulances and recovery vehicles. As well as different chassis, there was great differentiation in cab design as production progressed. For example, the number 13 cab was a complete redesign to allow more interior space and better positioning of the foot pedals. Other designs replaced the all-steel cab with a soft-top. The versatility of the range was remarkable and was reflected in the numbers in use.

Country of origin:	Canada
Crew:	1
Weight:	2100kg (4620lb)
Dimensions:	length 6.20m (20ft 4in); width 2.29m (7ft 6in); height 3.05m (10ft)
Range:	270km (168 miles)
Armour:	none
Armament:	none
Powerplant:	one Ford V-8 petrol engine developing 95hp (71kW)
Performance:	maximum road speed 80km/h (50mph); fording 0.5m (1ft 7in)

Krupp Kfz 81

The Kfz 81 was one of the most commonly used German light trucks during the early stages of World War II. The role in which it was most frequently seen was that of artillery tractor (it was the prime mover for the 20mm ant-aircraft gun), replacing the Kfz 69 purpose-built artillery tractor. The Kfz 81, or Krupp Boxer as it was known, had all-round independent suspension which allowed reasonable cross-country mobility. It was similar in many ways to contemporary six-wheeler British light trucks. In addition the indigenous light trucks, the Germans made extensive use of captured material such as the Czechoslovakian Tatra T92. Early German vehicles had stub axles amidships to carry the spare wheels, though there were never enough to go round even the élite field divisions.

Country of origin:	Germany
Crew:	1
Weight:	2600kg (5720lb)
Dimensions:	length 4.95m (16ft 2.9in); width 1.95m (6ft 4.8in); height 2.30m (7ft 6.6in)
Range:	300km (187 miles)
Armour:	none
Armament:	none
Powerplant:	one Krupp M304 4-cylinder engine developing 52hp (38.8kW)
Performance:	maximum road speed 70km/h (43.75mph); fording 0.4m (1ft 4in)

Opel Blitz

The Opel Blitz was one of the most successful products of an attempt by the Germans to standardise their vehicle fleet (100 different vehicles were in service by the late 1930s, leading to massive logistical difficulties). The Blitz had a steel cab and wooden body and was used in many roles, from field ambulance to mobile workshop to command vehicle. To improve cross-country performance, the vehicle was given four-wheel drive, these vehicles being designated 'Allrad'. They were used in all theatres of the war, with later models being constructed of pressed card to conserve steel. Production lasted until 1944, when Allied bombing and ground advances overtook the factories. The Blitz was well built, but suffered from being too complicated for reliability in rugged conditions.

Country of origin:	Germany
Crew:	1
Weight:	3290kg (7238lb)
Dimensions:	length 6.02m (19ft 9in); width 2.265m (7ft 5.2in); height 2.175m (7ft 1.6in)
Range:	410km (255 miles)
Armour:	none
Armament:	none
Powerplant:	one Opel six-cylinder petrol engine developing 73.5hp (54.8kW)
Performance:	maximum road speed 80km/h (50mph); fording 0.5m (1ft 7in)

Büssing-Nag

Germany relied heavily on modified civilian models for its heavy trucks as the war broke out when her rearmament programme was nowhere near completion. One of the types adapted was the Büssing-Nag 454 4 x 4 truck, designed to be used as a transporter unit for tanks. Only a small number were ever constructed as the 6 x 4 Faun was preferred for the role in most cases. Even this vehicle saw limited service as a tank-transport, as the German logistics system relied mainly on the railways for the movement of general supplies during World War II, with medium trucks taking on the task of distributing the equipment to the point of use. Heavy trucks were used most often for specialist roles such as carrying mobile radio stations for controlling armoured forces.

Country of origin:	Germany
Crew:	1
Weight:	9200kg (20,240lb)
Dimensions:	length 10.40m (34ft 1.4in); width 2.50m (8ft 2.4in); height 2.60m (8ft 6.4in)
Range:	270km (169 miles)
Armour:	none
Armament:	none
Powerplant:	one Deutz F6M517 six-cylinder diesel engine developing 150hp (111.8kW)
Performance:	maximum road speed 65km/h (40.62mph); fording 0.4m (1ft 4in)

Bedford Three-ton

The Bedford Three-ton truck was the British equivalent of the American 2.5-ton trucks, in other words the largest cargo vehicle which could be produced in large quantities. After the huge losses of equipment suffered by the British Army at Dunkirk in 1940, the British had been unable to concentrate on development of new vehicles and relied instead on current models and American imports. Once the crisis has eased, ie the threat of German invasion had subsided, new truck development could begin. The Bedford Three-ton was one of the most significant of the new vehicles produced. In addition to general cargo-carrying duties, the vehicle was capable of being converted to a fuel (as shown here) and water tanker with the help of a detachable superstructure.

Country of origin:	UK
Crew:	1
Weight:	7490kg (16,478lb)
Dimensions:	length: 6.7m (22ft); width: 2.3m (7ft 7in); height: 3m (9ft 9in)
Range:	300km (187 miles)
Armour:	none
Armament:	none
Powerplant:	one Austin six-cylinder petrol engine developing 72hp (54kW)
Performance:	maximum road speed 80km/h (50mph); fording 0.6m (1ft 11in)

Trucks and Prime Movers

M36

The M36 is the long wheelbase version of the M35 truck. The layout of the basic cargo version is conventional, with the engine at the front, two-door cab in the centre with a windscreen that can be folded forward onto the bonnet and a canvas top. The cargo area at the back has a drop tailgate, removable bows, tarpaulin cover and troop seats positioned down either side. Many trucks are fitted with a 4536kg- (9979lb-) capacity winch which can be used to the front or rear of the vehicle. It has a steel cable with two speeds forward and one speed in reverse. The truck itself has a manual gearbox with five forward and one reverse gears. A large number of kits are available for this vehicle, including ring mount for machine gun over cab, hard top for the cab and central seats for troops in the rear.

Country of origin:	USA
Crew:	1
Weight:	11,500kg (25,300lb)
Dimensions:	length 8.4m (27ft 6in); width 2.4m (7ft 10in); height 3.2m (10ft 6in)
Range:	480km (300 miles)
Armour:	none
Armament:	none (basic version)
Powerplant:	one LDT-456-1C six-cylinder inline diesel engine developing 140hp (104kW)
Performance:	maximum road speed 90km/h (56.26mph); fording 0.76m (2ft 6in)

Bedford QLD

At the outbreak of World War II, Bedford was contracted by the British War Office to produce a 3-tonnes (3-tons) 4 x 4 general service truck. The Bedford QLD was rapidly developed and the first production vehicles began to arrive in early 1941. Commendably, despite the speed of development, there were hardly any early problems with the vehicle. There were a number of variants on the basic design: the QLT troop carrier with room for 29 troops and kit, popularly known as the 'Drooper'; the QLR wireless truck; a vehicle adapted specifically to carry and fire the 6-pounder anti-tank gun from the body; and a fire tender. The Royal Air Force used them extensively as fuel tankers. An amphibious version, the Giraffe, was developed but never passed the prototype stage.

Country of origin:	UK
Crew:	1
Weight:	12,727kg (26,998lb)
Dimensions:	length 5.99m (19ft 8in); width 2.26m (7ft 5in); height 3.0m (9ft 10in)
Range:	370km (230 miles)
Armour:	none
Armament:	none
Powerplant:	one Bedford six-cylinder petrol engine developing 72hp (53.7kW)
Performance:	maximum road speed 61km/h (38mph); fording 0.4m (1ft 4in)

Fiat/Spa

The Italian Army in World War II was heavily reliant on trucks of somewhat dated design. Prior to World War II, though, some measure of standardisation had been achieved, with Fiat supplying the bulk of the vehicles. *Dovunque* means literally 'go anywhere', and the truck had adequate cross-country capability, being one of a range of Fiat and other Italian vehicles which saw extensive service, particularly in North Africa. The fact that most needed to be hand-crank started belied their effective performance. The Germans appropriated large numbers of Italian trucks for service in all theatres, and British troops valued captured Italian trucks highly because the vehicles did not rely on a carburettor, which tended to clog up in the dusty desert conditions.

Country of origin:	Italy
Crew:	1
Weight:	1615kg (3553lb)
Dimensions:	length 3.80m (12ft 5.6in); width 1.30m (4ft 3.2in); height 2.15m (7ft 0.6in)
Range:	250km (156 miles)
Armour:	none
Armament:	none
Powerplant:	one OM Autocarretta 32 four-cylinder petrol engine developing 21hp (15.7kW)
Performance:	maximum road speed 63km/h (40mph); fording 0.5m (1ft 7in)

GMC 6 x 6

The GMC 6 x 6 was built for the US Army as part of a standardisation programme, begun in 1939, which allowed for only two of each type of vehicle to be considered, and emphasised commonality of parts and accessories wherever possible. Known as 'Jimmies', the vehicles were supplied to Britain under the Lend-Lease scheme before America's entry into World War II, and the trucks served with distinction in all theatres, including in the Soviet Union, which also received significant numbers. The 'Jimmy' made an enormous contribution to the Allied victory after the D-day landings by ensuring a reliable method of transport for supplies to units at the front, all of which had to be trucked across France until ports nearer Germany had been captured.

Country of origin:	USA
Crew:	1
Weight:	11,939kg (26,265lb)
Dimensions:	length 6.82m (22ft 4.5in); width 2.44m (8ft 0in); height 3.01m (9ft 10.5in)
Range:	255km (165 miles)
Armour:	none
Armament:	none
Powerplant:	one Hercules RXC six-cylinder petrol engine developing 106hp (79kW)
Performance:	maximum road speed 64km/h (40mph); fording 0.75m (2ft 5in)

Mack 6 x 6

Mack was a well-established name in the truck manufacturing industry prior to World War II, and was thus well-placed to fulfil the transport needs of the US Army. The most prominent model produced, perhaps because of its size and power, was the 7.6-tonnes (7.5 tons) NO 6 x 6. This was mainly used by both British and American forces to tow heavy artillery pieces, such as the 155mm 'Long Tom' howitzers. The Canadians also used the truck widely for a variety of purposes. The truck was first seen in action in Italy. Despite their size, the Macks negotiated the difficult mountainous terrain to be at the forefront of the advance. The layout of the 6 x 6 was conventional, with the engine at the front, two-door cab in the centre with a fold-forward windscreen, and a cargo area at the rear.

Country of origin:	USA
Crew:	1
Weight:	19,813kg (43,588lb)
Dimensions:	length 7.54m (24ft 9in); width 2.62m (8ft 7in); height 3.15m (10ft 4in)
Range:	340km (212 miles)
Armour:	none
Armament:	none
Powerplant:	one Mack EY six-cylinder petrol engine developing 159hp (118.6kW)
Performance:	maximum road speed 84km/h (52.5mph); fording 0.76m (2ft 6in)

ACMAT VLRA

ACMAT has based their vehicle design on the premise that for full reliability, a military truck must be able to fulfil all requirements while remaining as simple as possible. The VLRA family of trucks all use the same tyres, axles and wheels to avoid the need for carrying different types of spares. All vehicles have long-range fuel tanks and sand channels for desert operations. The trucks can be fitted with a wide range of weapons including machine guns, mortars or Milan anti-tank guided weapons. The command and control version, the TPK 4.20 VCT, is fitted with extensive communications equipment and the many other variants include a fire-fighting truck and a type of armoured personnel carrier. Reliable and durable, the ACMAT VLRA is in service with more than 30 countries worldwide.

Country of origin:	France
Crew:	1 + 2
Weight:	6800kg (14,960lb)
Dimensions:	length 6.00m (19ft 8.2in); width 2.07m (6ft 9.5in); height 1.83m (6ft)
Range:	1600km (1000 miles)
Armour:	none
Armament:	basic version – none. Optional 7.62mm machine gun; Milan anti-tank weapon; 60mm mortar; twin 20mm anti-aircraft cannon
Powerplant:	one Perkins Model 6.354.4 diesel engine developing 120hp (89.5kW)
Performance:	maximum road speed 100km/h (62mph); fording 0.9m (2ft 11.4in)

DAF YA 4440

DAF produced around 4000 YA 4440 trucks for the Dutch Army between 1977 and 1980 for the initial order, and have continued to supply the Dutch since with several thousand more. Essentially a civilian truck, the YA 4440 has been modified for military use. The all-steel cab has a reinforced roof so that a machine gun can be mounted for anti-aircraft defence. The suspension comprises double-acting hydraulic shock absorbers to help with cross-country driving. The engine is mounted at the front of the chassis and power is transmitted to the two-speed transfer box via the five-speed synchromesh transmission. Optional equipment includes a manual crane and hydraulic crane (stabilisers are fitted to the sides and must be lowered when the crane is in use).

Country of origin:	Holland
Crew:	1 + 1
Weight:	10,900kg (23,980lb)
Dimensions:	length 7.19m (23ft 7.1in); width 2.44m (8ft); height (tarpaulin cover) 3.42m (11ft 2.6in)
Range:	500km (331 miles)
Armour:	none
Armament:	(optional) one 7.62mm machine gun
Powerplant:	one DAF DT615 six-cylinder turbocharged diesel engine developing 153hp (114.1kW)
Performance:	maximum road speed 80km/h (50mph); fording 0.9m (2ft 11.4in)

Sisu A-45

Sisu-Auto AB was a natural choice to fulfil the Finnish Army's requirement for a rugged truck capable of carrying considerable loads cross-country, as the company was well used to building trucks for the exacting local climate and terrain. The vehicle is unusual in having a steel lower cab but fibre glass upper. This is useful for airborne operations as it can be dismantled and reassembled quickly. The cargo body is attached to the chassis by special rubber mountings which give greater flexibility and thus reduce wear and tear. The vehicle can be fitted with a winch for vehicle recovery, or to drag itself out of trouble, and the engine has a special heater to cope with the extreme cold in Finland. The cargo area can be fitted with bows and a tarpaulin cover if required.

Country of origin:	Finland
Crew:	1 + 2
Weight:	9000kg (19,800lb)
Dimensions:	length 6.00m (19ft 8.2in); width 2.30m (7ft 6.6in); height (cab) 2.60m (8ft 6.4in)
Range:	700km (435 miles)
Armour:	none
Armament:	none
Powerplant:	one six-cylinder diesel engine developing 130hp (96.9kW) or turbocharged diesel, developing 160hp (119.3kW)
Performance:	maximum road speed 100km/h (62mph); fording 1.0m (3ft 3.4in)

Trucks and Prime Movers

M813

The M813 was part of the M809 family, all-based on a standard chassis, which entered production in 1970. This in turn was a development of the M54 series, the first range of trucks to be produced for the US Army after World War II. Capable of carrying 4.5 tonnes (4.4 tons) of cargo cross-country, and towing considerably more, the vehicle proved a durable workhorse. It was the standard vehicle in its class in use with US forces until being replaced in the 1980s by the M939. It had foldable seats in the rear which allowed up to 26 troops to be carried. Optional equipment included a deep-fording kit, essential when used by the US Marine Corps in amphibious operations, a winch and special cold-weather equipment. As well as a cargo carrier, the vehicle was used to tow artillery and various missiles.

Country of origin:	USA
Crew:	1 + 2
Weight:	14,294kg (31,446lb)
Dimensions:	length 7.645m (25ft 1in); width 2.464m (8ft 1in); height 2.946m (9ft 8in)
Range:	563km (350 miles)
Armour:	none
Armament:	(optional) one 0.5in anti-aircraft machine gun
Powerplant:	one NHC-250 six-cylinder diesel engine developing 240hp (179.0kW)
Performance:	maximum road speed 85km/h (53mph); fording 0.76m (2ft 6in)

M35

Developed after World War II, the M35, known as the 'Eager Beaver', became the standard US Army 6 x 6 truck and was the most widely used military truck in the West, with the US Army alone having 65,000 in use. By early 1980, AM General had produced over 150,000 M35/44 series 6 x 6 trucks. Initially equipped with a petrol engine, later variants were converted to multi-fuel and diesel systems to make them more fuel-efficient. Other improvements included a redesigned suspension, brakes and steering, and forward-tilting bonnet. Optional extras were a winch, special heating for cold-weather operations, deep-fording kit and centre troop seats for carrying personnel. The many variants of the M35 included the M48 tractor truck, M50 water tanker, M59 Dumper, M60 wrecker and M185 repair van.

Country of origin:	USA
Crew:	1 + 2
Weight:	8168kg (17,969lb)
Dimensions:	length 6.71m (22ft 0in); width 2.39m (7ft 10in); height 2.90m (9ft 6in)
Range:	483km (300 miles)
Armour:	none
Armament:	none
Powerplant:	one LDT-465-IC six-cylinder diesel engine developing 140hp (104.4kW)
Performance:	maximum road speed 90km/h (56mph); fording 0.76m (2ft 6in)

Trucks and Prime Movers

Ural-375D

Production of the Ural-375 series truck began in 1961. The most numerous version of the truck was the 375D. The truck was equipped with an all-steel, fully enclosed cab (an improvement on the initial 375 design) and, like most Soviet vehicles, carried a pre-heater for the engine to deal with the cold climate found in Russia. A tyre-pressure regulation system ensured that the truck was capable of carrying considerable weights cross-country. Variants included a recovery truck, fuel truck and one adapted especially for service in the tropics. The TMS-65 was a version designed as a decontamination vehicle. The body was replaced by a modified jet engine and decontamination liquid tanks. Vehicles were decontaminated by being driven slowly past while the jet was in operation.

Country of origin:	USSR
Crew:	1 + 2
Weight:	12,400kg (27,280lb)
Dimensions:	length 7.35m (24ft 1.4in); width 2.69m (8ft 9.9in); height 2.68m (8ft 9.5in)
Range:	650km (404 miles)
Armour:	none
Armament:	none
Powerplant:	one ZIL-375 V-8 petrol engine developing 180hp (134.2kW)
Performance:	maximum road speed 75km/h (47mph); fording 1.0m (3ft 3.4in)

ZIL-131

The ZIL-131 entered production in 1966 as the replacement for the ZIL-157. Capable of carrying up to 0.4 tonnes (0.4 tons) cross-country and towing about the same amount, the vehicle was fitted with a tyre-pressure regulation system as standard. Also standard was a 4.5-tonnes (4.4-tons) winch. The cab was fully enclosed with a heated engine, while the cargo area at the rear had drop sides and a drop tail-gate. In addition to cargo carrying, the truck was widely used to tow 122m guns, and the chassis was used for mounting multiple rocket launchers such as the 122mm BM-21. Variants included a dump truck, fuel tanker (including the MA-41 tanker which carried diesel, water, oil and petrol in specially heated tanks to refuel vehicles even in the coldest weather) and decontamination vehicle.

Country of origin:	USSR
Crew:	1 + 2
Weight:	10,425kg (22,935lb)
Dimensions:	length 7.04m (23ft 1.2in); width 2.50m (8ft 2.4in); height (cab) 2.48m (8ft 1.6in)
Range:	525km (326 miles)
Armour:	none
Armament:	none
Powerplant:	one ZIL-131 V-8 petrol engine developing 150hp (111.9kW)
Performance:	maximum road speed 80km/h (50mph); fording 1.4m (4ft 7.1in)

Bedford MK

Following a competition in the 1960s to find a successor to the Bedford RL (which continued in service up until the 1980s), Vauxhall was selected to build the Bedford MK based on the civilian 4 x 2 TK truck. Military modifications included a new engine, all-wheel drive and bigger wheels. The vehicle has an all-steel fully enclosed cab with a mounting for an anti-aircraft machine gun. The chassis is of the ladder type with six cross-members, two of the 'alligator jaw' design. Optional extras included a winch and rear dual wheels, while seats can be inserted in the centre of the cargo area for carrying passengers. The vehicles were used for carrying specialist repair systems, as recovery vehicles, for carrying portable trackways and general cargo-carrying duties.

Country of origin:	UK
Crew:	1 + 1
Weight:	9650kg (21,230lb)
Dimensions:	length 6.579m (21ft 7in); width 2.489m (8ft 2in); height (cab) 3.404m (11ft 2in)
Range:	560km (348 miles)
Armour:	none
Armament:	none
Powerplant:	one Bedford six-cylinder diesel engine developing 103hp (76.8kW)
Performance:	maximum road speed 77km/h (48mph); fording 0.76m (2ft 6in)

Mercedes-Benz U 1300

The Mercedes-Benz Unimog was designed for industrial and agricultural purposes in the years following World War II. Having undergone many modifications, the U 1300L vehicle was chosen to fill a West German Army requirement for 17,000 military trucks to be delivered between 1978 and 1989. A versatile vehicle, the 1300 L has been used as an ambulance, a dump truck and a pole erector. Many are fitted with winches and the chassis has been used as the basis for an armoured personnel carrier (the UR 416). The vehicle has seen service with the Australian and New Zealand Armies and is used by the RAF for towing Harrier jump jets in the field. For normal road use the vehicle is driven with only the rear wheels engaged, the front wheels being engaged for cross-country driving.

Country of origin:	West Germany
Crew:	1 + 2
Weight:	7500kg (16,500lb)
Dimensions:	length 5.54m (18ft 2.1in); width 2.30m (7ft 6.6in); height (including tarpaulin) 2.83m (9ft 3.4in)
Range:	900km (559 miles)
Armour:	none
Armament:	none
Powerplant:	one Mercedes-Benz OM-352 six-cylinder diesel engine developing 96hp (71.6kW)
Performance:	maximum road speed 80km/h (50mph); fording 1.2m (3ft 11.2in)

Trucks and Prime Movers

Stalwart

The Stalwart High Mobility Load Carrier comes from the same family as the Saracen armoured personnel carrier and the Saladin armoured car, and uses many of the same basic components as those vehicles. The Stalwart is fully amphibious and has excellent cross-country performance. In the water it is driven by two marine jets. It can carry up to half a tonne (0.4 tons) of cargo. Its main role is to supply the rest of the battle group with fuel and ammunition. Alternatively, the stalwart can be adapted to carry up to 30 fully equipped soldiers. The engine is under the cargo area, and the engine drive is taken through a twin dry plate clutch and five-speed gearbox to the transfer box with a no-spin differential. The driver is positioned in the centre of the cab with a single passenger seat either side.

Country of origin:	UK
Crew:	1
Weight:	14,480kg (31,856lb)
Dimensions:	length 6.36m (20ft 10in); width 2.6m (8ft 6in); height 2.64m (8ft 8in)
Range:	515km (322 miles)
Armour:	none
Armament:	none (basic version)
Powerplant:	one Rolls-Royce B-81 Mk 8B eight-cylinder water-cooled petrol engine developing 220hp (164kW)
Performance:	maximum road speed 63km/h (39.37mph); fording amphibious

Pegaso 3055

In 1982, the Spanish Army selected the Pegaso 3055 to be the successor to the 3050 as the standard military truck in its class. The vehicle is fitted with a removable canvas hood and fold-down windscreen which facilitates air transport (there is an optional metal top to the cab). The Pegaso 3055 is able to carry six tonnes (5.9 tons) of cargo cross-country and almost double that on roads. The many variants include a tractor truck, recovery and crane trucks, a fuel tanker, dump truck and fire-fighting vehicle. The vehicle is also used to tow field artillery. When used as a personnel carrier, there is capacity for up to 30 fully equipped infantrymen. The current version of the Pegaso 3055 is the longer-wheelbase Model 7323, which is powered by a Pegaso naturally aspiring diesel engine.

Country of origin:	Spain
Crew:	1 + 1
Weight:	15,000kg (33,000lb)
Dimensions:	length 6.956m (22ft 9.8in); width 2.406m (7ft 10.7in); height 2.765m (9ft 0.9in)
Range:	550km (342 miles)
Armour:	none
Armament:	none
Powerplant:	one Pegaso Model 10 six-cylinder naturally aspirated diesel engine developing 220hp (164kW)
Performance:	maximum road speed 80km/h (50mph); fording 1.0m (3ft 3in)

Trucks and Prime Movers
Oshkosh M911

Realising that using the combination of the M746 vehicle towing the M747 semi-trailer for transporting tanks was unnecessarily complicated and expensive, the US Army issued a requirement for a simpler, cheaper vehicle in 1976. The Oshkosh F2365 civilian truck was selected and designated the M911. A total of 747 were eventually delivered to the US Army, with a small number being exported to Thailand. Tanks are loaded with the help of two winches mounted to the rear of the cab, unusually, the M911 is an 8 x 6 vehicle, with the second axle being lowered to the ground when heavy loads are carried. Standard equipment for the cab includes an adjustable seat for the driver, heater and defroster. The brakes have a dual air supply system, one for the front and one for the rear axles.

Country of origin:	USA
Crew:	1 + 2
Weight:	39,917kg (87,818lb)
Dimensions:	length 9.38m (30ft 9in); width 2.89m (9ft 6in); height 3.658m (12ft)
Range:	990km (619 miles)
Armour:	none
Armament:	none
Powerplant:	one Detroit-Diesel model 8V-92TA-90 V-8 diesel engine developing 450hp (335kW)
Performance:	maximum road speed 71km/h (44.37mph); fording 1.0711m (3ft 6in)

Berliet GBU 15

For nearly a quarter of a century up to the mid-1980s, the Berliet GBU 15 was the standard 6 x 6 heavy truck of the French Army. It was capable of carrying a cross-country load of up to six tonnes (5.9 tons), and was capable of towing a load of up to 15 tonnes (14.8 tons). The engine was housed under the unusual four-door cab, which has a removable top and windscreen. The vehicle was able to run a variety of fuels including petrol, paraffin, JP4, gas oil, light fuel and mineral or vegetable oils in the lower power ranges. A winch was fitted as standard, which has a lifting capacity of 8000kg (17,600lb). As well as normal cargo-carrying duties, the GBU 15 was used to tow the 155mm Model 1950 howitzer. Variants included an artillery tractor, fuel tanker and recovery vehicle.

Country of origin:	France
Crew:	1 + 3
Weight:	20,500kg (45,100lb)
Dimensions:	length 7.974m (26ft 1.9in); width 2.50m (8ft 2.4in); height (cab) 3.00m (9ft 10.1in)
Range:	800km (497 miles)
Armour:	none
Armament:	none
Powerplant:	one Berliet six-cylinder multi-fuel engine developing 214hp (159.6kW)
Performance:	maximum road speed 75km/h (46.6mph); fording 1m (3ft 3in)

Fiat 6605

The Fiat 6605 stemmed from Italian development of a medium artillery tractor in the 1960s. The 6 x 6 6605 was subsequently adapted by the Italian Army to tow such heavy artillery pieces as the 155m howitzer. Known as the TM69, the vehicle had a very long cab which extended back to the centre of the chassis, carrying both the crew and the gun detachment. Charges, projectiles and general stores were kept in separate compartments within the hull for safety reasons, and a winch was fitted as standard. Variants included a cargo-carrying version with a hydraulic crane fitted at the rear of the cab, and a recovery version with telescopic crane and stabilisers. In addition to seeing service with the Italian Army, the Fiat 6605 series was exported to Libya and Somalia.

Country of origin:	Italy
Crew:	1 + 11
Weight:	17,000kg (37,400lb)
Dimensions:	length 7.33m (24ft 0.6in); width 2.50m (8ft 2.4in); height (cab) 2.92m (9ft 7in)
Range:	700km (435 miles)
Armour:	none
Armament:	none
Powerplant:	one FIAT Model 8212.02.500 six-cylinder diesel engine developing 219hp (163.3kW)
Performance:	maximum road speed 78km/h (48mph); fording 1.5m (4ft 11in)

Oshkosh HEMTT

Following a US Army requirement for a Heavy Expanded Mobility Tactical Truck (HEMTT), Oshkosh was selected to produce around 5000 vehicles to be delivered over a five-year period. The first production vehicles arrived in 1982, but problems occurred due to a lack of proper testing. The problems were soon overcome, though, and the truck saw service with US forces in West Germany and South Korea as well as within the United States itself. To keep down development costs, the truck used many standard commercial automotive parts. The basic model came fitted with a winch and cargo crane. Variants included a fuel tanker, and a tractor truck as well as a recovery truck which has a cargo platform between the second and third axle for carrying spare parts. Some 4536 vehicles have been funded.

Country of origin:	USA
Crew:	1 + 1
Weight:	28,123kg (61,870lb)
Dimensions:	length 10.16m (33ft 4in); width 2.39m (7ft 10in); height (cab) 2.565m (8ft 5in)
Range:	483km (300 miles)
Armour:	none
Armament:	none
Powerplant:	one Detroit-Diesel Model 8V-92TA V-8 diesel engine developing 445hp (331.8kW)
Performance:	maximum road speed 88km/h (55mph); fording 1.524m (5ft 0in)

M520 GOER

The GOER was based on vehicles designed for the civil construction industry in the 1950s. The designs attracted army interest and were adapted to fulfil battlefield requirements. The first production GOERs were delivered in 1964. They were soon deployed to South Vietnam, where their excellent cross-country mobility, especially in the rainy season where normal 6 x 6 trucks fared badly, prompted the US Army to expand their use. Despite being the heaviest truck then in use with the US Army, the vehicle was fully amphibious. Unusually, it had no suspension, relying on its huge tyres to absorb the shock. The vehicle has a windscreen and a removable canvas top with removable side curtains. Variants included a fuel tanker and a recovery vehicle. Around 1300 of all types of GOER were delivered by 1976.

Country of origin:	USA
Crew:	1 + 1
Weight:	18,500kg (40,700lb)
Dimensions:	length 9.753m (32ft 0in); width 2.743m (9ft 0in); height 3.404m (11ft 2in)
Range:	660km (410 miles)
Armour:	none
Armament:	none
Powerplant:	one Caterpillar D333 six-cylinder turbocharged diesel engine developing 213hp (158.8kW)
Performance:	maximum road speed 48.3km/h (30mph); fording amphibious

Foden 8 x 4

The Foden is a low-mobility truck, adapted from a civilian design and minimally modified to suit military requirements (the emphasis being on ease of maintenance). They were used mainly for carrying heavy cargo over long distances, the cargo being deployed to more mobile vehicles close to the point of use. For example, they were often used to transport cargo from the Channel ports to bases in West Germany before the unification of Germany. Typically the truck carried up to 6 tonnes (5.9 tons). Variants included two types of fuel tanker and a tipper truck for the Royal Engineers. In addition, some basic models were fitted with the French Ampliroll system, which allowed a vehicle to be quickly adapted for a number of roles such as tanker or armoured car transport.

Country of origin:	UK
Crew:	1 + 2
Weight:	27,000kg (59,400lb)
Dimensions:	length 10.287m (33ft 9in); width 2.489m (8ft 2in); height 3.327m (10ft 11in)
Range:	499km (310 miles)
Armour:	nonen
Armament:	none
Powerplant:	one Rolls-Royce 220 Mk 111 six-cylinder diesel engine developing 220hp (164.1kW)
Performance:	maximum road speed 76km/h (47mph); fording 0.914m (3ft 0in)

Bedford TM

The TM 4-4 was developed following a British Army request for a medium-mobility 4 x 4 truck to be based on a proven commercial chassis. Bedford delivered the first of over 2000 vehicles in 1981, with Marshall providing the rear cargo body. There were four basic models: the basic cargo vehicle; basic cargo with winch; cargo with Atlas hydraulic crane; and a tipper truck, this having a shorter wheelbase than the other versions. Military modifications included an observation hatch in the roof and a mounting for a machine gun for anti-aircraft defence. As well as seeing service with the British Army, the vehicle was exported to a number of countries including Oman, Abu Dhabi and Bahrain. Like all Bedford vehicles, this truck is rugged and able to operate in varied climatic and terrain conditions.

Country of origin:	UK
Crew:	1 + 1
Weight:	16,300kg (35,860lb)
Dimensions:	length 6.629m (21ft 9in); width 2.489m (8ft 2in); height (cab) 2.997m (9ft 10in)
Range:	499km (310 miles)
Armour:	none
Armament:	(optional) one 7.62mm machine gun
Powerplant:	one Bedford turbocharged diesel engine developing 206hp (153.6kW)
Performance:	maximum road speed 93km/h (58mph); fording 0.762m (2ft 6in)

Tatra T813

Developed in the 1960s, the Tatra T 813 range of vehicles included cargo trucks and prime movers for artillery systems. The basic cargo truck had an unusual four-door fully enclosed cab which was fitted with a nuclear, biological and chemical (NBC) defence system. Four-wheel power-steering and tyre-pressure regulation system were standard, giving impressive cross-country mobility. All vehicles were fitted with a winch for recovery of other vehicles, or to haul themselves out of trouble and some were fitted with a hydraulic dozer blade on the front. As well as moving cargo and towing artillery systems, the vehicle was also used as the basis for the M1972 122mm multiple rocket launcher. The vehicle saw service with Libya and East Germany, in addition to the Czech Army.

Country of origin:	Czechoslovakia
Crew:	1 + 6
Weight:	22,000kg (48,400lb)
Dimensions:	length 8.75m (28ft 8.5in); width 2.50m (8ft 2.4in); height 2.69m (8ft 9.9in)
Range:	1000km (621 miles)
Armour:	none
Armament:	none
Powerplant:	one Tatra T-930-3 12-cylinder diesel engine developing 250hp (186.4kW)
Performance:	maximum road speed 80km/h (50mph); fording 1.4m (4ft 7in)

KrAZ-255B

The KrAZ-255B replaced one of the standard trucks of the Soviet Army, the KrAZ-214, production of which ceased in 1967. The main improvements of the later vehicle were increased payload, a more powerful engine and the installation of a tyre-pressure regulation system to improve mobility. The 255B was used for a wide range of specialised roles, such as carrying engineers' cranes, laying the TMM treadway bridge and launching the PMP heavy floating pontoon bridge system. Other engineer versions included an excavator truck, fuel tanker, tractor truck and a USM pile driving set used for constructing bridges. The layout of the vehicle is conventional, with the engine at the front, two-door fully enclosed cab in the centre and the cargo area at the rear which could be covered with tarpaulin (as here).

Country of origin:	USSR
Crew:	1 + 2
Weight:	19,450kg (42,790lb)
Dimensions:	length 8.645m (28ft 4.4in); width 2.75m (9ft 0.3in); height (cab) 2.94m (9ft 7.75in)
Range:	650km (404 miles)
Armour:	none
Armament:	none
Powerplant:	one YaMZ-238 V-8 diesel engine developing 240hp (179kW)
Performance:	maximum road speed 71km/h (44mph); fording 0.85m (2ft 10in)

M4 High-Speed Tractor

The M4 was developed following a 1941 requirement for a new medium tractor for the US Army field artillery to be based on the same automotive components used in the M2A1 tank. The vehicle was standardised as the M4 in August 1943. Two versions were built, one to tow anti-aircraft guns, the other to tow howitzers, as well as carrying the gun detachment and all equipment. The latter vehicles were fitted with a crane to help with loading the heavy projectiles. After World War II, the M4 was supplied in some quantity to various countries including Japan, Brazil, Yugoslavia and Pakistan under the Mutual Defence Assistance Program. The M4 was the first in a long line of tractors in service with the US Army, and which can fulfil a wide variety of roles, from ammunition carriers to heavy load towing.

Country of origin:	USA
Crew:	1 + 11
Weight:	14,288kg (31,433lb)
Dimensions:	length 5.232m (17ft 2in); width 2.464m (8ft 1in); height 2.515m (8ft 3in)
Range:	290km (180 miles)
Armour:	none
Armament:	one 12.7mm anti-aircraft machine gun
Powerplant:	one Waukesha 145GZ six-cylinder inline petrol engine developing 210hp (156kW)
Performance:	maximum road speed 53km/h (33mph); fording 1.04m (3ft 5in); vertical obstacle 0.7m (2ft 3in); trench 1.5m (5ft 0in)

M5 High-Speed Tractor

Development of what was to become the M5 began in 1941 when the T20 and T21 were developed using the tracks and suspension of the M3 tank. In October 1942, the T21 was standardised as the M5, designed to tow 105mm and 155mm howitzers as well as their crew and equipment. Five different models were produced in all, differing mainly in their track and suspension. The vehicle entered production in 1942 and was built by International Harvester. A winch was fitted as standard and a roller under the winch allowed it to be used to pull vehicles to the front or to the rear. The vehicle did not outlast World War II by very long in the US Army, but it continued to serve with the armies of Austria, Japan, Yugoslavia and Pakistan for many years after 1945.

Country of origin:	USA
Crew:	1 + 10
Weight:	13,791kg (30,340lb)
Dimensions:	length 5.03m (16ft 6in); width 2.54m (8ft 4in); height 2.69m (8ft 10in)
Range:	241km (150 miles)
Armour:	none
Armament:	one 12.7mm Browning anti-aircraft machine gun
Powerplant:	one Continental R6572 six-cylinder petrol engine developing 207hp (154kW)
Performance:	maximum road speed 48km/h (30mph); fording 1.3m (4ft 4in); vertical obstacle 0.7m (2ft 3in); trench 1.7m (5ft 6in)

M8 High-Speed Tractor

The M8 was developed during World War II following the failure of the T33 cargo-carrier, which was based on the chassis of the M24 Chaffee light tank. The new vehicle was standardised as the M8 after the war had ended and was based on the chassis of the M41 Walker Bulldog light tank, production lasting from 1950 until 1955. As well as towing cargo trailers, the M8 towed a variety of weapons such as the 75mm anti-aircraft gun and the M59 'Long Tom' gun. The cargo area of the basic version could be quickly adapted for carrying projectiles and charges. Unlike many other such tractors, the M8's engine was at the front of the vehicle. Some M8s were equipped with a hydraulic dozer blade for clearing battlefield obstacles, and in the process having a useful engineering capability.

Country of origin:	USA
Crew:	1 + 1
Weight:	24,948kg (54,885lb)
Dimensions:	length 6.731m (22ft 1in); width 3.327m (10ft 11in); height 3.048m (10ft 0in)
Range:	290km (180 miles)
Armour:	none
Armament:	one 12.7mm anti-aircraft machine gun
Powerplant:	one Continental AOS-895-3 six-cylinder air-cooled petrol engine developing 863hp (644kW)
Performance:	maximum road speed 64.4km/h (40mph); fording 1.06m (3ft 6in); vertical obstacle 0.46m (1ft 6in); trench 2.13m (7ft)

M548 Lance Missile Carrier

The M548 was developed as a result of a requirement from the US Army Signal Corps for a tracked vehicle to carry specialised equipment. Using many of the automotive components of the M113 armoured personnel carrier, the vehicle was designed either for carrying cargo cross-country or for towing trailers or weapons. The M 548 was fully amphibious, propelled in the water by its tracks and was equipped with infrared night vision. The M548 has been used for many specialised vehicles including: the Vought Lance missile-launcher (as shown above); radar and electronic warfare vehicle; mine layer; 35mm self-propelled anti-aircraft gun; mine clearance and recovery vehicle. Over a dozen countries use variants based on the M548 chassis, including Germany, Spain and Italy.

Country of origin:	USA
Crew:	1 + 3
Weight:	12,882kg (28,340lb)
Dimensions:	length 5.893m (19ft 4in); width 2.692m (8ft 10in); height 2.82m (9ft 3in)
Range:	483km (300 miles)
Armour:	44mm (1.73in)
Armament:	one 7.62mm or 12.7mm anti-aircraft machine gun
Powerplant:	one Detroit-Diesel Model 6V-53 six-cylinder liquid-cooled diesel engine developing 215hp (160kW)
Performance:	maximum road speed 64km/h (40mph); fording amphibious; vertical obstacle 0.61m (2ft 0in); trench 1.68m (5ft 6in)

AT-S Tractor

The AT-S was developed in the 1940s and entered service with the Soviet Army in the early 1950s. The fully enclosed cab had room for six passengers and carried the gun crew when towing artillery. The open-topped cargo body was sometimes swapped for an enclosed hull when carrying specialised equipment such as communications and radar. The AT-S was used as the basis for the BM-24T rocket launcher and the AT-S also formed the basis for the Sbkh, which was used for transport in snow-covered terrain. The OTS was an AT-S fitted with a dozer blade for removing obstacles. The AT-S was widely exported, being used by nearly all Warsaw Pact countries as well as Syria, Egypt, Yugoslavia, Finland and China. A Polish version of this vehicle also exists.

Country of origin:	USSR
Crew:	1 + 6
Weight:	15,000kg (33,000lb)
Dimensions:	length 5.87m (19ft 3.1in); width 2.57m (8ft 5.2in); height 2.535m (8ft 3.8in)
Range:	350km (217 miles)
Armour:	none
Armament:	none
Powerplant:	one V-54-T V-12 water-cooled diesel engine developing 250hp (186kW)
Performance:	maximum road speed 35km/h (22mph); fording 1.0m (3ft 3in); vertical obstacle 0.6m (2ft 0in); trench 1.45m (4ft 9in)

Trucks and Prime Movers

Type 73

From its inception in the 1950s, the Japanese Ground Self-Defence Force relied heavily on American equipment. However in the early 1970s, the Japanese chose to develop their own artillery tractor to take the place of the American M4 and M8. Built by Hitachi, the first production vehicles were completed in 1974 but was never produced in large numbers as the emphasis switched to self-propelled artillery. There was a fully enclosed all-steel cab and a similarly constructed compartment to carry the gun crew. Ammunition was carried in a separate compartment at the rear. Used for towing weapons such as the 'Long Tom' gun and the 203mm M115 howitzer, the vehicle was sometimes fitted with a dozer blade to clear obstacles and prepare fire positions.

Country of origin:	Japan
Crew:	1 + 11
Weight:	19,800kg (43,560lb)
Dimensions:	length 6.13m (20ft 1.3in); width 2.95m (9ft 8.1in); height 2.30m (7ft 6.6in)
Range:	300km (186 miles)
Armour:	none
Armament:	one 12.7mm anti-aircraft machine gun
Powerplant:	one Mitsubishi ZF6 six-cylinder air-cooled diesel engine developing 400hp (298kW)
Performance:	maximum road speed 45km/h (28mph); fording 1.0m (3ft 3in); vertical obstacle 0.6m (2ft 0in); trench 2.0m (6ft 7in)

Index

Note: Page numbers in **bold** refer to main entries.